The Arrival of B.B. King

THE AUTHORIZED BIOGRAPHY

Charles Sawyer

DOUBLEDAY & COMPANY, INC.
GARDEN CITY, NEW YORK
1980

Library of Congress Cataloging in Publication Data

Sawyer, Charles.
  The arrival of B. B. King.

  Discography: p. 235.
  1. King, B. B.   2. Afro-American musicians—Biography.   I. Title
ML420.K473S3   784.5'3'00924 [B]
ISBN: 0-385-15929-3
Library of Congress Catalog Card Number 79-6085

Grateful acknowledgment is made for permission to include the lyrics
from the following copyrighted songs.

"And Like That," © 1965 Modern Music Publishing Co., Inc. Music by
B. B. King. "Nobody Loves Me But My Mother," written by B. B. King
© 1970 ABC/Dunhill Music, Inc. and Sounds of Lucille. All rights
reserved. "Let the Good Times Roll," by Sam Theard & Fleecie Moore ©
1946, 1947 Warock Corporation © renewed 1974, 1975 Rytvoc, Inc.

0 0 4 3 8 8

To my father

Contents

Preface

I FIRST MET B.B. King in 1968 at Lennie's on the Turnpike, a jazz club on the North Shore outside Boston. It was between sets, and B.B. was talking to admirers in a storeroom off the bar. When I entered, he broke off his conversation, reached over the shoulders of those around him, and greeted me, a total stranger, with sincere warmth, asking me to introduce myself to the others. By then I already knew something of his place in American music. But it was this simple setting that alerted me to the intrinsic interest of his personal style and his life story as well as his place in American race relations.

This book is a social rather than a musical biography. Much as I admire B.B. the artist, and much as I invariably thrill to the sound of his music, it is the social significance of his life story that I think is the more compelling aspect of his biography. I admit I have an ax to grind: in telling B.B.'s story, I want to celebrate the death of Jim Crow, the mythic personification of racist segregation, the cancer afflicting the American soul on both sides of the Mason-Dixon Line. I hope that while grinding my ax, I have also managed to do justice to B.B.'s art and portray his musical achievement.

Bielefeld, Germany, October 1978
CMS

Acknowledgments

IN WRITING THIS BOOK, I have been assisted by a number of people who contributed by giving raw material, strategic advice, and moral support. Without the cooperation of many who shared in B.B.'s story, and willingly, candidly, and in good cheer gave me uncensored interviews, this book would indeed be lopsided. To my private thanks, I add my public gratitude to Booker Baggette, Mrs. Johnson Barrett, Johnny Board, Clarence "Gatemouth" Brown, Wayne Cartledge, Elder Birkett Davis, Sue Evans, Bert Ferguson, Earl "Father" Forest—King of the T.N.T.s (turntables), Solomon Hardy (Sparrow), Mattie Fields, Mrs. Robert Henry, Mr. and Mrs. Edwayne Henderson, Luther Henson, Evelyn Johnson, Mr. and Mrs. Albert King, Shirley King, John Matthews, Andrew "Sunbeam" Mitchell, Mama Nuts (Evelyn Young), Jim Rooney, Sidney Seidenberg, Rufus Thomas, Willie Mae "Big Mama" Thornton, Laverne Toney, Jesse Turner, Eric von Schmidt, and the Walkers: Cato, Cato III and James "Shinny." Finally I owe thanks to all of B.B.'s road company, but especially to Eddie Rowe, Milton Hopkins, and Bert English.

Two institutions helped me by allowing me to use their facilities: the Center for Southern Folklore in Memphis, Tennessee, and the Mississippi Department of Archives and History in Jackson, Mississippi. I thank them both and add my personal thanks to Judy Peiser, director of the Center for Southern Folklore.

For strategic advice I am indebted to Professor Ian Jarvie of

York University in Toronto and Dominick Abel, both of whom gave extremely helpful criticism of an early, largely unsuccessful draft, and made constructive, helpful suggestions on how to recast the main ideas of the book. I am grateful to them both. John Wettersten, Judith Agassi, and Peter Guralnick read parts of the last draft and made valuable comments; Ester Kurz contributed a most helpful criticism. I want to thank them all for their contributions.

A special acknowledgment is due Professor Robert Cogan of the New England Conservatory for his help in transcribing the B.B. King guitar solo that appears in Appendix IV.

Special thanks are due to Doris Kimball for her moral support, to Polly Walker for her friendly help and advice in maneuvering through the dense networks of show business, to Bob Aude, for his editorial advice in selecting the photos in this book and for his extremely high standards of darkroom craft, which is my insurance that my photographs are seen to their best advantage, to Dick Balzer for suggestions in preparing the photos, and to Sandy Burrows, my typist, for her efficiency.

My greatest debt in seeing this book to its successful completion is to B.B. King, himself, who was always a willing subject, a gracious host, and a gentleman. His tolerance of my persistent attention with tape and cameras was far more than I had a right to expect—even from someone as cooperative as he.

Finally, I want to extend my deepest appreciation to my friend and collaborator, Professor Joseph Agassi, of Boston University and Tel Aviv University, who participated in every aspect and every phase of this book. Every page has been improved by his helpful suggestions, and his beneficial influence is felt in every line. My personal debt to him goes much further.

Prelude

"Have You Ever Seen Niggers Like Us?"

IT WAS HOMECOMING WEEKEND in Fayette, Mississippi, and the group called Stump was raging on the lawn in front of Evers Motel. The crowd stood four or five deep in a semicircle around them, clapping to the music, swaying with the tempo. Waves of polyrhythmic sound poured out of the speaker columns to the side. Around the edge of the adjacent blacktop, souvenir vendors were hawking costume jewelry and Charles Evers T-shirts. The smell of barbecued pork ribs and chicken hung in the still, humid air. From my vantage point under a canopy near the barbecue pit, the musicians were hidden behind the wall of bobbing celebrants. The surging R&B had so many melodic lines going at once that I left my shady spot to see exactly how many musicians were laying down all this delicious clamor. I wormed my way to the front and found just a three-man rhythm section plus one soloist sitting at the keyboard of a clavinet, which is like an electrically amplified harpsichord. His hands flew over the keys, and his left leg pumped furiously beside the stump of his right leg, amputated above the knee. He began to sing, and the other musicians joined in unison, singing the same refrain over and over as they closed the set:

> "Have you ev-er seen nig-gers like us?"
> "Have you ev-er seen nig-gers like us?"

The knot of people gathered around the band began to unravel. I returned to my spot in the shade but soon found the heat even there unbearable. Sid Seidenberg, B.B.'s manager, saw my discomfort and said, "Come on, I know where it's cool." He led the way inside through the jammed motel barroom and on through a door at the rear. Here, in Charles Evers' office suite it was cool, almost chilly. Mayor Evers was talking on the telephone to a journalist explaining that his campaign for U. S. Senate was more than quixotic. On the far wall a torn newspaper clipping describing the unsuccessful attempt of federal prosecutors to convict Evers on charges of income tax evasion flapped in the breeze from the air conditioners. Evers put down the phone and greeted Seidenberg.

"Little Milton goes on at eight P.M. and B.B. hits at ten-thirty. Okay?"

Seidenberg smiled and nodded. "Got a table for us?" he asked Evers.

"Sit anywhere you want," Evers replied. "I'm the mayor and the judge—and I own this joint."

I drove down to Natchez with my date for a quick bite. We were back at Evers' Motel just as Little Milton's band was taking the stage. The ballroom was nearly full. When the nine musicians hit the first note, the excitement around the tables was almost palpable. Little Milton, a veteran blues singer and guitarist, appeared after three warm-up numbers, and the joint began to jump. He ran his set long, and the intermission that followed dragged on so that it was nearly midnight when B.B.'s band hit. The crowd had its second wind, and the earlier, feverish mood that had held sway during Little Milton's set now gave way to a mellower ambiance. The King appeared from stage left in a double-breasted, white suit. The first note from his electric guitar was magic. Time flew.

An hour passed by, and now Little Milton appeared from stage right. He plucked a microphone from its stand and began employing his gift for mimicry by stealing every other lyric and singing it true to B.B.'s style.

B.B. nodded in his direction and the audience shouted delighted cries of approval. B.B. called out a command to his musicians, the tempo slowed to a crawl, and the volume dropped to a hush. Over the purr of the instruments, B.B. and Little Milton exchanged a running patter about blues and lovers, mixing in song titles and lyrical lines in their commentary.

On an impulse, I grabbed my date and joined the couples on the crowded dance floor. We were the only white couple—a fact that no one paid special attention to—until B.B. called out my name.

"There's Charles in the crowd," B.B. said in time with the rhythm. "He's doing a book on us," he added proudly after a bar or two. Umchaaah cha Umchaaah, Umchaaah cha Umchaaah. "Put up your hand, Charles. Look at that, he's actually dancing!" I proudly waved my hand as high as I could reach.

"You scared me, B.," Little Milton said. Umchaaah cha Umchaaah. "You said, 'Put up your hand, Charles,' and I saw this white hand waving above the people out there; I wondered for a second what had happened to the mayor [Charles Evers]!" Gentle laughter rippled through the crowd, and B.B. broke into the lyrics of "The Thrill Is Gone."

ANECDOTES like this appear in books of all kinds and are usually included to make a point or establish a mood; often they do both. This one is presented here to suggest a problem central to the very conception of this book; namely, the broad diversity of the intended audience. After all, the people who read a biography of B.B. King may include musicians and nonmusicians; academics and public readers in all disciplines, blues fans, and, of course, that brand of faithful readership, the success-story addicts. Some of the readers will be whites, other blacks; some of them will be Americans, but not all, for B.B.'s fame is worldwide. The details of his life story are full of the history of our times, and that story has much to offer anyone interested in the American South, in the changing economics and sociology of American race relations, and in the impact of technology on the social mechanisms of American society at large. Moreover, there is much to recommend the story of B.B. King as plain human drama. To speak solely to the concerns of any one of these groups of potential readers would be to fail in doing justice to B.B. King as the man of many roles that he certainly is: the artist of the first rank, the mainstay of a specific art form, the cultural figure of major importance in our time, the Horatio Alger of the modern South. This book, then, is a quixotic effort to speak at one and the same time to the broadest possible public—to all readers who might possibly find merit in the story told in the following pages. To aim so wide and hence be also so ambitious will mean requesting each subdivision of the whole readership to make some allowance in some way—which may be reasonable if members of each subdivision would be willing to benefit from understanding how the story appeals to other subdivisions, namely to readers with different tastes and interests. I therefore dare beg all my readers to cooperate with me so as to allow for my high ambitions in trying to reach such a diverse audience, to draw such a kaleidoscopic picture.

Part One

The Artist in Perpetual Motion

I

Living by the Odometer

SINCE 1951 when he had his first national hit, "Three O'Clock Blues," B.B. King has been in nearly constant motion. As soon as that first record reached the top of the black charts, B.B. left his job as disc jockey at WDIA in Memphis, turned over his band to his friend and pianist, Johnny Ace, and headed for his first engagement up North. True, for many years thereafter he kept a residence in Memphis, through the late sixties he had a plush apartment in New York, and now it's a thirteen-room house in Las Vegas, with a staff of three. But these are mere sanctuaries, temporary refuges. At one stage in his career, B.B. traveled entirely by bus and limousine, at another by air alone, and recently by both. When he first left Memphis in 1952, to go on national tour, he traveled alone; by the mid-1950s his entourage topped twenty. In recent years he has reduced his road company, which now consists of seven to ten musicians, two support persons, a road manager and a driver/valet.

The following chapter relates details from the daily routines of B.B. King and those around him during February and March 1978. The narrative is, I believe, an accurate portrayal of the life of modern day itinerant blues musicians.

CHICAGO: THE BURNING SPEAR

A gig in Chicago begins a five-week series of engagements east of the Mississippi. B.B. and his band have just finished a month in the western states and Canada ending with five days in Arizona. B.B. and three of his roadmen have homes in Las Vegas and so they passed through there on the way to Chicago, and thereby managed to spend a night at home. The others made their own ways. Fogg, the bus driver, would arrive with the bus in a few days.

The band checked in, one by one, at the three-star Essex House in downtown Chicago; B.B., his road manager, and valet checked in across the street at the four-star Conrad Hilton. All stay on B.B.'s tab.

The gig is at a club called "The Burning Spear," deep in South Side Chicago, one of America's biggest and ugliest black ghettoes. The floor of the main room at the Burning Spear seats roughly 800 and when it is jammed with high-spirited customers the waitresses must use speed, agility, and muscle to serve them.

By 10:00 all the musicians in B.B.'s band are in the club, some loitering in the lobby, others sitting in the dreary second floor dressing rooms, limbering up on their instruments.

"When do we hit?" asks one. No one answers. "Where's Bebop?" he shouts, calling for the road manager, Bebop Edwards, who just then enters carrying B.B.'s guitar in a soft black vinyl case.

"Hit at 11:00," answers Edwards, unlocking the heavy padlock on King's personal dressing room.

At 10:30 the soul group onstage closes their set and twenty minutes later Bebop, who, as road manager, is responsible to see that the show begins on time, rouses the musicians with gruff wisecracks.

"Get your asses down on that stage. When you finish this here parade, you don't get no cotton candy, you get dollars."

As the band is gathering onstage, B.B. enters the club and goes directly to his dressing room, unnoticed. His guitar, which he tuned roughly at the hotel, is already standing beside his amp onstage, another responsibility assumed by Bebop.

Bebop unlocks the padlock on the dressing-room door, opens the door for B.B., and stands aside, leaving the open padlock dangling from the metal loop on the door frame. As he passes through the open door, B.B. snaps the padlock shut on its loop. Bebop looks at B.B. quizzically, then toward the padlock, then back at B.B. pleadingly. "Let's not give some wise guy the chance to lock us in," says B.B. with a smile, handing him the key. Bebop grins and nods knowingly. He chuckles at the thought of the two of them locked in while the crowd downstairs stomps and hollers for their star to appear. He knows that even after twenty years as his boss's keeper, he still doesn't have the same sharp instincts as B.B. to guarantee the star's reliability as a performer.

B.B. peels off his camel's hair coat and opens a small valise from which he pulls a comb and a can of Afro Sheen. In the glaring light of a dozen bare bulbs, he sprays and combs his hair. As the band begins the second number downstairs, Bebop appears with a glass and a pitcher of ice water. B.B. pours a tall drink, downs it at one go, and pours a second.

"You want two or three tunes?" asks Bebop about how long to run the opening routine.

"It's opening night. Let's get into it good. Run three."

Midway through the third number, Bebop walks down to signal conductor Eddie Rowe to begin B.B.'s introduction. When B.B. hears the abrupt change of tempo a few minutes later, he downs his second glass of ice water and heads for the stage.

"Lock it up," he says to Bebop as they pass on the stairs.

The Burning Spear is full. Any fire marshal not on the take would stop the show. Every seat in the house is full, and the aisles are jammed with dancing, laughing, boozing patrons. The audience and the nightclub are almost timeless. This could be 1939 at Jones Night Spot in Indianola, Mississippi, or 1950 at the Club Handy on Beale Street in Memphis, or the Apollo Theater in Harlem, around 1960. The audience is comprised of no special age or marital status; two and three generations of the same family can be found at some tables. All imaginable variations of dress from casual to theatrical are visible in the soft light reflecting off the stage and shining up from candles flickering in colored glass cups at the tables. Wide-brimmed hats wag beside tall, glittering wigs fit for a Renaissance court. Only one trait unifies this audience: race. The dozen-odd white faces dotted among the eight-hundred-plus black ones look oddly like pieces of lint on dark cloth.

B.B. is facing a stiff challenge. This is no casual warm-up set, it's Friday and nearly midnight. The crowd has already heard two hours of music, and they are ready for the show, wound up tight. Moreover, the people here know B.B.'s music intimately, and most of them have followed him over the balance of his thirty-year career. In his first set of this three-day gig, he must give his best—if he doesn't, the fans will know.

The emcee, a bucket-mouthed, willow-legged gag man, begins B.B.'s introduction and quickly charges up the crowd. The music swells, and the emcee's last words blare out: "Mr. B. . . . . . . B. . . . . . . King!" As B.B. wriggles under his guitar strap, the band abruptly switches to a fast shuffle tempo. The crowd cheers louder. B.B. hits the first seven-note figure on his instrument, and the crowd goes haywire with excitement. Middle-aged women stand at their seats, hands over heads in ecstatic worship, shaking their broad, besequined buttocks, shouting cries of joy. Twenty-four bars into the number, the band stops abruptly and B.B., half-singing, half-shouting, dragging out the lines far longer than the shuffle tempo would ordinarily allow, introduces his performance with the lyrics:

> Hey everybody!
> [*Band strikes a chord*]
> Tell everybody!
> [*Another chord*]
> That B.B. King's in town.
> [*Chord*]
> I got a dollar and a quarter,
> And I'm rarin' to clown.
> [*Chord*]
> But don't let no female
> Play me cheap.
> I got fifty cents more than I'm . . .
> Gonna keep.
> So let the good times roll

The band resumes the quick shuffle tempo at the word "roll," and B.B. continues singing in a relaxed voice, loping over the choppy shuffle time laid down by the musicians.

> Let the good times roll.
> I don't care if you're young or old.
> Let's get together and
> Let the good times roll.*

* "Let the Good Times Roll" by Sam Theard & Fleecie Moore © 1946, 1947 Warock Corporation © renewed 1974, 1975 Rytvoc, Inc. International Copyright secured. All Rights Reserved. Used by permission.

Pandemonium.

Seventy-five minutes later, shortly before 1:00 A.M., B.B. closes the show to a tumultuous ovation. The dressing room is already half-crowded when he arrives back there, drenched and drained. With hardly a moment's pause between the roles of performer and host, he dries his face and neck on a towel handed him by Bebop and greets his dressing-room guests warmly.

"Call the lady up here, will you, please," he says to Bebop, who goes off dutifully to find the dressing-room waitress.

The dressing room is ill fit for entertaining. Besides a few plastic contour chairs, a lumpy couch is the only piece of furniture. Two Formica counters stand before mirrors rimmed by bare incandescent bulbs. The air is rank with the stale smell of smoky barrooms. B.B. begins to parcel out his attention to the seated guests. There is a nephew of one of B.B.'s distant Mississippi cousins with his wife, a Chicago musician who once played in a band that shared the stage with B.B. during a long engagement in another city, three women who describe themselves as "friends from the old days in Memphis," and a tall, striking, slender young woman with knee-length vinyl boots and rose-tinted glasses that cover half her face.

B.B. sits in a corner from where he has a clear view out into the upstairs lobby reflected in the mirror on the opposite wall. The lobby is filling up with people who have persuaded the uniformed sentry below that they are expected here above. From his corner vantage point, B.B. monitors the traffic and remains on top of the highly fluid situation. As new faces appear in the reflection of the open dressing-room door, he breaks off conversation and turns to welcome the newcomers. He treats them all graciously whether he knows them or not, making no pretense of remembering names and faces long forgotten.

Soon the dressing room is full and the air close.

"Can't we have the air conditioner on?" asks a lady who is poured into a dress with a snakeskin pattern.

"I'm sorry, madame," B.B. replies. "We can't do that. God gave us two of every part of our bodies 'cept the ones we use too often." She looks utterly perplexed. He looks impish. "In my case, it's my throat. I'm afraid I have to keep it warm in here; otherwise I'll lose my singing voice." When his meaning registers on the face of the lady in snakeskin, B.B. roars.

The waitress appears in the doorway loaded down with a tray of drinks for the guests whose orders B.B. took ceremoniously, one by one.

"Give this to my man out there," he tells her, pointing to the $43 check she holds. "Bop!" he shouts. Bebop shows his face at the door. "Take care of this, will you? And be generous with the lady, too." They are dismissed and the party resumes.

For two hours, until he takes the stage for the second set at 3:30 A.M., B.B. holds court. It is no casual party, but rather more like a ceremony. Everyone dotes on B.B.'s attention, which he distributes graciously, allowing no one to monopolize it, offending no one by requiring that it be shared. He is a celebrity and his guests, many of whom are virtual strangers to him, feel tremendously important to have this fleeting moment of ceremonious intimacy with a star. Orchestrating the proceedings, directing the human traffic, carefully observing etiquette require sharp concentration and considerable social skills. All in all, holding court is as demanding a task as performing onstage.

Several times B.B. diplomatically fends off insistent people who take liberties. A young woman repeats a story her father told her about the time he went coon hunting with B.B. King in Arkansas, but B.B. does not respond as she has anticipated by confirming the story. She insists; he declines politely to play the role of I - remember - your - daddy - well - we - used - to - hunt - coon - together - down - in - Arkansas. She pushes very hard. He says firmly that he has never been coon hunting in Arkansas. She looks distressed; he asks her to have a seat and offers her a drink.

An intoxicated man approaches and asks, not very politely, to have a word with B.B. *alone.* That would be rude to my guests, B.B. declares coolly. But it's *business,* the drunk protests. There's a time for business and it's not now, B.B. declares firmly but evenly. They go several rounds, neither raising his voice. Finally, the drunken hustler leaves with a swagger. No one seems to notice the episode.

Many visitors want their photos taken with the star. The house photographer, a middle-aged man with a young niece assisting him, has stationed himself in the lobby from where he is frequently summoned to officiate in the ritual picture-taking. B.B. never refuses to pose for photos, though he always directs the action ("Wouldn't you like your husband in the photo, too? Let's not leave him out.") and politely declines the unusual requests ("Mr. King, will you get your guitar for the photo?") and the bizarre proposals ("Will you play your harmonica while he takes our picture, B.B.?") which some people put to him. The photographer, perhaps convinced that a professional ought to have a special word to utter the moment he is ready to snap the shot, raises his Speed Graphic, checks the ready light on his strobe and focuses: "Downtown!" Flash. Zip (Polaroid back). The stream of supplicants is steady. The litany is repeated over and over again. Pose, focus, "Downtown!" Flash. Zip. Pose. Focus. "Downtown!" Flash. Zip. Nearly every supplicant returns with a fully developed Polaroid to get B.B.'s autograph in the little folio the photographer supplies to display the snapshot, or to retake the shot if it has turned out too dark or too light. B.B. favors every reasonable request.

There are frequent requests for autographs. One man in his twenties hands B.B. a shred of cardboard.

"Sure, I'd be glad to sign my autograph if you give me a pen," says B.B. The young man pulls out a roll of bills and peals off a crisp $10 bill. "I said, I'll be glad to sign if you give me a *pen*. A *pen*." B.B. is patient, the young supplicant embarrassed. Pen found, autograph signed, the money disappears back into the young man's pocket, and the proceedings resume.

For B.B. there are no real lulls in this routine. In moments when the gaiety is at an ebb, when the room is less crowded or the attention of the guests is not focused on him, people advance to put the touch on him. They pull his sleeve, squeeze his elbow, whisper in his ear. The requests are not usually extravagant: come to my house for dinner tomorrow, lend me twenty, and so on. Still, granting these murmured requests is cumulative and in the long run would be exorbitant, so ordinarily B.B. does not favor them.

At 3:10 A.M., when the band takes the stage for the second set, the crowd in B.B.'s dressing room thins out. When he sends Bebop down to signal the emcee, he is still entertaining the last hangers-on. At the sound of his intro theme, B.B. pours a glass of ice water down his open throat and takes his leave.

"Gotta go to work, folks. You'll excuse me, please." He slips downstairs to the wings just as the emcee shouts his name. It is 3:30 A.M.

IN THE DRESSING ROOM between sets on Saturday, squirrel-and-dumpling casserole is served from a hot plate. For nearly a half hour, the dressing-room company is entertained by a wise-cracking comic who gave a steady barrage of insults and slurs in the styles of Redd Foxx and Don Rickles. Samples: B.B. asks how are things out on the Coast. "The niggers in California are starving, B.—I did all I could for them, even sent back my rented Rolls-Royce." Then, turning and pointing to Bebop Edwards, "You did real well by this nigger, B.B. You put money in his pocket so he could buy those jive clothes. Yes sir, this nigger looks much better then he did when I first saw him. He walks like his feet don't hurt him anymore." Such humor is taken in good spirits, and the racial epithets here bring peals of laughter.

B.B.'s opening set is cut short when a woman rushes onstage and lunges at him. The horn players grab at her but fail to catch her before she seizes B.B. around the neck. The speed with which she crosses the stage, the desperate way she clutches him with un-mistakable force, the savage look on her face have all the distinc-tive characteristics of an assault. As the woman lays her hands on him, B.B. feels something sharp in his neck and a slicing sensa-tion behind his ear. The next moment, the horn players have her arms pinned behind her. B.B. reaches back to the spot where he felt the painful sensation. His hand feels something warm and wet. Blood? Sweat?

As he hurries off stage, he murmurs "I think she cut me."

The audience comes to its feet, the house lights go up. The emcee exhorts the crowd. "No one in show business is more open to his audience than B.B. King, and now this happens. The woman cut him and it's a damned shame!"

Backstage, B.B. discovers superficial fingernail wounds and no blood. In all likelihood, the woman had meant no harm—a zeal-ous hug or something of the sort—but by the following night, the popular version of the episode will evolve to include a new ele-ment: supposedly the assailant had returned to her table and bragged, "I cut him, I cut him," whereupon another woman sit-ting at the same table supposedly pulled a pistol from her purse and, pointing at the braggart, challenged her, "Try it just one more time, sugar."

MONDAY, following the three-day engagement at The Burning Spear, is an open day. B.B. decides to visit friends and relatives in the Chicago area, rather than make an urgent business trip to his Memphis office.

Tuesday, B.B. plays a one-nighter in Elgin, Illinois, traveling the forty miles from Chicago on his private bus which had arrived from Arizona on the weekend, and returning the same night to the Chicago Hilton.

Wednesday he plays in Milwaukee, returning again to Chicago without a layover.

Thursday is open. As on Monday, B.B. fails to make his business trip to Memphis.

Friday, B.B. is booked to begin a ten-day stand in Detroit, a 240-mile bus ride from Chicago. The band is given a 9:00 A.M. Friday-morning call to board the bus.

ON THE BUS

10:30. Bebop Edwards and Bert English, B.B.'s gofer, have just brought B.B.'s luggage out to the sidewalk. Most of the band is on board by then. Calep Emphrey, the drummer, sits in the front seat of the elevated rear deck staring at a bleary color television propped up in front of the skylight. Cato Walker, alto saxophonist, sits studying a book, *How To Succeed in the Big World of Music*. Bert English, who has left the two carts of baggage to Bebop, is teasing Walter King, B.B.'s nephew who plays tenor saxophone in the band. From his pocket Bert has pulled a plastic bottle containing a pair of casino dice. He pops the cap and spills the dice on the carpeted aisle. "Three and four makes seven, Walter. See what I mean? You can't afford to play with me."

11:00. Baggage loaded. B.B. boards the bus with Bebop close behind carrying a stereo turntable. Milton Hopkins, rhythm guitarist, is missing; no one has seen him all morning. He keeps a crib in Chicago—a small apartment for entertaining—and he stays there when in town. The bus pulls away without Milton. He will have to find his own way to Detroit.

12:00. Half the band is sleeping soundly; the other half is huddled behind B.B.'s seat at the front of the bus. The conversation consists of a kind of contest to see who can tell the most outlandish story of sexual exploits. Among the stories that brings the biggest avalanche of laughter is one they all contribute to, about a couple at a front-row table during a recent performance. Each describes the difficulty he had concentrating on the music while being distracted by their intimacies; relief came as they left when they could no longer carry their escapade further without creating a public sensation.

The conversation turns to music, and B.B. sends one of the band back to the lounge at the far rear of the bus to put an eight-track cartridge on the sound system which plays over speakers fore and aft. B.B. has been up all night listening to records and selecting cuts to make eight-track and cassette programs of music to suit his tastes and moods. He gives a running commentary on the songs, the artists, the arrangements. The music is mainly blues, some rhythm and blues, and just a smattering of jazz. There are several cuts of Lonnie Johnson, an Eddie "Cleanhead" Vinson cut called "Nigger, Shut Your Mouth," whose recurrent title lyric is greeted by hearty laughter, some Ray Charles ("He truly is a genius," B.B. comments), some Albert King ("He's a fine blues musician when he sticks to his basic material and they let him alone"), and some cuts from a new Brook Benton album. One cut from the Benton record attracts great interest—a song called "Makin' Love Is Good for You." B.B. says that it has "hit record" written all over it and begins discussing how it should be arranged for B.B.'s band. He explains how the recurrent title lyric of the song, which is sung on a catchy seven-note figure, could be woven into B.B.'s performance to form a leitmotif scattered among the familiar songs he usually sings. "You need always to be bringing something new into your material," he says emphatically. "You can't stand still." It is the central problem of every established performer: to remain true to the style that made him or her popular, while still appearing fresh. For a blues artist, the problem is especially difficult because blues is one of the narrowest forms of contemporary popular music.

"Maybe I'm crazy," B.B. says, continuing his running commentary on his personally edited tapes, "but nearly everything I hear I find something [that] sounds wrong with it. Like right here, it sounds draggy. It's draggin' right there. The drummer's not right on top of the beat, you understand?" He pounds the back of one hand on the palm of the other, trying to show what he would do. "And there—did you hear it? They introduced a major seventh where they shouldn't. You've got to keep it simple. Don't use more where less will do. That major seventh gave it a jazzy sound. . . . And there—they changed the voicing of the horns needlessly. . . . And there—they used a completely wrong chord. . . . I must be crazy—I find fault with everything I hear."

His fault finding seems not to detract from his obvious pleasure with the music he is hearing. He rocks to and fro in his seat, singing a line here and there. Meanwhile Barnett Fogg, the bus driver, has begun talking with truckers on the C.B. radio. "This is the Bluesman outa Memphis," he says to each new contact. He ends each transmission with a flourish of his microphone hand. He gives up competing with the blaring of the sound system and switches to earphones. Conversation dies down. The tape ends. B.B. is fast asleep.

DETROIT GHETTO GIG

Band Talk

The engagement in Detroit is another ghetto nightclub job: ten days at Phelps Lounge, smaller, classier and higher priced than The Burning Spear in Chicago, but otherwise more or less the same. Opening night has its own headaches. Will everyone arrive at the job safe and well, ready to go on? In this instance, there is Milton Hopkins, rhythm guitarist, who had not made the morning call for the bus. He arrives, bitching loudly, "Shit! Nobody bothered to let me know. How am I supposed to make the goddamn bus if no one calls me at my crib, man? I had to fly." Other headaches: What's the hit time? Has the equipment specified in the special riders to the contract—amplifiers, drums, organ—been faithfully supplied by the local promoter? After opening night, a routine will be established and minor details will take care of themselves, but until then there is a peculiar tension and concern in the air.

Phelps Lounge is located in a residential slum midway between a Chinese takeout and a dilapidated wood frame house that serves in the summer as an outdoor barbecue take-away and year-round as headquarters for a fundamentalist church. A legend scrawled in chalk on a slate hanging on the porch announces the time for week-night prayer meetings and Sunday services. The Chinese food service is a simple storefront; orders are taken and the food served out through an elaborate barricade—a deterrent to armed robbery—in the lobby which is empty of furniture and devoid of any decoration save graffiti. For the first few days of the gig, it becomes a habit that between sets, from midnight to one, the band goes next door to "The Chinaman" to bring back cartons of food and plastic spoons. When someone discovers a cockroach in the food, the practice rapidly loses popularity.

A ten-day job is a comparatively long layover in B.B.'s schedule, longer than all but the recording dates and Nevada casinos. Whereas the blazing pace of one-night stands has the tedium of a constant blur, the tedium of extended layovers gives the feeling of utter timelessness. The musicians and support staff cope with tedium and boredom by distracting themselves with television and the telephone and anything else. James Toney, the gentle, soft-spoken organist in B.B.'s band, talks to his wife Laverne in Las Vegas nearly every day; his average phone bill runs $200 per month. Alcohol plays only a minor role in the lives of the B.B. entourage, drugs even less, and hard drugs none at all: the demands of the road eliminate the junkie and the drunkard. Moreover, anyone discovered using hard drugs would be sacked.

Constant travel magnifies small problems. The electric outlets in the hotel walls will not accept the AC plug from a practice amplifier; finding an adapter in a strange city costs time and perhaps also cab fare to cruise around from one hardware store to another.

The bassist has pains in his lower back; it may be just strained muscles, but it could also be kidney trouble. The rhythm guitarist has lame shoulders; liniment might help, but it seems to be more in the joint and may require a cortisone shot.

Conversation among the musicians centers on sex, music, and strictly practical problems like the wall plug adapter. Politics and religion seldom come up but most exchanges are loaded with sociology: sociology of the music business, sociology of urban life, sociology of the family.

"Detroit is a *bad* place, man. I saw a dude in a Cadillac sittin' at a intersection get scraped on the rear fender by another dude in a new T-Bird. The first dude gets out, sees the scrape, reaches in his back seat, pulls out a tire iron and starts beatin' on the hood of the dude that hit him. He beat hell outa that motherfucker, man."

"Yeah, but it's not as bad as New York, man. I read about a woman that stepped on another woman's toe, waiting for the subway, and so the one woman pushed the other right in front of the subway car as it came down the track—just for stepping on her toe! Can you believe that?"

"But Chicago's the worst. In Chicago you carry your insurance papers with you when you go out to the supermarket so if you get mugged and killed, they'll know who to send the insurance money to."

"You done your taxes yet?"

"You crazy? It's only March. You do yours?"

"No, but I'm ready. I been audited every year for the last six years. Last time I had a book an inch thick. The dude that was doin' the audit didn't want to believe me because he said no one keeps such complete records. He thought I'd just made up all that shit. In the end everything was cool, though."

"I got my book, too, but it's a drag keeping it up to date."

"D'ju hear about Warren?"

"No, what'd he do now?"

"Jumped bail. He's a dumb motherfucker. He could've paid a $50 fine, 'stead he skipped bail. Now he's a fugitive."

"What was the charge?"

"Carryin' a concealed weapon."

"Jesus Christ! Wasn't he a cop before? Didn't he get in trouble for *not* having his pistol when he was supposed to?"

"No, it wasn't quite like that. As a cop he could buy a pistol with nobody askin' a lot of questions. So Warren bought a pistol for a friend, the friend got in some trouble, they traced the pistol to Warren, and zap! he was off the force."

"I remember once when he was workin' for B.B. We were riding in the bus when he asked how far it was to the next gig. We told him 600 miles. He says, 'That's too damn far to ride. Take me to the airport. I'm gonna fly.' So we drove the bus out to the airport and dropped Warren off. *A year and a half later* Warren shows up. Damn, that was a slow plane."

B.B.'s roadmen have a language which incorporates all the idioms of black America plus a few of their own. Besides common black expressions like "gig" for musical engagement, "joint" (pronounced "jernt" by some) for barroom or tavern, and "bad," said with heavy emphasis to mean "good," they speak of the "hit time" and to being "out here," meaning on the road. The last expression is analogous in use to the way in which G.I.s in Vietnam referred to their tours as being "over here," as opposed to being "back in the real world."

In fact, sometimes they put it in exactly those terms. "I been out here a few years now, man," said one, "and the chief problem, as I see it, is not to forget that it's not real out here. Nothin's real out here. It's a never-never land. If you start to think it's real, man, you're dead. That's what I think happened to Bobby Forte. He began to think it was real and then he went—" He began making a noise on his lips with his fingers. He was referring to B.B.'s tenor man of many years who is reputed to have suffered a mental breakdown.

"Out here" is anywhere the speaker is standing. It's everywhere and nowhere. The similarity between Viet-vet slang and road musician lingo is not an accident, in my view, because more than any other profession, road musicians resemble soldiers—not garrison soldiers, but cavalry soldiers; and not draftees, but career noncommissioned officers. Like professional soldiers, road musicians have a basic skill to offer and must have talent if they are to succeed. Yet the sine qua non for succeeding in either profession is durability.

The prestige a road musician holds with his peers depends largely on two factors: musical ability and longevity. "The longer the cat's been out here the heavier a dude he is." Among the musicians surrounding him, B.B. is unanimously acknowledged to be without rival by both criteria.

B.B. himself takes an attitude of paternal benevolence toward his employees. He considers it a point of honor to make life comfortable for them. "Like Johnson Barrett used to do when I was working on his plantation, I think I have to watch out for my men. I have to take care of their needs." This concern takes a few basic forms: making favorable working conditions, bestowing favors, responding to special pleading and coming to the rescue in emergencies. B.B.'s musicians' jobs are highly coveted, and there is a long line of experienced men waiting for them. Starting pay for members of the band is $500 per week, tops $675, plus a travel allowance (hotel and transportation); the bus is comfortably equipped; the hotels are middle grade ($20–$35) and everyone gets a single; and distant engagements are reached by air (economy class—B.B. flies first class). One year, when B.B.'s accountant advised him to shed some cash for tax considerations, he gave every roadman a few thousand dollars' bonus. Occasionally, on a two-day lull in the schedule, a band member may come to B.B. for financial help to fly home—an allowance not ordinarily included in his expense account.

B.B. at Home on the Road

B.B. has extraordinary resiliency. Every working day he runs a cycle from the supercharged state in which he performs onstage to a kind of living death, in which he recharges his internal batteries. It is a resurrection akin to Lazarus. He has the ability to wake from a deep sleep, answer the telephone, conduct business, then return straight to the same depth of sleep and wake later, not failing to remember the business transaction. Now, at the Holiday Inn two blocks from Tiger Stadium, he is fiddling with his videotape recorder. The timer allows him to set the machine to record prime-time programs that air while he is working. In addition to movies and musical extravaganzas like the Grammy awards, he records some sports (especially boxing) and a few favorite series ("Sanford and Son," "Kojak"). He has a sharp eye for style and craft which shows in his fascination with cartoons and commercials which he collects on the cassettes. ("It's amazing how in sixty seconds or sometimes thirty seconds they can tell a whole story from start to finish, at the same time promoting their product.")

Beside the two videotape units on the floor stand three tiers of sound equipment: eight-track, cassette, tuner, and amp. There's a portable version of the same unit on the dresser, and on one of the beds amid a thicket of paperwork in his pocket cassette machine. There are books on the dresser (Eldridge Cleaver and self-help books) and on the counter in the bathroom a small, open suitcase with an elaborate assortment of toiletries, and tools for repairing electronic equipment. His wardrobe is spread out on the beds in the next room.

"What I'd really like," he says, putting a fresh cassette into the two-hour Betamax, "is the new RCA video recorder that can record up to four hours. With the Betamax, I have to set the timer to go off twenty minutes into a two-hour, twenty-minute movie. Yes, sir, I'm going to get that four-hour machine as soon as I have some money. I have the bread, actually, but it's a question of priorities.

"I have a heavy 'nut' to carry—that's the amount of money it takes just to keep my show going. Counting all my expenses, salary and travel for me and my band, and maintenance on the bus, it comes to $15,000 per week. Less than that, and I begin to lose money."

At that moment there is a rap at the door. B.B. admits a slightly stout black woman in her late twenties. She is cradling a very large brown paper bag from which come the rich, sweet smells of hot food. She begins setting out dishes of fried rice, cornbread, and meat casseroles. B.B. dispatches someone with a five-spot to get milkshakes. The bed becomes a table.

"People wonder how entertainers making good money can ever die broke," B.B. says, digging into his impromptu meal. "I'll tell you. Out of every dollar I make, I pay ten cents to the booking agency and ten cents to my manager—off the top. I haven't done a damn thing, haven't put a drop of gas in my bus, and I've spent twenty cents already. By the time I pay the overhead and my taxes, you know what I've got left over for myself? A dime. Maybe two."

He goes on to explain why in his opinion he has never achieved genuine wealth and why he probably never will. He has chosen the basic moral code of human decency rather than taking unfair advantage of the world. First, he considers it a point of honor that he is a good employer. He is known among musicians for his generosity and fair-mindedness. Hardly a month goes by that he doesn't get a few calls from musicians who want to work for him. His reputation as a good employer is a source of considerable pride and self-esteem. Second, he considers it immoral to take advantage of others by insisting on the letter of the law. "I would never pull a tech [technical violation] on someone," is how he puts it. "Like if I made a contract with someone to pay them so-and-so much money on Friday, the tenth, and I come with the money that Friday afternoon and they tell me 'but it says here by *noon* on the tenth or you pay x-amount more.' That's a tech and I don't think that's right. I would never do that. Maybe I'll never be rich because I feel that way, but that's the way I am."

His assets, he goes on to explain in response to my prying, consist of an apartment house in Memphis, a private home on a house lot in California, his own home in Las Vegas on which he still owes most of the purchase price ($200,000 in round figures) and a few bonds. "Not that much, really, when you come down to it," is his overall appraisal of his off-the-cuff statement of net worth. Besides the mortgage on his house, his liabilities include back alimony to his second wife, who has remarried since their divorce.

There is a knock at the door, a new interruption. Nothing in B.B.'s daily activities is immune to interruptions, unless one counts performing (he can sing his way through changing a broken guitar string): not sleeping, not eating, not talking, not even, presumably, sex. On rare occasions, when he has three or four days free, he deliberately disappears and then even his private secretary in Las Vegas doesn't know where to locate him. Only at such times is he interruption free.

"Would you get the door, sugar?" he says to the woman who had brought the food and who now lies across the corner of his bed watching with adoring eyes as he eats with conspicuous pleasure. She crosses to the door and admits an old crony of B.B., a stout middle-aged man with no upper teeth.

"I got a good deal for you with my man out there," he says resolutely to B.B.

"Yeah? Has it got the wire wheels?" B.B. asks in reply.

"It's got everything. *Every*thing."

"What's the sticker say?"

"Sixteen."

"And how much will he take for it?"

"Twelve."

"When've I gotta tell him by?"

"By six tonight."

"Right. I'll tell you later what I decide."

"I haven't bought a new car since 1968," B.B. says to me.

Later that evening, I see a new Cadillac Brougham with wire wheels and temporary plates sitting in front of the hotel.

The Master Plan

On Tuesday, Sid Seidenberg, B.B.'s manager, comes to Detroit overnight to confer with his artist. Three years have passed since B.B. dissolved his partnership with Seidenberg because Seidenberg was neglecting B.B.'s career in favor of Gladys Knight and the Pips, the other main act he was handling. Things stand differently now. B.B. is short of cash and his career has lost significant momentum. Seidenberg is still managing the Pips and a stable of other performers, but Gladys has acquired a new husband with imperial ambitions, and now she is trying to make the transition to a single without Seidenberg or her blood kin, the Pips. In late 1977, B.B. and Seidenberg renewed their arrangement of personal manager and artist. The 1978 meeting in Detroit is not their first face-to-face meeting since renewing their partnership; nonetheless, fence mending is still the basic objective beyond matters of routine business.

Seidenberg, once a Manhattan accountant, has changed with the times and with his switch of professions at least in matters of appearance. Once given to pinstripe suits, dark ties, and wingtipped cordovans, at fifty-two he now dresses more casually: a shin-length leather coat, above-the-ankle boots, occasional denims. His hair comes down over his collar, and he sports bushy sideburns. Passing through the lobby I spot him buying a paper from a machine. He hails me and invites me to come up to his room to kibitz while he does business on the phone.

Upstairs he takes out three cigars from his jacket, props his feet up on the bed, and leans back. He selects one cigar, puts the others aside and lights up.

"I make a game of it—finding a good cigar," he says, blowing out a cloud of smoke. "When I'm in Miami, I spend all day going from cigar shop to cigar shop. That's where you find the best cigars in this country—Miami. Lot of Cubans in Miami . . . best cigars."

He opens a notebook, empties his pockets of slips of paper, and begins telephoning. The TV plays, sound off. He calls a Columbia Records V.P., head Pip Bubba Knight, his office, and a few dozen other high muck-a-mucks. Throughout his conversations his voice never rises far above a whisper. While he talks, he nudges the slip of paper around on the bedspread in front of him, and while he listens he pulls on his cigar. Between calls, he mutters, "This is such a lousy business I'm in. See that singer on the TV screen?" He points to a tight shot of a singing face that belongs to a well-known pop crooner. "The Mafia made him big. He has no voice, no talent." He picks up the phone for another call. That call finished, he begins a running commentary on B.B.'s career and his theories of show biz management.

"The important thing is to have a long-range plan, a master plan," Seidenberg says. "If I hadn't had a master plan when I met B.B., he wouldn't be where he is now. The booking agency doesn't have a master plan; the record company doesn't have a master plan. That was B.B.'s mistake when he walked out on me three years ago; he thought he could continue to thrive without someone taking a deep personal interest in his career. Record-company executives usually haven't the vaguest idea how to promote a record. *Someone* has to know and then has to get to the right people at the record company and threaten, cajole, sue them until they do what's necessary. But if you don't do these things, nothing happens.

"The consensus in the industry is that it was a mistake for me to take B.B. on again. People say, 'Why do you want to start over again with a man of his age? The blues market is cold now.' But I think I can heat him up again. He's got as much potential now as he had in 1968, when I first took him over. He's still got the appeal for young college kids. The old college kids that are grown up now—they'll still buy his records *provided he's promoted properly*.

"I was flying back from Miami recently, sitting beside a guy with a beard, wearing beads and denims. He told me he had seen B.B. play the Fillmore in 1969 and wanted to know where he was now. 'He played to two sellout crowds in Radio City just a few months ago,' I told him. He said he hadn't heard about it, even though he lives in New York. Now, *that's* bad promotion. *He'd* buy B.B.'s records now if they were promoted right. You know what this grown-up hippie is doing now? He's a dentist.

"The things we can do with B.B. are fantastic. He can make an indelible mark on the music industry and the public. He can become an institution—like Satchmo, when he was living. His career will be an annuity for him. Me, too."

He pauses for a moment and reflects. Before resuming his telephoning, he adds one last thought:

"I don't know why he has that bus now. Maybe it's ego, maybe it's his return to familiar things. The first thing I did when I took over in 1968 was to get rid of the bus. The first thing he did when he went out on his own in 1975 was to buy another bus. Right away it broke down; he had to get a new engine."

At the Joint

The ten-day gig at Phelps spans two weekends, and the audiences are generally all-black, teeming, and raucous.

As the second weekend approaches, a Detroit television station does a live three-minute minicam spot from the Phelps stage. The segment is smooth beyond words. A portable TV on an empty table shows what the viewers at home see. B.B.'s face appears behind the late-evening newscaster in the studio while he makes the intro; then the location switches from the TV studio to Phelps with B.B. in mid-song. Zoom back, on-the-scene-reporter steps center stage, band continues softly cooking, reporter chats with B.B. who continues tickling his instrument, B.B. invites the folks at home to come down and join in, reporter departs, music surges, pan to audience nodding and finger popping, close shot of reporter for close out, back to studio, B.B. again playing behind the newscaster at his desk. End segment.

On the weekend following, unlike the opening weekend, the audience is mixed white and black. Moral: only good promotion through the racially indiscriminate media will broaden the performer's audience.

AFTER Detroit, B.B. and the band have three days off. From the last note of the gig to the first of the next, it is every man for himself. Some ride the bus back to Chicago; one takes a 7:00 A.M. flight to Nashville. B.B. calls his Memphis office to tell them he is going to the dark side of the moon and will call in at some point. Then with a few buddies—old friends from Detroit and Chicago —he climbs in his gleaming new chariot and rolls out of Detroit.

BIG APPLE BASH

New York affects different people in different ways. Some get wax buildup in their ears. Perhaps it's the survival mechanism of the body responding to the clamor of the city, trying to protect the delicate parts of the hearing which were evolved for detecting minute sounds of alarm in the primordial jungle, not for the roar of the New York subway. For B.B., a visit to New York must be something like a ride on a bucking bronco. The heavy concentration of media and show-business headquarters there make the city a prime opportunity for him. Every available minute of time during his stay is allocated, with Seidenberg the choreographer. On the agenda for this visit were trips to the recording studio to complete a series of commercials for Panasonic and to the physician for a general examination for a new insurance policy. There were several interviews with journalists of one kind or another. B.B. told the editor from *High Times,* the glossy drug-paraphernalia magazine, that he never used to smoke much dope, never could seem to get high any way except from sympathetic intoxication—the so-called "contact high"—and stopped smoking dope altogether many years back when the law cracked down on dope smokers, though he was careful to add that he had no personal disapproval for others who do smoke. On this subject B.B. has the same public posture as Satchmo, who said, "I used to light up with the other cats, and to me you'd have a better session with gage, as we called it, than getting full of whisky. But the judge started throwing all of them years at us for just a roach. So, well, I didn't see nothing funny in that. Truth is, it's all in your mind and you play better without anything. . . . So anything that'll hinder me—out—automatically."† There were interviews with two radio correspondents. B.B. flirted with chic-and-trendy-syndicated-rock-commentator Alison Steele politely and benignly, treating her like the sophisticated groupie she is. With a matronly woman from Voice of America, B.B. shifted gears and treated her the way Elvis would have treated any grandmother who was a devoted fan of his. The main engagement is a three-night stand at The Bottom Line, Manhattan's most prestigious small nightclub

† *Louis Armstrong—a self-portrait,* The interview by Richard Meryman (New York: The Eakins Press, 1966), p. 51.

for the under-forty set. The showcase appearance during his stay in New York is a three-hour party in his honor held at Studio 54, the city's most celebrated disco, sponsored by ABC-Dunhill records at a cost of $10,000 to promote his latest album, *Midnight Believer*. Studio 54 had been much in the news as the place to be seen in, a reputation greatly enhanced by its arbitrary policy of admissions which barred many celebrities including, according to gossip, Aretha Franklin ("I didn't recognize her," the doorman is supposed to have said.) and the president of Cyprus, who was in town to speak at the UN ("I thought he ran a lumber company not a country—how was I supposed to know?" was the arrogant quip attributed to the maître d'.). The three nights at The Bottom Line are a smashing success. The music press turns out in force and each night has its surprise: Johnny and Edgar Winter sit in on one set the first night, Jacqueline Onassis is a surprise visitor the second night, and on the third night guitarist George Benson joins B.B. onstage for a friendly game of one-upmanship. (Benson falls into a blues style to mesh with B.B. and holds his own.) The visit by Jackie O., reported in Earl Wilson's gossip column and flashed around the world, is a publicity coup worth at least as much as the extravagant bash at Studio 54.

BRIEF RESPITE

B.B. King's rambling one-story stucco house is not especially opulent by Las Vegas standards. It is located on a corner lot with a large, flat lawn, and tall shade trees—one very distinctive feature in this city, where most residential areas were scrub lands a decade or two ago. Arriving several hours after B.B. as I pull in under the broad carport I recognize Hampton Reese, B.B.'s musical arranger.

Reese has been a satellite of B.B. for at least ten years. He is a kind of small planet circling the blazing star in a tight orbit and is seen only for a few moments during the whole year—when it crosses the face of the star. This metaphor may be a bit unfair to Reese, and surely it is not one he would choose; he would undoubtedly be more content to be described as an orbiting comet or even the lesser of a pair of twin stars, rather than a small dependent, warmed and lit by the other. It is not my aim here to cast him this way or that, which is really quite unnecessary as there are no villains in this piece. However, Reese does play the difficult and not very appealing role of friend and confidant to a celebrity, inevitably frowned at by nearly everyone else in the circle. He is roughly B.B.'s age, and, like him, he is a child of the Deep South; unlike him, and significantly so, he is conservatory trained. He writes the charts for his band, a fact that annoys most band members who regard him as a pompous, high-handed meddler.‡ It is easy to see where he gets the reputation for pomposity: he speaks in a highly affected manner, full of worn-out clichés and doubtful erudition. His speech is like the gestures of a beauty queen who throws rose petals to the crowd. Among some members of B.B.'s circle, he is reputed to be responsible for B.B.'s being fully literate. For years he was a kind of tutor to B.B.—indeed, until B.B. got hooked on books. The details of the relationship between Reese and B.B. escape me—I suppose I was reluctant to or discouraged from investigating too closely.

I confess I am not enthusiastic when I see Reese; on those few occasions that I had met him over the years, I had not found his company very pleasant. I am not surprised to see him here since I had heard gossip that B.B. had sent his bus to the East Coast to bring his furniture and belongings out to Nevada. I had wondered if he was moving in [on him?]. Still, whatever the case, B.B. is entitled to his friends, of course. Moreover, loyalty counts for a great deal with him—and perhaps with me too—and the ethic of loyalty is a two-way street. B.B. has his reasons for being friends with Reese, and any dislike that others may hold for the man is strictly not to the point.

"Hello, Reese," I say cordially, extending my hand and reminding him of my name.

"Oh yes. Hello there," he replies. We shake hands. "Didn't I bend an elbow with you once in Boston?" He strokes his scraggly Ho Chi Minh beard.

"Close. New York. But never mind. I hear you're moving out here. Is that right?"

"Posthaste, pronto, and just as quickly as possible."

I wince inwardly.

‡ After this account was written B.B. appointed a new arranger/conductor for his band, Calvin Owens, a contemporary of B.B. from Memphis, who played in the first B.B. King road band.

He holds a fistful of keno tickets which he was stuffing in his jacket pocket. "My homework," he says, flapping the tickets.

"Have you found a place to live, Reese?"

"I found an apartment in the general environs, and yonder vehicle contains my worldly goods and chattel." He points to B.B.'s Scenicruiser bus parked on the street. We head inside the star's house.

B.B.'s house inside is dark, spacious, thickly carpeted, and furnished with deep, soft chairs that envelop the sitter. The walls are crammed with memorabilia—citations, plaques, photographs—from the many stages of his career. The house spreads out in many directions from a central room which opens onto the terrace and pool at the rear. There are four guest rooms, an office, a very large living room with a dining area, a large kitchen, a master bedroom at the extreme end, and the central room connecting the others. B.B. is out when we arrive. I am introduced to his secretary and housekeeper, Laverne Toney. She is in her mid-thirties, very shapely and very sexy; her face is lovely, kindly, and intelligent, her manner confident and highly competent. She is just finishing her day of answering the persistent telephone and pestering her boss with nitty-gritty affairs that require his personal attention. I stroll out on the terrace to have a look; the deep-water, L-shaped pool has a film of leaves on the surface, on which the shadows of the two diving boards, high and low, make an interesting pattern. Floating near the edge of the water is a lone keno ticket. The pool skimmer stands on a long pole against the fence, its wire mesh torn in several places. Beyond the pool stands a neglected tennis court, its torn net casting a lacy shadow on the dirty tarmac. I sit by the pool to relax with a book. Soon B.B. comes and welcomes me graciously. We sit together briefly, and he speaks about his house with obvious satisfaction. He is proud that the previous owners were a casino manager, and before that, a banker. Besides Laverne, his secretary, he employs two maids who alternate nights, cleaning and guarding the house—the house is thereby never empty, though sometimes ill-tended—and a gardener who comes a few days a week. There is also a pool man, though he comes heaven knows when. There is no cook, and everyone fends for himself in the kitchen; the fridge is well stocked, and there is a supermarket nearby.

B.B. has a look of physical discomfort on his face. From his pocket he takes a small plastic medicine vial and pokes it into the back of his mouth. "Throat?" I ask. "Tooth," he replies. "Dentist tomorrow," he adds, excusing himself with a plea that he still hasn't touched his stack of waiting bills. I go to raid the icebox.

During the three days I stay with B.B., his house is a bachelor pad. In residence are his son Willie, at twenty-eight the oldest of his eight children, Leonard, his younger son, Tim, the bus driver, Reese his arranger and me, his biographer. Willie, an amiable, intelligent man, is part owner of a Las Vegas nightclub; Leonard, a good-natured country boy, is B.B.'s current valet. B.B. comes and goes. The phone rings often; the driveway is clogged from time to time. Late on the morning of his dentist appointment, B.B. comes out to the pool where I am reading and, with a look of deep relief, shows me the elephantine molar which had caused him such discomfort; cradled in his palm, it looks an ugly, twisted monster. His jaw is swollen, and I make a mental note that he will probably be out of commission most of the day. However, within a few hours, his speech is normal, his swelling is gone and he shows no sign that earlier that day he had endured minor oral surgery. I make a mental note never to underestimate his recuperative powers. Whenever B.B. is in sight, he is busy either on the phone or fiddling with his videotape recorders. A majority of the time he is out of sight back in his master bedroom which is really an apartment within the house; it is located at the end of a corridor in the far corner of the house and the door has its own lock. His bedroom is his retreat within his retreat. It is L-shaped and has a partially enclosed bathing area with a deep tub in the center of the room behind the king-sized bed. There is more than ample counter and closet space around the perimeter, yet all of it is filled to overflowing with belongings of all sorts, especially clothes and records. In one corner stands a small mountain of guitar cases, all of them full, I was told; seven or eight, at least. In another corner a stack of suits slouches; discards, bound for friends and relatives, he explains.

Although his bedroom is his haven, it is not off limits to others; he is not reclusive and while I stay as his guest, I come and go from there freely, engaging him in conversation and pestering him with pertinent questions. The lock on the bedroom door, he explains, is to discourage well-meaning souls who borrow his things with every intention of returning them, yet never manage to bring them back. He shows me closet after closet full of records and tapes, stacks of 78s, piles of tape spools—7″, 10″, and 12″ spools, yards of 33-rpm albums and racks of 45s. He estimates his record collection at 20,000 records. It is his pride, his joy, his preoccupation. Hours and hours on end he sits at the tall bank of Panasonic stereo equipment—his compensation for making a series of Panasonic ads—transferring music from disc to tape. It soothes him and appeals to the archivist in him.

When he is not sitting at his audio or videotape recorder, he is busy with some other project. He is constantly puttering. Evidently he is acquisitive; he never buys one of something if it might possibly break or wear out. He returns from his road trips with luggage bulging at the seams from all the goods he has acquired. It is probably a compensation for his harsh childhood, so fraught with deprivation, but whatever the reason, B.B. is a pack rat who hoards belongings as if he were expecting a famine. Some of his hoarding makes sense, like his record collecting, but other times he packs things home that defy explanation—like stationery and office supplies that surely must be available at the local office supply store. Perhaps Boy Riley, ever worried where the next pound of lard and sack of flour will come from, still lives in the heart of this man.

Late on one of my three nights at B.B.'s, I find him in his room, dressed up to go out. "I'm fixing to go downtown on business," he says. "You asked if I might ever go back to Memphis to live—like Elvis did. And this is the reason why I would never do that. In Memphis at this hour, things are closed. And besides, if this was Memphis, I wouldn't feel entirely safe out on the streets now. I'm very content here. Of all the things in my life right now, today, I think I'm proudest of this house. I love it. I hope I can keep it."

The morning that B.B.'s brief vacation ends, the house is in turmoil. He and son Leonard are booked for a 9:30 A.M. flight to Minneapolis, where he is scheduled to play that evening. He is a master caboose-catcher, watching the clock carefully, marshaling his garment bags, suitcases, and the aluminum trunk containing his videotape recorder, and habitually arriving at the terminal gate with barely minutes to spare. My flight back home to Boston is scheduled to depart thirty minutes before B.B.'s caboose, so son Willie offers to drive me out to the airport with the first load of B.B.'s luggage. As I step out at the terminal, the nearby porter spots the luggage; his eyes light up and he smiles. "B.B.'s taking off again!" he calls to the other skycaps lolling around by the door.

CODA: ♯17

B.B. King has much to offer any ambitious person as a model. The concluding incident in this chronicle of B.B.'s daily working life as a study in perpetual motion was one such occasion.

Months after we parted company in Las Vegas, B.B. was scheduled to play a three-day gig in Halifax, Nova Scotia. By coincidence it came after another of his rare respites at home in Las Vegas. A telephone call from his office tipped me off that he would change planes at Boston's Logan Airport on the way to Halifax. There was less than an hour's time to reach the airport on the far side of town, if I was to catch him between gates. I was wedged in a snarl of commuter traffic on Storrow Drive before discovering that my gas gauge showed I was driving on little more than fumes. Ahead of me lay the Callahan Tunnel under Boston Harbor, not a place I would like to run out of fuel. There was one last exit before the tunnel; yet, if I left the stream of traffic, I would surely miss B.B. at Logan. This is how things are with B.B., I thought to myself. If you want to catch up with the man, even for a few minutes, you must be ready to burn up all your reserves. Presented with the same dilemma, I reasoned, B.B. himself would prefer to run out of gas in a tunnel at rush hour, than to arrive at the airport with a full tank of gas yet too late to make his connection. I entered the tunnel, coasting with my engine switched off on the down side.

At the Air Canada check-in at Logan, no one had seen B.B. when I reached the counter, panting, ten minutes before the plane to Halifax was due to take off. He was not on the passenger roster as the flight pulled away from the boarding ramp. Wondering if he had somehow managed to make another earlier flight, I nonetheless strolled down to the baggage-claim area, where a mob of passengers were pressing around the mouth of the baggage conveyor. Just as I gave up hope to catch him, I was nearly knocked down by a charging black bear in a hulking sheepskin coat, carrying an oversized cassette recorder. It was B.B., dashing for the already departed Halifax clipper. When I blurted out that it was already too late, he seemed to shrink physically, as if the news of failure caused him to deflate. Dejected and guilt-ridden, he shuffled to the Air Canada counter, explaining on the way that he had missed the flight out of Las Vegas the night before and had been unable to find any combination of flights anywhere on earth that would get him to Halifax with more than the twenty minutes' time between planes here in Boston. It was his misfortune that the flight into Boston was just twenty minutes late. Now there was nothing to be done. He was expected onstage in Halifax in two and a half hours; not even a chartered plane, gassed and waiting, could get him there in time. After making reservations for the morning plane, he called his Memphis office to give instructions for notifying the promoters in Halifax. Then he checked into the airport Hilton and ordered a fried shrimp platter with baked potato and cheesecake from room service. While he waited for his meal to arrive, he drew back the curtain and gazed on the Boston skyline.

"This is only the seventeenth time in thirty years that I've missed a gig," he mused. "I was taught as a child that whatever happens, happens for the best. Well, at least now I'll be well rested when I get there tomorrow."

B.B. PLAYED the last two nights of his scheduled three-night stand in Halifax. Nonetheless, local promoters brought suit against him claiming $30,000 damages for his failure to appear the first night. The suit is still pending. I expect out-of-court settlement, perhaps in the form of other engagements.

Part Two

A Black Horatio Alger

II

Mississippi Sharecroppers

B.B. KING spent all his formative years, from birth until age twenty-one, in the alluvial plain of the Yazoo and Mississippi rivers, known locally as the Delta, and in the hilly part of northern Mississippi, a short distance east of the Delta. The rich, dark Delta soil laid down by centuries of sedimentation from the flood waters of the two rivers is some of the best growing ground anywhere on earth, and in those days, life in Mississippi was dominated by King Cotton. Many early blues musicians—perhaps even a majority of the originators and of the founders of the blues —came from this region of the South, a couple of hundred miles long and roughly sixty miles across at its widest. The blues style is known as southern, yet the Delta area just described is just a dot on the map of the continental United States. The Delta is sometimes described as running from the lobby of the Peabody Hotel in Memphis to Catfish Row in Vicksburg, Mississippi. No other place—save New Orleans—can rival the Mississippi Delta for its impact on American popular music.

ALBERT AND NORA ELLA KING

Albert King, B.B.'s father, was an orphan, raised by a black sharecropper named Love. Albert's family was scattered by misfortune. In quick succession, his mother left her husband (he disappeared to parts unknown), and his mother and sister both died. Albert's only other kin, a brother named Riley, left infant Albert with the Love family and disappeared. When they went out to chop and pick cotton, the Loves carried Albert to the fields in a tub and draped a cotton sack over it to give him shade and keep the insects away. When he was seven, word reached Albert that his brother was in a Texas prison. That was the last he ever heard of brother Riley.

B.B. King's mother, Nora Ella King, was slightly more fortunate in life than her husband, in that she had kin to fall back on in hard times. Nora Ella came from Kilmichael, Mississippi, in the hills to the east of the Delta, where the kudzu vines creep up any standing thing, smothering young trees and obliterating road signs. She met Albert in her mid-teens, when her family moved to the Delta in search of better working conditions. They were married after a brief, puritanical courtship. (Her entire family was religious.) They moved into a sharecropper's cabin near the tiny Delta town of Itta Bena and began raising a crop. Albert drove a tractor on the nearby plantations. Tractors were too valuable during planting season to leave them idle, so they were used in the fields round the clock. Albert often worked two consecutive double shifts—forty-eight hours, at 50 cents a shift. Nora Ella became pregnant in the winter of 1925 and gave birth on September 16, 1925.

A neighbor went on foot to summon a midwife—there was no other available means of transportation or communication—but she arrived too late to assist in the routine birth. The child was named Riley, after Albert's missing brother. It was this Riley— Riley B. King, the son of Albert and Nora Ella King—who later became widely known as B.B. King.

A second child born to Albert and Nora Ella King died in infancy. For Riley's parents, life consisted of unremitting hard physical labor, scratching out a living on a few acres not their own. The day began well before sunrise around 3:30 A.M., when the plantation bells rang in quick succession. Albert could recognize the pitch and timbre of the different bells starting the work day at each plantation. They rang once more at midday to signal lunch. The end of the day came when it was too dark to tell a black mule from a brown mule.

MATRIARCH, PATRIARCH, AND PREACHER

When Riley was four, his mother left his father for another man. She moved back up into the hills east of the Delta and sent

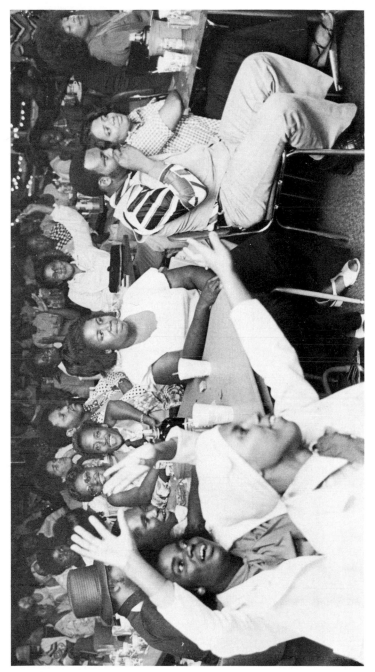

"Have you ever seen niggers like us?": Homecoming Day, 1978, Evers' Motel, Fayette, Mississippi. *Photo by Charles Sawyer.*

Old friends from Memphis in the dressing room at The Burning Spear, Chicago, Illinois. *Photo by Charles Sawyer.*

Willis "Bebop" Edwards, perso[n] aid to B.B. King since one day in t[he] mid-1950s when he left his cab at [the] curb of a Texas airport and boarde[d] plane with his new boss. *Photo [by] Charles Sawyer.*

"Downtown!" Flash, rip, zip. In the dressing room at The Burning Spear, an admirer poses with B.B. for a Polaroid portrait. *Photo by Charles Sawyer.*

On the bus, swapping ribald yarns. In the middle, alto saxophonist Cato Walker III; on the right, trumpet player Eddie Rowe; to the rear, tenorman Walter King. *Photos by Charles Sawyer.*

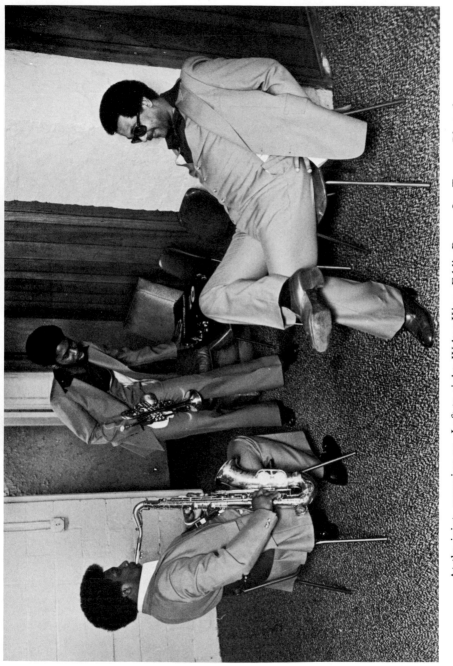

At the joint, warming up. Left to right: Walter King, Eddie Rowe, Joe Turner. *Photo by Charles Sawyer.*

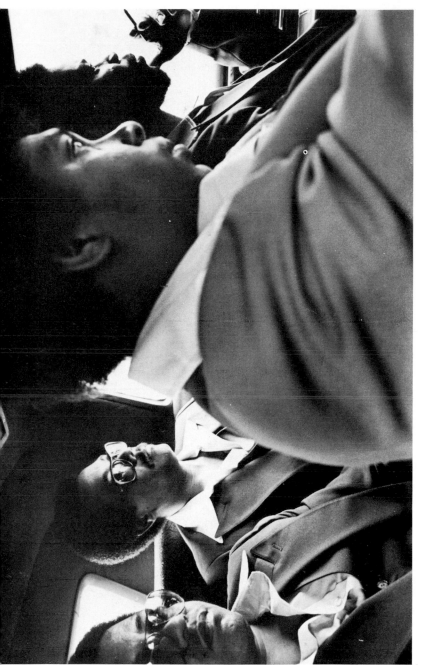

On the road. Four members of B.B.'s band from the mid-1970s: (left to right) Calep Emphrey, Jr., Joe Turner, Walter King, Eddie Rowe. *Photo by Charles Sawyer.*

Detroit, March 1978. *Photos by Charles Sawyer.*

B.B. with George Benson at The Bottom Line, New York, June 1978. *Photo by Charles Sawyer.*

Taping Panasonic commercial, New York, June 1978. *Photo by Charles Sawyer.*

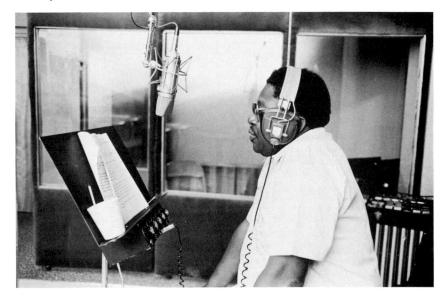

An interview with Alison Steele, New York City rock deejay. New York, June 1978. *Photo by Charles Sawyer.*

B.B. with manager Sidney Seidenberg, New York, June 1978. *Photo by Charles Sawyer.*

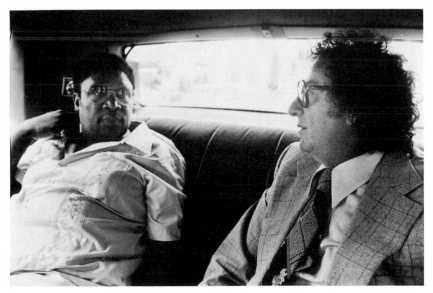

New York, June 1978. *Photo by Charles Sawyer.*

New York, June 1978. *Photo by Charles Sawyer.*

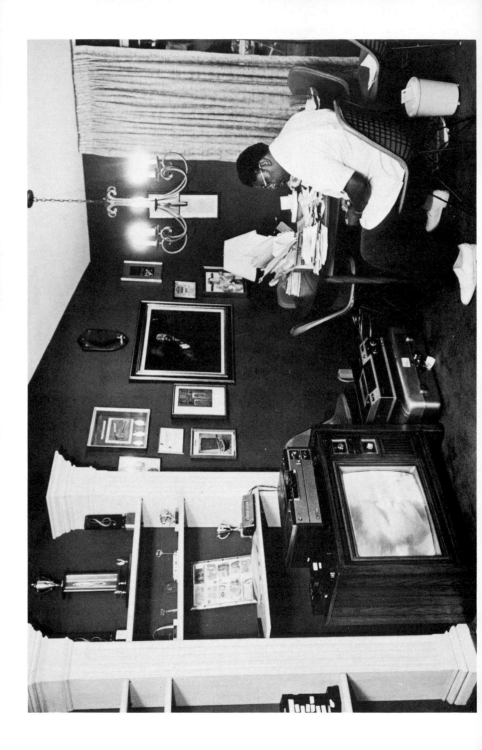

At his home in Las Vegas, B.B. taping records from among his 20,000-disk collection. *Photo by Charles Sawyer.*

In a rare slip-up, B.B. missed the last plane to Halifax and rushed to repair the damage. In thirty years, this was only his seventeenth no-show. *Photo by Charles Sawyer.*

Riley to live in nearby Kilmichael with his grandmother. Albert made no effort to interfere and quickly lost touch with both his wife and son. The situation then for blacks in Mississippi made it difficult and often imprudent to try persuading a fugitive spouse to return. Without telephones or automobiles, distances were greatly exaggerated by modern standards. Albert didn't even own a horse. Indeed, a black man who owned a horse or a mule was considered quite affluent.

There was always the prospect of violence over marital disputes. In one episode which happened in the Delta during the 1930s and is still remembered today, a black sharecropper on the Woodburn plantation complained to his landlord that another black man had come to his house accusing him of trying to steal his wife. The landlord told his tenant to shoot the intruder on sight if he was bothered again. The tenant did precisely that the next time the man came around his house, then reported to the landlord. The punishment meted out by the landlord: get some cypress boards at the cotton gin, make a coffin for the dead man, and bury him on the plantation. The dead man's kin were warned not to seek reprisals or even the return of the body. In such a case of violence by one black man against another, the law took little or no interest and always deferred to the planter or white landlord, never intervening without his sanction.

After leaving Albert, Nora Ella King had two other husbands. Riley lived intermittently with her and his nominal stepfathers, but most of the time he lived with his maternal grandmother, El-nora Farr, who sharecropped on the land of Edwayne Henderson, a white dairy farmer in Kilmichael. During boyhood and early adolescence, his most formative years, his most vivid impressions and recollections which shaped his character in adult life were of fundamentalist religion, economic privation, and his mother's affection, abruptly denied him by her death when he was nine. These experiences left him in maturity with an addiction to hard work, an insatiable need for the approval of others, a heightened sense of morality, a dedication to the idea of fair play, and an idealized gossamer image of his mother as a symbol of goodness and human kindness.

One childhood episode suggests both the difficulty of his early circumstances and the way in which his mother came to stand symbolically for certain values. A neighbor had recently died, and to signal the end of their mourning, the dead man's family invited friends and relatives for a meal. The family was concerned about laying out an ample spread of dishes to show the world a good face despite the loss of a productive family member, and the guests were just as concerned about not taxing the weakened productivity of their hosts. In particular, Nora Ella worried that Riley, young and ravenous, would eat too much and would spoil the occasion.

She warned Riley, "When I give you a long, hard look like this, that's the signal to stop eating. After you see that look, stop— that's all." Then, apparently, she entirely forgot her instructions. Riley did not. For him the meal revolved around the imminent signal that was finally flashed unintentionally when Nora Ella happened to momentarily stare blankly into Riley's face—just as he checked her eyes for permission to begin eating the sweet potato pie that had come hot from the oven. In her blank face he saw the signal to stop. For several minutes, he studied the steaming pie intently; the table conversation drifted into a remote corner of his mind; he forgot everything but the pie. Potato pie was his favorite. He was not to be denied his pie. In a flash, the pie was down behind the bib of his overalls. No one saw him put it there. But it was there—the hot plate against the bare skin of his belly. It was too late to put it back—she was looking again. It was hot; scorching hot. Tears appeared in his eyes.

"What's the matter with you, child?" Nora Ella asked her son.

He stared at her, the tears still running. She took him aside from the table and repeated her question. Riley unfastened his suspenders and cradling the pie, he dropped the bib of his trousers. He gently took the pie plate away from his belly and with it came a neat circle of skin the same size as the plate. His mother looked, incredulous. When Riley explained that he had seen her signal and so he had stuffed the pie in his trousers, she was shaken and apologized strongly. The incident made a deep impression on Riley. An adult had apologized to him—a child not even nine years old. His mother had found her treatment of him unfair and had asked his forgiveness.

All Nora Ella's kin around Kilmichael were related by blood or marriage to one patriarchal figure: Pomp Davidson, Riley's great-grandfather, who had been born in slavery. By time Riley was old enough to remember him, Pomp was a gruff old man who rode a mule and carried a jug of homemade liquor in one hand

and a shotgun in the other. He was known to be prone to violence, a reputation that had its advantages. His landlord had the same reputation. "Mr. So-and-So and that nigger of his, Pomp Davidson, are just alike," people said of them. "They're both crazy. Don't mess with them 'cause you could get yourself killed."

Pomp Davidson's reputation as a "crazy nigger" was probably well deserved, but it served as a defense mechanism in a social order where there was no recourse to the law. For instance, there was the time that one of his granddaughters ran off from her husband after a quarrel and fled to the sanctuary of her own kin. As the ultimate head of the extended family, Pomp could not remain indifferent in case trouble should start. Trouble did start, but it wasn't trouble of the sort in the Woodburn plantation incident mentioned earlier. That kind of trouble Pomp could easily have handled by enforcing his granddaughter's decision with his shotgun.

But the estranged husband was cagy. He knew better than to show up at that crazy nigger's place alone. That might earn him a blast of buckshot. Instead he took his grievance to his own landlord who, in his capacity as paternal guardian over the interests of his tenants, was obliged to try helping the aggrieved man. Besides, the landlord had his own interests at stake: the feuding couple had a crop in his ground which needed all available hands to tend it. As far as he was concerned, Pomp Davidson's granddaughter was one of *his* niggers. Still, it would not be easy. Nothing short of a showdown could win the young woman's return to what they considered her rightful place: chopping cotton with her husband. The landlord, too, was no fool. He understood that showing up at Pomp's with his black tenant demanding the woman's return would challenge the authority of Pomp's landlord. Hence the high sheriff would have to be consulted. The trouble culminated when a party of three arrived at Pomp Davidson's place: the estranged husband, his landlord, and the high sheriff.

The high sheriff—"high" to distinguish him from his deputies —was the chief law enforcement officer of the area. Southern sheriffs of the time differed from their counterparts in the urban North and the Old West. In the North, the sheriff generally took a subordinate role to the police in law enforcement. The frontier sheriff of the Old West was employed mainly to protect the permanent interests of the community against the highly mobile, often desperate opportunists who roamed the vast countryside. It was the frontier sheriff's job to see that local cattlemen, merchants, mine owners, and saloon keepers were not pillaged by saddle tramps, rustlers, and armed gangs. In the 1930s, the Deep South was more primitive than the urban North and had a social order not nearly as freewheeling as that of the frontier West of the previous century. The high sheriff in Mississippi was chiefly responsible for maintaining the social order (the race-caste system) protecting vested interests (landowners principally), enforcing the law (Jim Crow included), and seeing to it that no nigger trouble got out of hand. The situation was ticklish—to say the very least—when the party of three came to Pomp's place looking for the rebellious wife.

First, the high sheriff checked with Pomp's landlord. "Don't go down there high-handing him, if you know what's good for you," he advised, then gave his permission for the intruders to go ahead. The aggrieved husband and his landlord waited at a safe distance while the sheriff went on. Pomp was not around, but the sheriff found the woman at home. But soon the husband lost his patience and joined them, his boss following, to join the fray. The woman refused to return to her husband, who for his part refused to leave without her and insisted that she be taken by force. The husband's landlord, and in turn the sheriff, would have no part in kidnapping her, as the husband proposed.

Then Pomp arrived on the scene. He took his granddaughter inside the cabin to hear her side of the story in private. Arguments broke out in every direction. Then Pomp appeared in the door, shotgun in hand.

"She ain't goin'," he said, jabbing the air with his gun muzzle. "She ain't goin'. That's all there is to it. She ain't goin'." The situation was near the flash point and might well have ended in violence had not Pomp's landlord appeared and broken the spell, allowing tempers to cool. Negotiations began again with the two white landlords as advocates and the high sheriff as arbiter. They arrived at a compromise which, although not fully satisfactory to any of the black parties, was sufficient to resolve the immediate crisis while protecting the interests of the white landlords. According to the compromise, Pomp's granddaughter would remain there with Pomp and her kin, the intruders would leave empty-handed, and then, after a face-saving grace period, she would return to her husband and finish raising the crop they had in the ground.

Religion was an important part of young Riley's environment both psychologically and musically. Both his mother and grandmother were pious, prayerful women, good Christians and church members. They were both Baptists, though they belonged to different sects. But the biggest impact on young Riley came from the Holiness Church near Kilmichael where his uncle's brother-in-law was a Sanctified preacher.

Archie Fair was called "Sanctified" because he preached the message of the Pentecost. In the story of the Pentecost, Jesus and His disciples were gathered together praying when the Holy Spirit descended on them; tongues of fire flickered above their heads, and they began speaking unknown languages. The Pentecostalists took this as the ideal of spiritual fulfillment. To be thus filled with the Holy Spirit was to be Sanctified, and hence briefly united with the Spirit of God. Holiness Church services, besides being worship services, were also part séance and part conjuring act as the preacher would try to bring the Spirit into the congregation and perhaps actually into the hearts and souls of some individual members of the congregation.

Music was the Sanctified preacher's principal means for bringing the Spirit and the congregation together—loud, foot-stomping, emotionally charged, ferocious, overpowering music sung with complete abandon by the entire congregation, led by the preacher and often accompanied by guitars and piano. Pentecostal churches varied according to how far they carried their message. In some such churches, the faithful would simply shout and sing their praises to the Lord, whereas in others the Holy Spirit would seem to take control over individuals in the congregation who would shake, dance, and throw themselves against the floor, the pews, or their brethren. Those so completely filled by the Spirit acted as if possessed by an external will and had to be restrained to prevent injury. The Pentecostal sect called the Holy Rollers was known for this kind of ecstatic worship.

Another part of Pentecostal worship was the religious experience called glossolalia, or speaking in tongues. When one of the faithful spoke in tongues, it would sound like some unknown foreign language. The Spirit takes control of the tongue and vocal cords of the faithful and speaks to the congregation through the host's mouth. The preacher at the Pentecostal service is a sort of medium who by half-singing, half-shouting, and in some cases strumming a guitar, leads the congregation and controls the energy dynamics of the group in successive surges of higher and higher energy. The services gave the faithful complete catharsis, and they came away feeling purified and Sanctified.

Riley's uncle, William Pullian, was married to Archie Fair's sister. Riley often went to Archie's services, sometimes with his mother, sometimes with his grandmother. Riley had an unusually strong voice for a boy, and he sang with special feeling that made him a star of the congregation. He became the piston in the engine Archie Fair stoked on Sunday mornings at the Holiness Church near Kilmichael, Mississippi. The sound of Preacher Fair's electric guitar and Riley's clear, strong, poignant voice never failed to conjure the spirit feeling. The important fact for Riley's later development as a blues singer was the experience he had while still a boy of eight or ten of leading people in a group purge of worldly troubles. Often, after the services at the Holiness Church, Archie Fair went to visit his sister at William Pullian's house. Then Riley would have a chance to fiddle with the Sanctified preacher's guitar which was left on his uncle's bed. He was mesmerized by Archie's polyrhythmic strumming and tried to imitate it. Archie taught him the E, A, and B chords basic to all gospel and blues music. While his singing came to him naturally, trying to coax the instrument to give up its secrets was hard, frustrating work. But he was hooked. B.B. King's first musical debt is to Sancified Preacher Archie Fair.

In the summer of 1935, Nora Ella sent word to her mother to bring nine-year-old Riley from Kilmichael to where she was living at French Camp a dozen miles away. She was ill and wanted the comfort of having Riley nearby. A doctor visited her and found her jaundiced and anemic. Her strength waned. After roughly two weeks she realized her time was short and she summoned Riley to her bedside.

Psychologists tell us that emotionally powerful experiences in childhood, such as the sight of one parent beating another, the return of a long-absent parent, or the death of a family member, can be a strong influence on our behavior over the course of a lifetime. Whether Riley King's deathbed scene with his mother had such an impact on him is difficult to say for certain. However, there can be no doubting its dramatic tragic quality or the deep, vivid, and lasting impression it made on him—one he carries today as if it happened yesterday.

The dying Nora Ella told Riley that she would be leaving him very soon. Most important, she told him, he should not forget what she had tried to teach him, namely that if he was always kind to his fellow human beings, his kindness would never fail to bring him good in his life, even in cases where the person who benefited from his kindness made no effort to repay it. Riley took this moral precept that the milk of human kindness was the key to fulfillment as his guiding principle of life. Later he broadened it to a belief that striving to meet a high moral standard is the best attitude toward life, and later broadened it further still to apply to all standards moral and otherwise. (Sometimes this principle has boomeranged.)

When Nora Ella died later the same day, the hearse was summoned to carry her body away for embalming and dressing. In the evening, the body was returned to her home and laid out on the cooling board for viewing. The body was waked all night. The hearse returned in the daytime, her body put into a coffin and carried to the graveyard at Pinkney Grove for burial.

The scene at Nora Ella's deathbed as B.B. King described it is strikingly close to the opening scene in Somerset Maugham's classic story *Of Human Bondage,* which was, in turn, a close variant of the death of Maugham's own mother. Maugham's own experience and that of his fictional alter ego, Philip Carey—the abrupt and tragic denial of maternal affection—were the key to the adult character of the men who were called to their mothers' bedsides hours before their mothers died. By B.B.'s own appraisal, the experience of his mother's death was important to his world view, if not dominant in shaping his character.

BLACK SCHOOLMASTER

After his mother's death, Riley lived with his grandmother, Elnora Farr, in Kilmichael. During the winter months, he attended the Elkhorn School, a one-room schoolhouse maintained by the Elkhorn Primitive Baptist Church. The wooden frame building stood in a clearing beside the Elkhorn Church on a knoll behind a swamp. A third building, a two-hole privy, occupied the clearing, and beyond the church was a graveyard with a handful of simple headstones and several dozen tiny iron placards for grave markers. The schoolhouse itself was maintained entirely by contributions from the families of attending children. There was one teacher for the fifty-odd students, grades 1 through 8, a black man named Luther Henson, the son of a slave. The sole state and county support for the school consisted of Henson's $25 a month salary.

Luther Henson was a remarkable man and had a profound effect on Riley King. He managed somehow to give young Riley a positive self-image, get him hooked on the idea of self-improvement, and give him an optimistic idea of his prospects in life, which was no small accomplishment when dealing with an orphaned black boy in Mississippi in the 1930s. Luther Henson was the twentieth of twenty-one children, born September 26, 1899, the son of Syrus B. Henson who was twenty-eight years old when the Emancipation Proclamation declared him a free man. Syrus Henson understood that owning land was crucial to establishing the black man's new status and therefore bought 120 acres around Kilmichael in the 1860s. When he died in 1909, he was able to leave all his surviving children with some land to call their own. Luther, the next to youngest, was determined to raise himself through education. His determination to better himself was strengthened by the deaths of two sisters from pellagra, a form of malnutrition; he carried one sister to the madhouse in Jackson, Mississippi, before she died. He wanted desperately to attend high school and college, but his only source of income was farming and that left little more than subsistence. He settled for correspondence courses from Rusk College in Holly Springs, Mississippi, a Methodist-sponsored black college. When he was twenty years old, he took the job teaching at the Elkhorn School, and his formal education stopped.

The school season lasted only during the five or six months between harvest and planting. During the other months, anyone old enough for school worked at making a crop. As many as sixty children jammed the one-room Elkhorn School, where Henson juggled eight grades at once. Besides the basic skills of reading, writing, and arithmetic, Henson tried to educate his pupils in practical skills that would improve their lot in life and social ideas that would build self-esteem and a positive idea of being black. He taught self-sufficiency and prudent management of one's own resources however meager they might be. He held out economic independence as a worthy goal. To fight malnutrition, he told his students how vitally important it was to plant fruit trees and taught them how to can the fruit; he encouraged them to raise chickens and hogs, a practice discouraged by some white landlords who considered livestock a distraction from their tenants raising cotton, and showed them how to preserve meat with salt. Henson preached positive racial identity decades before dark-skinned people called themselves "black" and before words like "black pride" and "black power" had entered the American vocabulary. He showed his pupils copies of *The Black Dispatch,* a weekly newspaper covering black affairs published in Oklahoma City, Oklahoma by Roscoe Dungee. In *The Black Dispatch,* which sold for a nickel a copy, Henson's classes saw photographs of black personalities like Louis Armstrong and Joe Louis. For Riley King and most of his classmates, this was the first time they had seen black faces in the newspapers anywhere except on the crime page. Henson told his class about black musicians of the time, like Roland Hayes and Buddy Johnson, and read aloud the poetry and prose of black authors Harriet Tubman, Phillis Wheatley and Druscila Houston.

Henson believed rightly or wrongly that some whites in the area resented his efforts to raise up the young black people in his class and though he was never threatened or harassed, he lived in constant fear of reprisal. It is easy to see how he would be afraid for his life since violence against blacks was common, and self-righteous whites had little to fear from the law for imposing their ideas of social justice, however bizarre, on local blacks, even if they included terror tactics.

Luther Henson's impact on young Riley is hard to gauge precisely, but B.B. credits Henson as a major influence in building his character. As an adult, B.B. has many of the traits Henson tried to cultivate; most conspicuous among these is his great enthusiasm for self-improvement programs running from speed reading to flying lessons, and at least one trait which he may have gotten unintentionally from his old teacher, namely, the tendency to see his lack of higher education as a kind of character defect.

When word reached Albert King of the death of his former wife Nora Ella, he became concerned about what had become of his son Riley. Albert had remarried and moved to Lexington, Mississippi, where he was working as a tractor mechanic. He had children by his new wife, who had been a child of thirteen when she married Albert. With no phone and no car, it was not easy for him to check on Riley. Months passed before he found someone to lend him a car for the trip. When at last he found Riley, Albert told him he could come to Lexington and join the new King family anytime he decided he was ready. But Riley was reluctant to leave Kilmichael because he would have to leave Luther Henson's school, and the new gospel singing group he had started together with a cousin, Birkett Davis, and a schoolmate, Walter Doris, Jr. So he stayed on in Kilmichael, singing and going to school.

Riley absorbed the legacy of the race-caste system of the Old South. Jim Crow was a real person to young Riley in much the same way that Santa Claus is real to other children, and the Mason-Dixon line was a boundary beyond which lay a land where Jim Crow had no say in how blacks lived. His elders schooled him in how to talk to whites (always with deference and extreme courtesy) and how to do business with them (never questioning their authority or honesty, always striving to please). Perhaps owing to Henson's influence, the Jim Crow code of conduct was little burden and no badge of shame; in fact, as an adult B.B. even took parts of it—elaborate courtesy and heroic efforts to please one's employees—as models for human relations, regardless of race. Some grown-ups around him preached that the prevailing social order was divinely ordained, that some people were destined to serve others. This and other religious notions, like the account of the origin of man given in Genesis, he rejected; his efforts to discuss religion critically with his elders were treated as impiety, and he became a private sceptic on matters of doctrine.

WORKING ON HALVES WITH THE MAN

During his time in Kilmichael after his mother's death, Riley lived with his grandmother on a farm owned by Edwayne Henderson, whose own grandmother had come to Mississippi from North Carolina before the Civil War in an ox-drawn wagon driven by her slave, Syrus Henson, teacher Luther Henson's father. Edwayne Henderson operated a dairy farm with a herd of thirty or forty cows. In addition, he raised some corn and hay on his spread of a few hundred acres, and raised cotton on fifty-odd acres farmed by seven or eight sharecropping families including Elnora Farr (Riley's grandmother), Mimy Stells (his aunt) and William Pullian (his uncle, married to the sister of Archie Fair, the Sanctified preacher). Cotton, in both the Delta and the hills, was farmed by one of four types of labor: sharecroppers, share tenants, cash tenants, and day-wage laborers. Under the sharecropping system, a landowner would provide the sharecropper with an allotment of land (5 to 10 acres depending on the platoon of labor the sharecropper could field with his family), free housing, water and wood for heat, farming tools and usually, but not always, space for a vegetable garden and small livestock. In return, the sharecropper raised and harvested the crop on his land allotment and shared the cost of seed and fertilizer, ginning and baling (if the crop was cotton), with the landlord. The landlord and sharecropper split the proceeds from selling the crop, 50-50. Most sharecroppers were black, penniless, and landless, owning nothing but the clothes they stood up in. To support them while they worked raising the crop, the landlord customarily advanced them a monthly living allowance, called a "furnish," and paid all the expenses for seed, fertilizer, ginning, and baling. When the crop was sold, the landlord deducted the sharecropper's share of these expenses, plus interest in some cases, from the sharecropper's half of the proceeds. If the harvest was poor because of drought or flooding, the sharecropper might end the season just breaking even or, even worse, owing the landlord money. When that happened, the sharecropper might be forced to take an additional loan from the landlord to tide him over the winter months. (The first furnish was usually doled out in the spring, in March or April.) The result for many sharecroppers was a hopeless spiral of debt which left them bound to the landlord. It was the plight of the landless, and it left them in bondage to the land.

The share tenant was in a better position than the sharecropper. Share tenants—or "fourth tenants"—supplied all the labor and equipment, including mules and/or horses to work the land, plus 100 per cent of the cost of seed and three-fourths of the expenses for fertilizer, ginning and baling, and received in exchange three-fourths of the price the crop brought after harvest, plus free housing for their families, and working livestock as well as water and wood.

Cash tenants rented the land outright for a flat rate which covered housing, wood and water; they received all 100 per cent of the proceeds from the crops.

Riley's kin were sharecroppers on the Henderson farm. Edwayne Henderson was no Simon Legree, but rather a God-fearing farmer who worked as hard as his sharecroppers and took an abiding, paternal interest in their welfare. Like them he was often forced to borrow money to get his crops in the ground, and like them he was at the mercy of the weather; but unlike them he could borrow from the bank, mortgaging his land to finance the next crop. The land had been in the Henderson family since the 1800s, except for a brief period in the 1920s, when it passed into other hands with a provision for buying it back. Riley's kin could mortgage only their labor.*

While he lived with his grandmother, Riley worked with her raising cotton on the few acres allotted her. He was not paid either by her or Henderson; children were expected to contribute their labor without pay. Grandmother Farr was allotted a furnish of only $5 which was not easy to stretch over a month, even in those days when $1 bought a new pair of shoes.†

Henderson kept meticulous records of all his transactions; on a separate page in his ledger, he recorded the details pertaining to each of his sharecroppers for each year. According to his ledger, Elnora Farr drew $30 furnish between March 1, 1939 and the harvest in September of that year; her share of the three bags of fertilizer for her crop came to $4.61; her account was credited twice, one credit for $10.00 (no date) marked "Bank," signifying that Henderson borrowed the money from the bank to lend to her, and one credit marked "cridit [sic] acct" for $25.27, leaving her with a net balance for the season of 66 cents. The $25.27 credit is probably her share of the proceeds from selling the cotton which she and Riley had raised, and the other $10 may also be crop proceeds, but given the round sum it is

---

* The situation is reflected in the lyrics of primal Delta bluesman Robert Johnson who sang, "She's got a mortgage on my body and a lien on my soul."

† For photostats of the original Henderson farm records pertaining to Elnora Farr and grandson Riley, refer to the photo section following page 224.

more likely that it was wages for working for the Hendersons. In November she drew an advance of $1 and in December an additional $7, plus 5 cents for some lemons, 10 cents for lamp oil and 30 cents for wicks. Not only was she sliding into debt, she was in poor health. She was coughing blood, and her strength was low. She paid 10 cents for some pills and 20 cents for a bottle of "black draught," a popular health tonic. When her condition worsened a physician was summoned; Henderson paid the doctor and charged her account $8 for the visit(s). On January 15, 1940, Elnora Farr died, probably of tuberculosis. Henderson paid the Lee Funeral Home $5 for preparing her body for burial and charged her account accordingly. In May 1940, he received a check from the U. S. Government as part of the federal farm support program which applied to her crop of 1939, credited her account $18.12 accordingly, and closed the account with the word "Died" written across the lower part of the page. Elnora Farr died owing her landlord, Edwayne Henderson, $3.63.

Riley King was now more alone than ever. His uncle, William Pullian, and his aunt, Mimy (Jemima) Stells, both sharecropped on the Henderson place, but his aunt had an invalid husband, and his uncle a crowded house. Both relatives were in debt to Henderson. The prior year had produced an exceptionally poor crop and Pullian, who began the year owing $110.70, earned only $21.48 for his share of crop sales, ending the year $125.35 in debt. Mimy Stells began 1940 owing $8.31. Riley, now fourteen, stayed in his grandmother's cabin and in the spring accepted Edwayne Henderson's offer of the use of 1 acre of land to raise a cotton crop and drew his first $2.50 furnish on March 1, 1940.

For the five months of March through July, Riley drew a total furnish of $12.50. In June, Henderson bought Riley a pair of trousers and a wrench and charged his account $1 and 50 cents, respectively, for the two items. Sometime between July 1 and September interest at 8 per cent was debited; 40 cents was charged for 3 yards of cotton sack material at picking time; $4 credit entered "by work across canal," and $1 credited "by work." An undated unspecified debit of $1.20 follows—perhaps a second interest charge of 8 per cent on the subtotal rounded off to $15. On November 9 a credit of $4.18 was entered in Riley's account for his share of cotton sold. Net for 1940: $7.54 debt. Henderson closed the account with the notation "Paid in full by Rental

Check [Federal Farm Support]." In the fall of 1940, fifteen-year-old Riley moved to Lexington, Mississippi, in the Delta to live with his father.‡

Riley lived with his father and his new family for two years until 1942, when, age sixteen and heartsick for his gospel group and the Elkhorn School, he rode his bicycle the fifty-odd miles from Lexington to Kilmichael. He arrived in rags, a waif. Flake Cartledge, a white cash tenant in Kilmichael, who once had employed Riley's mother for day labor, heard about his plight and sent for him. Cartledge, an uncle of Henderson, bought Riley new clothes and fixed up a shed near his house as a dwelling for him. For the next year, Riley, age sixteen, lived with the Cartledge family, sharing their table and working for his keep.

Flake Cartledge's generosity and sense of justice made a deep impression on him. "Mr. Flake," as Riley called him, seemed blind to racial distinctions. Riley never heard him use the word "nigger" or even the white Southern locution "negra," and it seemed to Riley that Cartledge was visibly uncomfortable around others who did. He never called Riley "boy," but rather called him either by his first name or simply "son." Both Riley and Wayne, Cartledge's nine-year-old son, had daily chores tending the ten cows and five acres each of corn and cotton raised on the farm; both went to school. Riley walked to the Elkhorn School, a bus carried Wayne to the all-white school maintained by the county. Flake Cartledge himself was an ordinary man, except, possibly, for his ideas on race; he was deeply religious, like most of his neighbors, and worked long hours, running a road grader for the county, maintaining the dirt roads that crisscrossed the hills around Kilmichael. For Riley, his benefactor, the white cash-tenant farmer Flake Cartledge, became a model of the just man. The fact that he had any such figure to focus on is, in itself, remarkable when taken together with his circumstances in life and the social landscape he looked out on as he arrived at age sixteen.

During 1942 alone, three black men were lynched in Mississippi, two of them fourteen-year-old boys; and between 1885 and 1925, there were 530 men lynched in Mississippi, over 90 per

‡ For a tabular summary of the Henderson records for Riley's sundry kin and a detailed portrait of Henderson in retirement, plus a discussion of the morality of sharecropping refer to Appendix I: Requiem for Jim Crow, p. 183.

cent of them black. Besides the cases of flagrant mob lynching of the accused, which by the 1930s were uncommon, there were other clandestine acts of violence against blacks; cases where a black man would disappear only to be found months later at the bottom of a pond tied to a large-blade fan discarded from a cotton gin. Investigations of such crimes were cursory, at best. To these cases of open, defiant murder of blacks by lynch mobs, and the clandestine murders of blacks by night riders must be added the harsh penalties inflicted on blacks by the law. Not all high sheriffs were cruel, but, whether benign or malicious, they could use their authority with impunity in treating blacks, and cases of blacks committing violent crimes against whites especially the crime of rape, were adjudicated with medieval vengeance. Among Riley's vivid childhood memories was the sight of a black man's body electrocuted by the State of Mississippi and placed out on the courthouse steps for public viewing, his normally light brown skin turned dark by the electricity that had killed him.

This was the social landscape that Riley King saw stretching out ahead of him. As a black man he was poor, landless, disenfranchised, and subject to arbitrary violence without the protection of the law. Growing up without bitterness and despair, finding some ground for optimism, and building a positive self-image not fraught with shame were difficult at best and near impossible for many. When Riley decided to leave the Cartledge farm at the end of 1942 and move down to the Delta to look for work, his character had grown under the combined influence of three people: Archie Fair, the Sanctified preacher, who taught him how to spellbind people with soul-stirring music and lead them in group catharsis transcending their worldly cares; Luther Henson, who gave him a positive self-image as a black man and hooked him on self-improvement; and Flake Cartledge, who stood for the just man. Despite all his troubles, life had not dealt Riley such a bad hand after all.

DOWN IN THE DELTA: PLANTATION PLOWBOY

Birkett Davis, Riley's cousin and former singer with Riley's gospel group before Birkett left Kilmichael, told Riley about the better cotton farming down in the Delta and the day wages available there when he visited him at the Cartledge place in 1942. In the back of his mind, Riley was thinking about forming a new and better singing group with cousin Birkett. He had bought a guitar from a Kilmichael man, Denzil Tidwell, for $2.50 borrowed from Flake Cartledge, and continued singing spirituals with his chum Walter Doris, Jr., who often came to his cabin. In the winter of 1942–43, he wrote to Cousin Birkett asking him to help him move to the Delta. His cousin came to the rescue in a borrowed car, carrying sufficient cash to pay what Riley owed Flake Cartledge. In the spring of 1943, not quite eighteen years old, Riley moved to Indianola, Mississippi, in the heart of the Delta.

The Delta was just coming into its full power as one of the richest agricultural regions in the world. Most of the Delta was reclaimed from swampland, canebrakes, and pine forests. In the first third of the nineteenth century, it had been a wilderness; only a small portion was arable. Now, in the middle third of the twentieth century, the land was cleared, the swamps dried up, and the danger of flooding greatly reduced by work under the Flood Control Act of 1928, which diverted the Mississippi River in many places to eliminate the tortuous crooks and loops. The shortened river deepened its bed, lowering the water level by up to seven to fifteen feet. By 1943, when Riley came looking for work, a majority of Delta acres were in crops, and most of it was in cotton.

Riley got work with an Indianola planter, Johnson Barrett, who owned slightly less than 350 acres and rented more than he owned, for a total of around 1,000 acres under cultivation. This was a modest operation, hardly qualifying to fit the romantic image of the plantation as an empire of 2,000 acres or more spreading out for miles in every direction from the pillared manse. The Barrett plantation was a farm, larger than the average (56 per cent of all Delta farms of the time were less than 80 acres), but considerably smaller than the truly large plantations of 2,000 acres and more which controlled 21.5 per cent of the arable Delta land. Barrett was called a "planter" by custom, but that name calls up images quite different and less appropriate than does the term "farmer," which pictures him in bib overalls rather than wearing a white suit and holding a mint julep on the manor porch. The plantation in Indianola, comprised of four contiguous tracts bought from four different owners in 1936, was not the first attempt by Barrett to establish a substantial farm in Mississippi. In the years before, he had twice gone broke; and a third time, in 1935, he had been burned out of his house in Philip, Mississippi.

Working the Barrett plantation in Indianola were roughly fifty families, all but two of them farming on shares—the other two were cash tenants—plus six tractors and six mule teams. All these were under the direction of a black man, Booker Baggett, who had started working for Barrett in 1940 as a tractor driver. Baggett had worked his way up to a position of responsibility unprecedented for a black man in that area of the Delta. When Barrett fired his nephew for mismanaging the little general store he kept on the plantation to provide for the families farming his land, Barrett went out to the field and called his top hand, Baggett, off the tractor and told him to take over running the store. Inside two months, Baggett brought the store into the black, and Barrett was so impressed that he promoted him to plantation manager. Both the pay—$2.50 a day—plus housing, food, and an automobile, and the responsibility were unheard of for a black man at the time. His responsibility went far beyond what was ordinarily given to the black "straw boss," also known as the H.N.I.C. for "Head Nigger In Charge." He kept the plantation accounts and was authorized to do all hiring and firing, to make withdrawals from the bank, and to charge equipment and materials with local merchants. Often whites came on the plantation and refused to take Baggett's word that he was the boss—only to be sent back to him by Barrett who told them unequivocally, "Booker's in full charge." It took a cool hand on Baggett's part to handle such people when they came back with their feathers ruffled.

Like his benefactor in Kilmichael, Flake Cartledge, Riley's new employer, planter Johnson Barrett, was an ordinary man in most regards, with a few progressive ideas about race. Barrett was a plain-spoken, self-made man who was easily irritated by what he considered needless mistakes, and expected his employees to work with unflagging strength and no complaints. He took an abiding interest in the welfare of his employees, and was known to write off the debts of his sharecroppers in bad years At the same time, some tenants believed that in good years Barrett gave them less than the true market price he received for their share. According to one employee, who saw Barrett's record books, their suspicions were well founded. Among blacks in the Indianola area, Johnson Barrett was reputed to be unusually liberal for the time, yet no saint either.

Fifteen and twenty years before Riley arrived in Indianola, two events took place that profoundly changed plantation management, and had a subtle but important effect on his life personally. These were the mass production and marketing of row tractors by International Harvester, begun in 1922, and the design of a moistened-spindle mechanical cotton picker. These two machines— the row tractor and the mechanical cotton picker—changed cotton farming from a labor-intensive to a capital-intensive business, and abolished small-plot sharecropping by hand. The change took thirty years to accomplish, and Riley arrived at the Barrett plantation just as the swing was gathering momentum.

Riley worked on the Barrett plantation as both a sharecropper and a tractor driver, for which he was paid day wages of $1. As a tractor driver, he had a skill—albeit a modest one—though less modest in those days than it is now. He no longer worked with his muscle alone. Moreover, he was especially good with his machine and became highly valued by both Barrett and Booker Baggett. Before many months had passed, Riley had a crop in the ground, a skilled job working for a tough, fair-minded farmer under a black man, a new singing group, and a sweetheart. The singing group was a five-man chorus including Riley and cousin Birkett, led by John Matthews. They called themselves "The Famous St. John Gospel Singers" and patterned themselves after well-known groups like The Famous Golden Gate Quartet, The Trumpeteers, and The Dixie Hummingbirds. Riley accompanied them on his guitar when they sang at dozens on dozens of local churches. Occasionally, they gave live performances broadcast on WGRM in Greenwood, Mississippi. Meanwhile, Riley was moonlighting on his spiritual music by playing blues on street corners Saturday nights. (Blues was not a new musical interest for him; he had listened to blues records back in Kilmichael and had heard bluesman Bukka White, his mother's cousin, when Bukka came on rare occasions to visit his kin in Kilmichael.) He discovered that by using his weekly wage as traveling money to go to other Delta towns and cities, he could double or triple his net profit working the streets, singing blues and playing his guitar. His profits singing blues, plus his exposure to many leading blues and jazz musicians who played in Indianola, turned his musical interest away from spirituals.

Indianola was a main stop on the network of roadhouses and juke joints that dotted the landscape of the Deep South. The local joint there was run by Johnny Jones and called simply "Jones' Night Spot." At Jones', he saw Sonny Boy Williamson, Robert "Junior" Lockwood, and Louis Jordan, to name a few of the leading black musicians that passed through on the "chitlin circuit," as it was called. He managed to strike up an acquaintance with some of them and became afflicted with the malaise that strikes every provincial youth who comes in contact with highly mobile outsiders: envy of their sophisticated ways, their style of dress and, in this case, their musical proficiency and versatility. Riley's feet began to itch, his ears to burn, his heart to pound. He began practicing blues in earnest, listening to recordings purchased from a local fix-it shop proprietor named Willie Dotson. From the very first his taste was eclectic, running a spectrum from old-style bluesman Blind Lemon Jefferson to the pioneering jazz guitarist, Charlie Christian.

In 1943, soon after coming to Indianola, Riley registered for the draft and in 1944 was called to Camp Shelby for his physical exam. He stayed several days before being pronounced physically fit for service and allowed to return home. Johnson Barrett was short of hands then and was concerned that he not lose a good tractor driver; he told Riley he would apply to the draft board for an occupational deferment on his behalf and advised him that getting married would improve his chances of being deferred. Riley promptly married his sweetheart, Martha Denton, on November 26, 1944. He was nineteen; she was slightly younger. Riley's deferment as an employee in an essential industry was granted, and Riley and his new bride moved in with cousin Birkett Davis. Like millions of other men of draft age, Riley faced the alternative of remaining at his job—like it or not—or facing the draft. It was an unpleasant predicament for many, but people accepted such unpleasant circumstances as normal for wartime and not an injustice made especially for them. Riley's case was no different from the cases of steelworkers in Pittsburgh or doctors, providing medical care over vast remote areas of the country, except in one respect: he was a sharecropper, now obliged by the conditions of his deferment to go on sharecropping for the duration of the war. At times he felt that his status was little different than that of the convict laborers employed in public works projects, though he realized his conditions were dramatically better than those poor souls. It might never occur to the deferred steelworker in Pittsburgh and the G.P. in Idaho that they were indentured servants; but to black sharecroppers in Mississippi, deferment from the draft sometimes looked like a degenerate form of slavery.

While he waited out the war, Riley's musical ambition grew steadily, fueled by the radio programs he heard broadcast from Memphis. At this time, there still was no major radio station in the country that tailored its programming to black audiences, but stations KFFA in Helena, Arkansas, KWEM in West Memphis, Arkansas, and WHBQ in Memphis, Tennessee, had occasional programs of black music, usually performed live in the radio studio or at talent night on the stage of one Memphis theater or another. When he was released from the hold of selective service, Riley tried vigorously to convince the St. John's Gospel Singers to leave Indianola in search of fortune. Soon it became clear that if he was to make the break, it would have to be alone; his singing partners had families and worried, with good reason, that their children might suffer from their ambitions if they joined Riley on the road. Martha King, Riley's wife, had suffered a miscarriage and they were still childless.

When Riley boasted of his musical ambitions to the other tractor drivers on the Barrett plantation, Booker Baggett baited him: "You'll never do any of those things, Riley, so long as the earth stands."

"Mr. Booker," Riley replied, "someday I'm going to drive up in a brand-new car and give you a dollar. Then you'll know I wasn't jivin' when I said I'd do these things."

Memphis stood as a beacon. It was a main center of black entertainment in America; more active, perhaps, even than New Orleans, and unlike New Orleans to the south, it was a stepping stone to the North. Memphis, only 120 miles north of Indianola, must have seemed as though it was off the edge of the earth to a young black man of twenty who had never set foot out of Mississippi. It stood there hounding him to come: the southernmost outpost of the elusive mysterious North, center for black nightlife, home of Beale Street, where the best bluesmen alive played in crowded dives.

In May 1946, around the time when his cousin Birkett and the other sharecroppers on the Barrett plantation drew their first furnish of the season, the final straw came Riley's way and sent him north. It happened on payday, when Riley put his tractor under the shed for the night. Impatient to get his pay, he bounded off the machine as it came to rest; but the hot engine gave a few extra churns, and the tractor lurched forward, knocking the tall exhaust stack against the edge of the roof and breaking it off. Realizing that planter Barrett would be furious, he dashed home, told Martha to move in with her relatives, that he was going straight to Memphis, slung his guitar over his back, and walked out to Highway 49 without collecting his pay. Along the way, he met a pal, Walter Kirkpatrick, and persuaded him to come along. Riley carried his guitar and had $2.50 in his pocket. Walter had half a sausage for the two of them. Riley had only the vaguest idea of what to do once in Memphis. His plan boiled down to one thing: find cousin Bukka. He had no address for bluesman Bukka White (who was actually his mother's cousin). In fact, he wasn't even positive Bukka was still living in Memphis. But that was where he'd last had word from him. Twenty years old, Riley King left the Barrett plantation, heading north up the Mississippi Delta, bound for Memphis.

III

Memphis Blues Boy

LIVING WITH BUKKA

THE FIRST PLACE Riley looked for Bukka was Beale Street, capital of black entertainment for the Middle South. Memphis is located on the Mississippi River at a point where three states—Mississippi, Tennessee, and Arkansas—converge, a natural focal point for culture and commerce, and Beale was the main strip for black entertainment. This hodgepodge of pawnshops, nightclubs, theaters, and cheap hotels ran twenty blocks east from the Tennessee bank of the Mississippi. Some of the best music in America was played on Beale; prostitution and gambling were not uncommon. Beale Park on the north side of the street, opposite the Club Handy, named after W. C. Handy, the "Father of the Blues," was a gathering place for itinerant musicians. Riley asked after Bukka there. He slept one night in a railroad car, another in an all-night gambling joint. It took a few days' legwork before he found him. Bukka took young Riley in and for the next ten months schooled the young tyro in the art of blues. Memphis was a shock to Riley, a cold bath on his ambition. On every corner he found musicians able to play every bit as well as he. Like most provincial youths, he imagined himself as pure murder in his craft —until he came to a place where the standards were as high as any on earth. Then he suffered a flipflop in his self-appraisal. He fell back on Bukka's help.

Riley listened carefully to Bukka's playing and they played together often, though never in public. Riley's playing improved dramatically and he profited from impromptu exchanges and street-corner jams with the dozens and dozens of musicians he met around Memphis. He profited in other ways, too, from his association with Bukka. Booker T. Washington White was a hard man, sceptical, even suspicious of his fellow man, and assertive. His abrasive exterior had been hardened by bitter experiences. When he was a young man, he was involved in a fracas in a Mississippi juke joint. Someone was killed and the police suspected Bukka. Rather than face Mississippi justice, he fled to Chicago. In Chicago he met record-company talent scouts who knew his music from Mississippi; they offered to record some of his songs, and he went to the studio to cut some sides. According to legend, while he sat in front of the microphone in a Chicago recording studio, the sheriff's deputies from Mississippi appeared, arrested him, and took him to the train bound for Mississippi. Eventually he landed in Parchman Farm, the Mississippi penal colony celebrated in many old blues songs. Parchman was an old-fashioned prison farm where the prisoners lived in barracks at night and worked by day on chain gangs, wearing striped prison clothes. After more than a year at Parchman, Bukka White was released, allegedly through the efforts of record-company officials who appealed to state officials to shorten his term.

Bukka had many things to offer Riley to prepare him for life as a bluesman. First, he was a highly personalized stylist. He seemed to have his own way of doing everything from picking up his instrument to phrasing lyrics, and all these personalized wrinkles fit together in a way that was seamless, despite the coarseness of the fabric. He was cocky, defiant, mischievous, charming in a rough sort of way, and delicate with his guitar, appearances to the contrary (he always seemed to assault it). Bukka possessed one quality that was indispensable to every bluesman: durability. Bukka was a survivor, if nothing else. Without durability, B.B. King would not have been possible. How much of these qualities—a sense of style and the capacity for survival—Riley acquired from his older second cousin is impossible to say, but some of them must have rubbed off on the twenty-year-old youngster, fresh from the Delta.

After ten months, Riley decided he was getting nowhere. Perhaps he had learned enough to hold his own in Beale Park, but he hadn't begun to make a career as yet. The responsibilities he had left behind in Mississippi troubled him, too. There was his wife to consider. Had he abandoned her, he wondered to himself. He owed Johnson Barrett some money, and he felt badly about that. This was evidently not his time to make it in Memphis. Partly out of frustration, partly out of a sense of responsibility, he reurned to Indianola to meet his obligations and prepare himself for another bid at Memphis.

IN 1947 Riley and his wife Martha raised a crop on the Barrett plantation. Riley drove tractor again for Booker Baggett. He continued with his music as energetically as ever and found opportunities to play with other musicians, local and itinerant. By now gospel music had taken a feeble second place to blues in his repertoire. His objective was to pay his debt to Barrett and save enough money to return to Memphis, where he would look for steady work as a musician and perhaps form a band of his own. In the spring of 1948 he planted another crop at Barrett's. Between his sharecropping, tractor driving at $22.50 a week, truck jockeying at the trucking depot in town, and street-corner guitar playing, he managed to make enough to leave Mississippi free and clear with a small stake for Memphis. In late 1948 he headed north again, determined to take Memphis by storm.

BLACK RADIO PIONEERS

Upon arriving in Memphis, Riley made straight for West Memphis, Arkansas, immediately across the Mississippi River from downtown Memphis, looking for Sonny Boy Williamson, who had a daily fifteen-minute radio program of live blues music on station KWEM. Sonny Boy was an accomplished bluesman who played mouth harp (harmonica) with a small band around the tri-state area (Tennessee, Arkansas, and Mississippi). His real name was Rice Miller, but he took the name "Sonny Boy Williamson" to identify himself with the late, legendary harmonica player of that name. Riley had met Sonny Boy (II) in Indianola and there had struck up a friendship with one of Sonny Boy's musicians, guitarist Robert "Junior" Lockwood, "stepson" of Robert Johnson, who more than any other single man was the founder of Delta blues.* Riley asked Sonny Boy to let him play one song on his show that day.

Sonny Boy was an old fox. He was in a bind and saw that Riley might be a way out. Earlier he had accepted bookings for two separate engagements on the coming weekend—as insurance against one of them canceling. Now it was beginning to look as though both saloonkeepers were going to expect him to live up to his conflicting commitments. "Let's hear what you can do," he told Riley. Riley played a song for Sonny Boy, who judged him fit for the air and, perhaps, fit for filling in on one of his conflicting gigs. When they went on the air, Sonny Boy introduced him as a promising new talent and asked the listeners to telephone the station if they liked the youngster's stuff. When the station was flooded with calls, Sonny Boy was in the position to call one of the two places where he was scheduled to play and offer in his stead a "new sensation" who had "burned up the phone wires" with listeners calling in to rave about his guest appearance on Sonny Boy's show. After calling Miss Annie, proprietress of The Sixteenth Street Grill, the poorer paying of his two gigs, he sent Riley over to her West Memphis saloon to work out the details. Miss Annie's saloon featured dancing and gambling on the side, which was legal then in West Memphis. She agreed to take Riley in place of Sonny Boy for the coming gig and, further, offered to make him the regular featured artist provided he could get a regular spot on the radio to plug his engagements there. It was beginning to look to Riley, barely a day in the Memphis area, that his timing was right now to get a start as a bluesman.

RILEY KING'S timing on his second bid for success in Memphis was even better than he appreciated and better yet than anyone could then have understood. A revolution in radio broadcasting was brewing. On June 7, 1947, a new radio station began broadcasting in Memphis with a meager output of 250 watts, licensed under the call letters WDIA. The station was owned by two white

* Lockwood's musical kinship to the legendary Delta blues singer is solid, but his familial connection with Johnson is tenuous. Actually, Lockwood's mother was not married to Robert Johnson. Today, at sixty-five, Lockwood remains active. His music can be heard on Trix Records and Rounder Records.

Memphians, John R. Pepper and Bert Ferguson, both experienced in broadcasting. Pepper handled the financial end of things, and Ferguson was in charge of managing the station, determining what listening audience the station would cater to and what character the station would try to project. Ferguson had worked for Memphis radio station WHBQ during the 1930s and had learned both the management problems of radio broadcasting and the makeup of listening audiences in the Memphis area. Initially, Ferguson chose a very conventional programming policy, which included only a smattering of black music. Like the other Memphis stations, WREC which broadcast from the Peabody Hotel, WMC, WHHM, and WNBR, Ferguson's WDIA played music tailored to white audiences. Some stations, like KWEM which gave Sonny Boy his daily fifteen-minute spot, had short segments devoted to jazz, blues, and gospel, but as yet there was not one truly black-oriented station in the entire United States. On radio stations around the country, Guy Lombardo and even Xavier Cugat were given more air play than Duke Ellington and Louis Jordan, and Kate Smith and Bing Crosby dominated airtime that gave irregular exposure to artists like Ella Fitzgerald and virtually none to the likes of, say Wynonie Harris.

In 1948 Bert Ferguson recognized that the neglected black audiences offered him a virgin commercial market and an opportunity to perform a community service hitherto entirely overlooked. First he hired Nat D. Williams, whom Ferguson had known at WHBQ in 1937 when Williams was emcee for a weekly talent show featuring amateur black musicians broadcast over WHBQ from the stage of the Palace Theater on Beale Street. He gave Williams his own show which first broadcast on October 25, 1948. When the engineer gave him his cue that opening night, Williams' mind went blank. Struck by the absurdity of the situation, he began to laugh and continued laughing until he regained his presence of mind; that laugh became his trademark known all over the tri-state area.

The audience response to Nat Williams, called "Professor" because he had once been a high school teacher, was strong and favorable and, contrary to the fears of some, few of the station's advertisers complained. Ferguson made a convincing case to existing and prospective advertisers that black people used other products besides hair straighteners and cheap wine and that whether their product was soft drinks or automobile tires, there were tens of thousands of black customers who could be persuaded to buy their brand, if their attention were held by the smooth blues of Jimmy Rushing and the fast chatter of Professor Nat Williams, and, if the pitchmen touted their brand in the idiom of black listeners in the area covered by WDIA's new 50,000-watt transmitter, they stood to reap a whirlwind. That audience stretched down the Mississippi River into the Delta and, atmospheric conditions permitting, WDIA was heard as far south as New Orleans. In a short time, Ferguson transformed WDIA into a black-staffed, black-managed organization. He hired a black station manager, Charles Scruggs, and a bevy of colorful, hip, slick-talking black disc jockeys including Theo Wade, A. C. Williams, Rufus Thomas (who became a rhythm and blues recording artist, best known for his hit "Walkin' the Dog"), and Maurice "Hot Rod" Hulbert, who went on to be one of the best known, most influential DJs in America.

There was no equivocation in setting the style of the station. When Rufus Thomas began working as a DJ, he tried first to imitate the deep, pear-shaped tones of the white announcers he was accustomed to on other stations. Program director David James Mattis chastised him vehemently for discarding the up-beat sassy style he used when hosting talent-night shows on the stages of several Beale Street theaters. He told Thomas to visualize his Saturday-night theater audiences while he stood before the studio microphone. After the transformation of the station was complete, Ferguson solidified his audience by distributing 40,000 flyers to the mailboxes of black neighborhoods in the Memphis area.

The station became more than an outlet for black music and a medium for advertisers to reach black markets; it became a clearing house for black community affairs. Not infrequently, long-lost relatives of Memphis families would appear at the WDIA offices, asking the station to announce their arrival over the air so that their families, whom they could not find at old addresses, would call in and give their new location. Lost-children and lost-pet announcements were a routine feature, given like time and temperature readings. Such services which would be taken for granted now were a revolution then simply because they were completely absent in black communities prior to WDIA.

After Miss Annie made her offer, Riley rode a local bus back across the Mississippi to Memphis and went to WDIA, which he knew by reputation as the "new black station." There he saw Nat Williams in the lobby. He had his guitar slung over his shoulder. The Professor asked him if he could be of assistance.

"I want to make a record," Riley replied, incredulous at his own answer. Williams called Ferguson out of his office.

"You play that thing?" asked the general manager. Riley looked a little perplexed until he remembered he had his guitar on his back. He promptly belted out a solid blues while accompanying himself. Ferguson thought he sounded unpolished, looked like a Delta bumpkin, but his voice was poignant and he had an earthy, wholesome air about him.

A brainstorm hit Ferguson. The station had just won an advertising acount for a health tonic called Pepticon, a new competitor for the widely known tonic, Hadacol, advertised by Sonny Boy Williams on KWEM, and he needed a show on which to hawk it. He gave Riley a daily ten-minute spot on which he could sing and play anything he liked. A jingle was composed for him to sing:

> Pepticon, Pepticon, sure is good
> You can get it anywhere in your neighborhood.

Riley King became the Pepticon Boy.

With the Pepticon program scheduled for daily airing, the job in West Memphis was his and he moved in upstairs at Miss Annie's. He played The Sixteenth Street Grill as a solo with no accompanying musicians. Miss Annie paid him $25 a week; he did the Pepticon show gratis for the chance to plug his West Memphis engagement. On weekends the sponsors of his radio spot used Riley to promote their product by driving a truck around residential areas of Memphis and West Memphis with Riley King, The Pepticon Boy, sitting atop the cab, playing and singing while someone sold bottles of the patent medicine off the back of the truck. Riley had a formula for modest success: he advertised his tavern gig on his radio show and vice versa. His fledgling career had a feedback mechanism in the two jobs. He sent word to Mississippi for Martha to join him.

The radio station recognized his growing popularity and expanded his radio program, converting him from a tonic peddler to a full-fledged DJ. His new show was called the "Sepia Swing

Club"; he played recordings by black musicians with both local and national followings, and during the final fifteen minutes, he played his guitar and sang requests called in by his listeners. Now that he was a DJ, he needed a catchy name that would give him an image and stick in the minds of his listeners, like "Hot Rod" Hulbert had. Variations based on Beale Street, the main symbol of blues, were bandied about; "Beale Street Blues Boy" won out. For a time, Riley King was billed as "The Beale Street Blues Boy"; it was a little clumsy, and it excluded his own proper name; later he was called "Blues Boy King"; finally that was shortened to "B.B. King."

With his spreading reputation came new offers to play around Memphis and small towns in the tri-state area. For these engagements, he needed a band to back him. He befriended a saxophonist, Richard Sanders, who introduced him to other Memphis musicians, including drummers Earl Forrest and Solomon Hardy, and pianists Ford Nelson and John Alexander. Robert "Junior" Lockwood, Sonny Boy Williamson's guitarist, agreed to gig with him. He had no set combination of musicians at first, but improvised according to their availability. For their part, the Memphis musicians found difficulty playing with him because inclined as he was to the freewheeling Delta style of solo musicians, he varied his tempos unpredictably, at will, and even added bars here and there to the standard twelve-bar blues form. From their standpoint, he was musically unschooled, and more than one of them wondered how such a rube straight off the plantation could be garnering so much attention. They tried gently to teach him how to play *with* his musicians rather than *against* them; some confessed privately their embarrassment at playing with him in public, he was so musically crude. But even these Memphis slickers had to admit he had something going for him because his popularity grew so steadily.

In 1949 B.B. King made his first recordings: four sides for the Bullet Recording and Transcription Company. Bullet was the brainchild of Jim Bulleit, a onetime broadcaster for CBS and Grand Ole Opry announcer over WSM in Nashville. Bulleit began his label when a distributor selling records to jukebox operators told him that the operators were crying for country music. Soon he branched out into the race-record market by starting a line of gospel records and one for blues called the Sepia series.

Scarcely a year in business he further diversified into mainstream pop and hit it big when a song called "Near You," the flip side of a record Bulleit was pushing very hard, took off and shot to the top of the charts where it remained number one for six months. Bulleit obtained B.B.'s recordings from Sam Phillips, who sold Bulleit a piece of his fledgling Memphis record label, Sun Records. Bulleit later sold back his interest in Sun to Phillips and Phillips became the godfather of rock-and-roll with his "Million Dollar Quartet" comprised of Carl Perkins ("Blue Suede Shoes"), Jerry Lee Lewis ("Whole Lot of Shakin'"), Johnny Cash, and Elvis Presley. Bulleit's best known R&B artist was blues shouter Wynonie Harris.

B.B.'s four sides for Bullet enhanced his local reputation but none attracted national attention. However, they did produce one highly favorable result by soliciting the interest of the Bihari brothers, Jules, Saul, and Joe, who controlled Modern Records, which eventually issued three labels: Kent, Crown, and RPM. In the summer of 1949, B.B. signed a contract with the Biharis to record for their forthcoming label, RPM. His association with the Biharis was to extend over the next ten years.

During the last six months of 1949, RPM released six B.B. King singles in quick succession. They were local best-sellers, further enhancing his reputation in the tri-state area, though none of these six made the national rhythm and blues charts. His radio appearances, the air play of his new record releases, and his public appearances continued to feed on each other. He built up a steady circuit of cabarets and roadhouses where he was the top attraction. These included "Slackbritches" in Birdsong, Arkansas, owned by Slackbritches Warrens, where B.B. King played every other Sunday; Dizzy Vance's "Club Casablanca" near Blyville, Arkansas on the Missouri side of the Arkansas/Missouri state line; Ned Edan's "Blue Flame" in Covington, Tennessee, a steady money maker for B.B. King every Saturday night. There were "Loftie's Place" in Summerville, Tennessee; "The White Swan" in Brinkley, Arkansas; "Black Willie's Place" in Osceola, Arkansas; "Stevens Lounge" in Jackson, Mississippi; and "Jones' Night Spot" back in B.B.'s hometown, Indianola, Mississippi. [On one return trip to Indianola, B.B. made good on his promise to Booker Baggett. Driving a new Chevrolet, B.B. found Baggett standing in the driveway of the Service Implement Company, jumped out, and, wearing a grin as wide as the grill on his new car, he reminded his former boss of his promise and gave him a crisp dollar bill.]

These places ran the gamut from tiny roadside hash houses, where two hundred people would cram into a space no bigger than a woodshed, to large dance halls, in which six or seven hundred customers jammed together. Prostitution was not common but gambling, both legal and illegal, thrived in this social milieu. One standard format on this circuit was the "Gamblers' Ball," an affair that ran two or three days, often nonstop, and drew professional gamblers from great distances because they knew that they could find high-stakes games at these affairs. The most popular card games were fast tempo draw games that allowed for sudden large wagers, games like "kotch balls" and "coon can." Craps was popular, too.

Growing success made B.B.'s business affairs more complex and fueled his ambition. This created an ever more urgent need for someone with experience in show business to look after his financial interests and guide his developing career. He was no star yet, but he was moving up fast and needed a manager. One man seemed to have his finger in every aspect of show business in Memphis: a Beale Street pool hall and shine parlor proprietor named Robert Henry. Robert Henry had done about everything there was to do in the night life of Memphis, save taking to the stage himself. He had been a ticket taker at the old Daisy Theater on Beale Street in 1911, when tickets were a nickel apiece. Later he was a promoter of shows at several Memphis theaters: the Harlem, the Ace, the Church Park, and others. He had connections with big-city booking agencies in the North and handled arrangements for appearances by such renowned musicians as Earl "Fatha" Hines, Duke Ellington, Fletcher Henderson, and Fats Waller. He was also the "walking delegate" for the musicians' union, though not himself a musician; as walking delegate, he collected the dues visiting musicians were expected to pay to the local for performing on its territory. Over the years, he operated a number of businesses: a record shop, an amusement park, a few restaurants. His wife ran a small hotel on Beale Street which catered to itinerant musicians. Henry was a good-natured, smooth-talking businessman with a shrewd nose for what would please Memphis audiences and a soft heart for musicians. He was a man who always had a small percentage of every corner of the action, but by dint of character was destined never to make a big killing. In his lifetime, two nascent stars passed through his mitts. He signed one—the scrawny Delta blues singer, B.B. King—to a personal-management contract. He gave short shrift to the other: a surly-looking, rubber-legged white boy with a rosebud mouth, pompadour hairdo, and long sideburns, who came into Henry's Record Shop and Shine Parlor asking for introductions to black musicians in Memphis and for tips on starting a career as a rhythm and blues singer. The surly-looking kid was Elvis Presley.

In his first step to prepare his new artist for bigger and better things, Robert Henry took B.B. King a few doors down Beale to Nate Epstein's pawnshop and got him some decent stage clothes. From Epstein's racks he chose two outfits: trousers, jacket, shirt, and tie of matching color, two-toned shoes, black vest for both. One maroon, one light blue.

B.B. King was by now a local celebrity, but outside Memphis and the tri-state area, no one had as yet heard his name. Already, though, his career was inflicting a heavy penalty on him: his marriage was beginning to sag under the strain. Still childless after three miscarriages, the Kings faced the dilemma of every show-biz couple: to travel together on the road, or to separate during road tours. Even for engagements in the immediate Memphis area, the choice for Martha King was not easy: staying home or hanging around at the gig. Both Martha and B.B. were given to fits of jealousy. When he was on the road and she stayed at home, they both tormented themselves with thoughts of the other's infidelity. She knew that as an entertainer he was the natural target of adoring young women; he knew that without children to occupy her attention, she was footloose and prone to boredom. It was a matter of a few years before the growing tension had its inevitable result in divorce, but for a while they remained husband and wife—at least in name.

THE BIG BREAK

A few days after Christmas 1951 RPM's seventh B.B. King single, "Three O'Clock Blues," a Lowell Fulson tune often heard around Memphis in those days, made its appearance on *Bill-*

board's R&B hit record chart. In early 1952 it reached the number-one position and stayed there for fifteen weeks. For the moment, at least, B.B. had captured a national audience. It remained to be seen if he could capitalize on it. The history of popular music is littered with one-hit wonders: artists who have one smash hit and drop from sight never to be seen again. For that matter, there are many two-, three-, and four-hit wonders. A hit record is an opening in the overgrown swamp of show business, which may swallow the aspirant in obscurity as quickly as it opened to shine down the limelight. Now B.B. King had an opening which paid instant dividends. Offers poured into Memphis from the major booking agencies in the North. Under Robert Henry's tutelage, B.B. signed a six-month probationary contract with Universal Artists in New York City, which began with engagements in the three major theaters for black entertainers in the country: the Howard Theater in Washington, D.C., the Royal Theater in Baltimore, and the Apollo Theater in Harlem.

His contract with Universal called for him to perform with the Tiny Bradshaw Band, which was the backup band booked for all the artists on the tour. Now B.B. would have to leave his own band behind. At that moment, the piano player, John Alexander, was showing great promise. He had a good voice which, as B.B.'s sideman, he had little opportunity to use, and his good looks left the girls swooning. It was natural for B.B. to turn the band over to Alexander when he left Memphis for his first big gig in the real urban North at the Washington Howard. John Alexander put the opportunity to good advantage. He made live appearances on WDIA, where program director David James Mattis saw his potential and began promoting him, after coining a new name for him: "Johnny Ace," to suit his obvious glamour. When he died tragically and violently four years later of a self-inflicted gunshot wound, Johnny Ace's popularity was slightly ahead of B.B. King's, though both artists were only beginning to come into their own.

Less than eighteen months since the day he arrived there and played on Sonny Boy Williamson's radio show, and a scant two years since he had raised his last crop in the Delta, B.B. King took a leave from his job as DJ on the WDIA Sepia Swing Club and left Memphis for Washington and the start of his first national tour.

IV

Chitlin Circuit Rider

RUNNING THE GANTLET

B.B. KNEW THE BIG THREE THEATERS by reputation and facing them he felt like a young brave about to run the gantlet. The audiences at the Howard, Royal, and Apollo theaters were the most critical that any black entertainer could face in those days; their standards were the highest, and they took no pity on performers who failed to measure up to them. There was no one standing in the wings with a long hook to snare the unfortunate off the stage, but if an audience took a dislike to an entertainer, he would have been thankful to have a hookman there to pull him off. These audiences took pride in the abuse they could muster for substandard acts. On the other hand, they spared nothing in expressing their enthusiasm for the ones they liked. A new entertainer who went over well there had a good start on a national career. This applied across the spectrum of black show biz from singers to gag men. The Big Three were an acid test. If B.B. failed, he might be back in Memphis spinning records and gigging around the tri-states in just a few weeks' time; if he succeeded, he would get steady bookings around the country.

B.B. arrived in Washington in a state of shock. He had never been this far north before; he had never performed before *any* large metropolitan audience, much less the crowds at the Howard; he had never played with a large band before. He made friends with one of the Bradshaw Band, Tiny Kennedy, who treated B.B. like a "home boy"; according to the code that any old hand was supposed to help out any newly arrived home boy who had just "come up" from "down home." B.B. was greatly relieved to be adopted by Tiny, who looked at him in his maroon suit right off Nate Epstein's rack, and said, "Oh, Homey. . . . Not that, Homey. . . . You can't go on with that, Homey. This is no jive carnival, man. This is the big time. We got to get you into some clothes that make you look hip, not like you still got Delta mud on your heels."

B.B.'s panic mounted.

"And what you got for charts, man?" Tiny continued, asking about the musical arrangements he had brought for the band to accompany him. "Arrangements for seven pieces," B.B. confessed sheepishly.

"Shit," Tiny said contemptuously, "we got eighteen pieces to play behind you. We got to get you some decent charts, too, man. I can see we got a lot of work to do on you, Homey, before you can step out on the stage of the Howard."

On the same bill with B.B. was another new face, a singer named "H. Bomb" Ferguson, whose only talent seemed to be his ability to sound very much like the widely known and much liked singer Wynonie Harris. What H. Bomb lacked in original talent, he made up for in unbridled conceit. Seeing him made B.B. realize that his own insecurity was an asset in this situation and he feared the worst for H. Bomb, who might receive his comeuppance at the hands of Bradshaw's musicians, eager to put him in his place. B.B. went with Tiny Kennedy to a clothing store downtown and bought a black tuxedo and some "Mr. B." shirts. He stopped at the package store and picked up several fifths of liquor as gratuities for the band. Then he found the best arranger in the band and hired him to write expanded charts for his material. He talked to the band members and expressed his fears frankly, appealing to them for their help. By the time he stepped from behind the curtain on opening night, he had the full sympathy of the band and he looked every bit the seasoned performer. With the Tiny Bradshaw Band playing solidly behind him, he sounded like a million bucks. He took the audience with him like a Pied Piper.

H. Bomb lived up to his name—if not his image of himself.

GETTING ESTABLISHED

B.B. stayed with the tour for six months, and over the succeeding eighteen months, alternated between stints on the road and layovers in Memphis, where he resumed broadcasting over WDIA and playing his old haunts with his status much enhanced now that he was a nationally known artist. He continued recording for the Bihari brothers. His income soared, leaving him bewildered and giddy. The first Universal Artist tour paid him $2,500 a week. To a kid who had made $22.50 a week driving a tractor in the Delta barely three years before, the experience of making so much money destroyed his sense of proportion. Some of his new wealth he spent with wild extravagance, some he gambled away, some he showered on friends and relatives, and some he spent with sound common sense—most notably in purchasing a farm on the outskirts of Memphis where he installed his father. In the decades that followed, his income fluctuated and increased sporadically, eventually to levels much higher than his first boom, but his attitude toward money and his spending habits changed little. Throughout his career he has been a spendthrift, a gambler, and a man of extravagant generosity who, contrary to his basic disregard for security, has nonetheless managed to make a few sound investments.

WITH INCREASING national recognition and the advance of his career came the dissolution of B.B.'s first marriage. When word reached him on tour that Martha had left Memphis and planned to file for divorce, he was crushed. Following a pattern that was to be repeated a few times in his life when accumulated grievances reached an intolerable level causing his wife or lover to quit in despair, he took the rebuke as a breach in personal loyalty, a violation of trust and friendship, and a deep personal rejection. But one fringe benefit was the inspiration to express his despair in a new song. In the case of Martha King, the song was "Woke Up This Morning," his first big hit after "Three O'Clock Blues." In 1952, after eight years of marriage, Martha and Riley King were divorced, still childless.

ROBERT HENRY, the Beale Street entrepreneur, was still managing B.B.'s career two years after B.B. had won national recognition, but the partnership was bound to come apart; Henry was ideal for handling a Memphis based artist but ill equipped to manage a nationwide career. He was unwittingly the instrument of his own loss when he introduced B.B. to Bill Harvey, leader of the house band that played at the Club Handy on Beale Street. B.B. and Harvey struck a deal under which Harvey's band became B.B.'s steady road group. Later, Don Robey, a booking agent in Houston, was brought into the picture to handle their engagements through his agency called Buffalo Booking.

Harvey was a learned musician with a passion for teaching, and the Club Handy was a kind of Academy of Rhythm and Blues. The club was managed by Andrew "Sunbeam" Mitchell, a hard-driving local impresario, and his wife. The joint was small, and it was combined with limited hotel accommodations: in fact, some of the sleeping rooms opened directly into the barroom itself. Harvey's musicians lived in the hotel and ate in Mrs. Mitchell's kitchen while Harvey schooled them in basic musicianship. Over the years, dozens of young musicians cut their chops in Harvey's makeshift school.

Around 1953, B.B. broke his contract with Robert Henry and turned over management of his career to Maurice Merrit, another Texan, who had provided financing to equip the new road company with instruments, two station wagons for the band, and a Cadillac for the star. B. B. King was now a Texas-based blues-man.

BIG RED

Three years after he joined forces with B.B. King, Bill Harvey was forced to retire from the road because of poor health. B.B. took over responsibility for the band. For $5,000, a Memphis friend, Cato Walker, bought a used bus from Greyhound—one on which the bus company had completely abandoned hope. An additional $3,000 for parts, plus Cato's mechanical talent, made the bus roadworthy. The preparation of the bus, dubbed "Big Red," marked the beginning of B.B.'s career as an independent road musician, a star attraction who could also serve as musical bulwark of a road tour, providing a house band for other artists, plus transportation and housing. It also marked his association with Cato Walker and Cato's kin which has extended as long as B.B.'s career as an autonomous road musician. The B.B. King Band consisted of thirteen musicians and included, among others,

Shinny Walker, Cato's brother, on bass, Johnny Board on alto saxophone, (formerly the leader of the band that backed the semisuicidal Johnny Ace), and a woman saxophonist (formerly with the Bill Harvey Band), Evelyn Young. Cato Walker was bus driver and the retinue included a valet for the band, a road manager, and a valet/driver for B.B., who traveled separately in his Cadillac.

A total of eighteen comprised the traveling road company. The number of musicians varied, but remained close to the average of thirteen through the 1950s. At times the touring company was as few as fifteen; it never rose above twenty.

Keeping order among so many people was not easy. A list of rules was posted inside the bus, among them "Don't leave the bus with a do-rag on your head." (A "do-rag" is a bandanna worn on the head to preserve one's "process," also called a "conk," i.e., the hairdo after the hair was straightened.) "All guests traveling with the bus must have bus fare home." "Don't give a band member's seat to a guest." "Guests traveling with the band must have a change of clothes." "$25.00 fine for missing rehearsal." "Uniforms must be clean and pressed." And the most celebrated rule: "Don't Mess with Nu'."

The last rule referred to the featured artist with the band, saxophonist Evelyn Young, called "Nu'," which was short for "Mamma Nuts." Her prodigious talent and capacity for hell raising gave her a formidable reputation; for a brief period, she played with Dizzy Gillespie. In 1954, when Bill Harvey and the band came down to mid-Manhattan to Birdland from Harlem, where B.B. was playing the Apollo Theater, Evelyn Young was the only one among Harvey and his musicians to take the bandstand alongside Dizzy Gillespie and Charlie Parker for an impromptu jam. Harvey was slack-jawed and told her afterward, "You've got some nerve, Nu', stepping up there with them." The famous rule—Don't mess with Nu'—was mainly for her protection. Her erratic mood and penchant for alcohol made her vulnerable; hence Harvey made it clear that he would fire anyone who started her on a bender.

By 1955, B.B. had established the main components of a self-sustaining career: a reliable road band that supported and accommodated his musical style; a bus, Big Red, to carry the road company; a booking agency, Buffalo Booking in Houston, with a nationwide clientele; a recording company, Modern Records, that released a steady string of modest hits (100,000 copies, average); and a national circuit of appearances that gave him the sine qua non of success: long-term exposure to audiences who dependably patronized his music. However, the cost in strictly personal terms was heavy, and the combination of components that made his career at this point had a built-in ceiling. Modern Records and Buffalo Booking were marooned in a corner of the music business called "race music," because that part of the music market was strictly circumscribed by racial lines. Modern sold its records to ghetto record shops and small merchants called "rack jobbers," i.e., grocers, druggists, and sundry sellers who sold records from a counter-top rack at cut-rate prices. Modern, Duke, Peacock, and a few dozen other record labels were the successors to Okeh, Vocalion, and other earlier labels openly and explicitly called "race records." Both generations of recording companies depended on marketing mechanisms exclusively beamed at the lower economic strata of black American society. Buffalo Booking dealt with clientele who served the same market—ghetto theaters, small-town cafés, country dance halls and roadside joints—called the chitlin circuit. In the mid-1950s, these built-in limitations were not yet a burden to B.B. King, his burning ambition notwithstanding. He was in his early thirties, in good health, a dynamo of energy and full of himself; the demands of the road he bore in good spirits.

But the chitlin circuit was a ruthless pacemaker. Successive one-night stands were often 800 miles apart. Days might pass before the pace allowed a night's rest in a hotel: play five hours, dismantle the bandstand, load the bus, ride fifteen hours on the nod, set up the bandstand, play five hours, dismantle the bandstand, and so on. In 1956 B.B. King played 342 one-night stands.

There were racial indignities to contend with, too. Finding accommodations in segregated states was often extremely frustrating. The road manager and bus driver learned to use their need to fill up the bus's 150-gallon gas tank as an incentive. They would patronize gas stations with restaurants attached. "We need gas *and* food," they would say. Yet often they settled for sandwiches handed out the back of the kitchen. Willis "Bebop" Edwards, B.B.'s valet of twenty-five years' service, still speaks today with indignation about one hash slinger who ceremoniously broke the coffee cup from which Bebop had just drunk, as if to declare that some breach of the law of racial kosher had defiled it.

Over the years, the personal hazards mounted up. It is frightening to examine them. Most of the incidents that threatened life and body—such as sixteen auto wrecks—B.B. dismisses as the routine danger of steady travel, but a few have left deep impressions and one—the story of Lucille—has become a romantic legend. The episode that spawned the romantic story of how B.B. came to call his guitar Lucille took place in Twist, Arkansas, in 1949; while he played in a dance hall, a fight broke out between rivals for a lady named Lucille. As they fought, the two men knocked over the kerosene space heater in the center of the dance hall, setting the place on fire. B.B. fled with the rest of the crowd, but once outside, he realized his guitar was still inside and impulsively rushed back, snatching it on the run and fleeing a second time. The blaze claimed two fatalities.

Another time violence was directed at B.B. himself. A fracas took place around 1956 in Houston, at an auditorium named after a black serviceman among the first casualties at Pearl Harbor. During intermission, B.B. stayed on the bandstand to talk to fans and flirt with girls. The trouble started when a jealous man saw B.B. flirting with his girlfriend. He waited until B.B. crossed the stage to sit at the piano, then yanked the piano stool. B.B. took a pratfall, and the band members rose to their feet, ready to defend their collective honor against the ridicule of their star. An open clash was avoided; somehow the tension was resolved and the show resumed. Not for good, though. After the show, when the band pulled out aboard Big Red, the disgruntled locals sprung an ambush at the first intersection. In a scene reminiscent of the Old West and fully worthy of Texas' reputation, the locals opened fire and the musicians on board the bus returned the shots. The air was full of lead. The bus roared away in a hail of gunfire. No one was hurt. The upshot was a new rule for the band: no weapons on the bus.

The finances of touring on the road were precarious at best and more often cut-throat. The economic scheme offered no more security than sharecropping, and the psychology for everyone, including B.B., at the top of the pyramid, was virtually identical—the amount of money entailed notwithstanding. More often than not, B.B. worked for a percentage of the gate, without any guaranteed minimum. The result was a profound, lifelong impact on B.B.'s attitude toward money and on his financial prospects in later years. The quantity of plain cash that left the consumers' pockets for any given engagement was large compared to, say, the average small business of the time, and was enormous to a young man less than ten years off a Delta plantation. But accountability was hit-or-miss. The phrase "a piece of the action" just barely hints at the complex play of shadowy figures involved in handling the proceeds. Unlike working for a flat fee, which may have its own opportunities for cheating, banking on a percentage of a variable, indeterminate sum opens the performer to bilking from every direction. The following people are entitled to a piece of the action: the performer, the performer's personal manager, the club owner and the promoter (sometimes the same person), the booking agency, and Uncle Sam. The crooked club owner wants to conceal the total gate from all other parties because he or she can keep 100 per cent of the hidden gate; the dishonest performer wants to conceal his or her share of the gate from both the personal manager and the booking agent who take their percentage from the performer's share; the booking agent and personal manager, who may both take part in negotiating the performer's contract, may be taking kickbacks for not driving too hard a bargain; the performer must rely on his road manager to keep the club owner honest by watching the gate, a fact that invites suspicion of collusion beween the watchdog and the thief. Uncle Sam wants full disclosure and a piece of everyone's piece of the action.

During the mid-1950s, B.B.'s road manager was James "Shinny" Walker (brother to bus driver Cato Walker) who started out as bassist in the band but gave up his musical job to take on more responsibility and draw more pay not long after going "out there" on the road with B.B. To keep the gatekeeper honest, Shinny would post a man—sometimes brother Cato, sometimes one of the valets—at the door with a counter in hand and assign others to watch elsewhere for a clandestine entry. Some club owners objected vehemently and offered as verification of the gate the serial numbers of the first and last tickets sold. Disputes were common.

As often happens to people trying to conduct affairs in an industry fraught with duplicity, B.B. and his associates tried to combat the double-dealing with overriding bonds of loyalty—

strictly personal, unspoken covenants that stood apart from the
shaky, shadowy world they moved in. In the case of B.B. and
Shinny, Shinny showed his loyalty by doing countless unpleasant
tasks ranging from beating down club owners, to firing errant musicians, to bilking the booking agency (always done under the
conviction that the skimming was reciprocal); B.B. in turn
showed his loyalty by awarding Shinny with frequent, almost
nightly bonuses, anywhere from $25 up to a few hundred dollars.
The daily demonstrations of loyalty were all they had in their mutual affairs to combat the tendency toward mistrust made inevitable by the system.

Alas, such countermeasures are frail weapons against the system. Eventually, for many complex reasons, the relationship between star and road manager fell apart; Shinny was sacked and
he returned to Memphis to open a gas station.

The economic psychology of B.B.'s career resembled plantation
life in other ways besides the financial insecurity. From the beginning, B.B. took ultimate responsibility for "The Company," as
people called his road operation. Unlike some fragile, tempera-
mental, dependent artists who leave all decisions to others, and
unlike some who languish in a narcotic fog and are led from stage
to stage by caretakers in charge of everything except their performance before the microphone, B.B. ran his own affairs. He absorbed financial disasters and adopted a paternal, protective attitude toward his employees. B.B. saw the strict parallel beween
the way his employees depended on his fortunes and the depend-
ency of sharecroppers on their landlord, and between himself
and the Delta landlord. In some respects, his employees had it
worse: at least the land could be parceled out, but B.B.'s fame
was indivisible and intangible, though just as vulnerable to misfortune as a crop is to bad weather. He began to emulate his
model of the good planter, Johnson Barrett, by acting as the concerned benefactor, the compassionate patriarch, the generous
padrone, who takes care of the needs of his people. Those needs
were simple: minimizing the hardships of travel and paying bills.
He attended to the first by making an extra effort to provide crea-
ture comforts for the band and coped with the second by becoming an easy touch. Whether the bills were family medical expenses
or gambling debts, B.B. was quick to lend money to his employees, often without terms.

B.B.'s posture as Old South patriarch went further: he became fanatic about his reputation for reliability. His word was his bond, and he believed that he had to keep it regardless of the cost. Not so seldom he was faced with the prospect of operating at a loss; the bus broke down many times for weeks on end, and to meet his engagements he would be forced to rent a small fleet of cars to carry the eighteen people in his entourage, which meant running up costs over profits. When this happened, he always declined the option of canceling dates and took the loss as the price of keeping his word. When sudden emergencies struck, a breakdown on a highway, or a blizzard, he drove the band to the edges of endurance to make the gig on time. In such situations, whatever could be done—chartering a plane, getting a pawnshop owner out of bed to replace lost instruments—B.B.'s self-esteem was jeopardized if he didn't do it.

Taking up the role of good planter, Patriarch of the Old South, with its rigid code of ethics, gave B.B. a few things, internal and external, in the bargain: an air of aloof detachment, a feeling of lonely isolation, a tendency toward intractable stubbornness, and a long line of petitioners waiting to plead their cases.

B.B.'s family life during these years living on the chitlin circuit was peculiar by Middle American standards. Over a ten-year period, by his own account, he sired eight children. Partly through luck and partly through caution, he was never accused of paternity by casual lovers or total strangers, and whenever one of his paramours announced that she was pregnant, he accepted responsibility and was personally very pleased. His attitude on the matter seems to stem from two sources: his determination to be a moral man, which had no basis in religion but rather grew out of his lifelong struggle to win and hold his self-esteem; and his boyhood as a foundling, which left him in his adult years yearning for close kin he could call his own. As he puts it now, "When a lady says the baby is yours, the only question to ask is 'Was you in there?' If the answer is yes, then it's yours." Contraception in those days among B.B. and his peers was a vague, slightly mysterious idea. "We didn't have the knowledge then that you do now. I knew that if you didn't leave the sperm in the woman, you wouldn't make her pregnant. But that was asking an awful lot of a young man." With each of his children, B.B. accepted full responsibility by providing for them financially, including a college education in some cases, and giving them his name. His one main regret in life is that he never made a family for his children.

Of his eight children, only one, his daughter Shirley, grew up with B.B.'s own kin. Shirley lived on the farm in Memphis with B.B.'s father, Albert, and his family. Shirley and her cousins knew B.B. as a voice on the radio and a jovial visitor to the farm; all of them, Shirley included, called him "Uncle B." On rare occasions, B.B. would manage time enough from his traveling to take his daughter and her cousins—they were really half-cousins, being the children of B.B.'s half-siblings—to the drive-in movie. As Shirley remembers it, more often than not he would take his shoes off and fall dead asleep, driving the kids to distraction with the sound of his snoring and the smell of his feet. As she reached adolescence, she began to take his neglect as a sign of personal rejection and finally resorted to feigning an attempt at suicide simply to gain his attention. Today Shirley King is an entertainer, the only one of B.B.'s offspring to try a career in show business. She works the clubs around Chicago as a combination erotic dancer and contortionist.

FIERY CRASH ON A TEXAS BRIDGE

In 1958, on a road near Dallas, Big Red with B.B.'s entourage aboard had an accident. As the bus was crossing a bridge, a car began to pass it. When an oil truck entered the bridge from the far end, headed toward the two vehicles, the car sped up to overtake the bus. At the wheel of the bus, Millard Lee, known as "Mother" after his conversational habit, applied the brakes. The driver of the car grew desperate and pulled in so perilously close to Big Red that Mother Lee swerved to the right to avoid being clipped. Lee's maneuver caused the bus to carom off the bridge wall straight into the path of the approaching truck; the bus struck the truck head on. Miraculously no one on the bus, including Mother Lee, was seriously hurt. But the truck burst into flames. As the stunned band members crawled out the back windows of the bus, they saw a ghastly sight: one of the two riders from the truck running down the bridge, flames trailing from his clothes. Two people died of burns from the wreck; one died in the cab of the truck, the other as he reached the water's edge below the bridge where he had stumbled, hoping to put out the fire that killed him.

B.B., who was not on the bus and not even at the scene, heard news of the crash by telephone. He was so horrified by the grisly details that it was a while before he realized that the accident couldn't have happened at a worse time. It was a weekend, and on the Friday before, B.B. had been notified that the insurance company holding the liability policy on the bus had been suspended for violating regulations, following an investigation by government authorities. The notice meant that the insurance on the bus was suspended, along with the company. B.B. had made a decision consistent with his fanatic determination to meet all commitments, to operate through the weekend without proper insurance; come Monday, he had reasoned, new coverage could be arranged. He had taken a calculated risk that nothing untoward would happen during those two days, and now the worst possible sequence of events had transpired.

The legal aftermath of the fiery Texas crash was a nightmare. B.B.'s liability was finally set by mutual agreement at a figure not far below $100,000. It was years before he managed to pay the debt. In addition to the cost of settling the liability, there was the expense of replacing Big Red. This time B.B. bought a brand-new bus. He paid the Skyliner Company in Laundonville, Ohio, $26,934.90 for a new Flexible Starliner Coach which Cato Walker took to Brown City, Michigan, where a motor-home company outfitted it with a toilet and other conveniences for the band. The new bus, which was considerably more comfortable than Big Red, was a nameless Titan that served B.B. and the band for seven years until, like its predecessor, it met with ill fortune.

V

The Fallow Years

THE FIERY CRASH of Big Red, the jalopy bus, and the purchase of the new Starliner Coach as a replacement marked a transition in B.B.'s life and career. By 1958 it was well established that he was no flash in the pan, but a major artist in his field. His stable appeal with his audiences was demonstrated; there could be little doubt that he now had a loyal, devoted following. He could go on indefinitely, even without more big hits, and as long as he did not slacken the pace, his appearances would be well attended and his new record releases would make a modest profit for the Bihari brothers. On the strictly personal side, the new phase of life consisted of his second marriage to a young Mississippi woman fifteen years his junior; on the professional side it consisted of growing frustration, and later despair, over the limitations imposed on his career by the impenetrable racial boundaries that circumscribed his musical genre, limitations made all the more conspicuous by the breakthrough of the neighboring genre, black rock-and-roll.

MARRIAGE #2

B.B. met his second wife, Sue Carol Hall, in his home town of Indianola, Mississippi. He was playing at Jones' Night Spot, the same place where he had heard many idols play before he left the Delta bound for Memphis twelve years earlier. The place had changed hands and been renamed Club Ebony. The new manager was Sue Hall's mother, a Leland, Mississippi woman whose romance with a white family man of Irish descent from the other side of the tracks in Leland had produced the light-skinned girl who caught B.B.'s eye. Sue Hall was an exceptionally bright woman with ambitions high by any standard and dizzying by standards usually applied to women of her racial mixture in that place in time. When she married B.B., she was eighteen, a college girl, and an unmarried mother. They married on June 4, 1958, in a Detroit hotel with two guests present: Goose Tatum of the Harlem Globetrotters, and a friend who hawked souvenirs at B.B's gigs.

For about six months, Sue King traveled constantly with B.B. and the band, sharing with B.B. every aspect of his roller-coaster road life except the performing. She was young, resourceful, and flexible. During that first half year, the new couple looked for a place to settle down, and they bought a house in Los Angeles that appealed to both of them. She began making a home there between stints on the road. They wanted children but failed; she had test after test to diagnose the difficulty, but none revealed any reproductive dysfunction. At last B.B. underwent tests and was found to have a sperm count too low to conceive; according to B.B., the specialists attributed his disability to an illness in 1949 which had resulted in a diminishing sperm count.

B.B. was rarely home. When Sue wanted to be with her husband, she had to travel with him. The tension in their marriage increased. The conflict was basically objective. She was very young when they married, and, as she matured, her objectives and life goals began coming into focus at cross purposes to B.B.'s. For his part, B.B. could see no way to maintain his career without constant travel. Only by staying on the move and on top of the heap could he make the income necessary to support his road show. Cutting back his retinue would lose him his top position. Moreover, few club owners would take the chance of booking him for long engagements—say, ten days, two weeks, or even a month, as they might with a small jazz combo—for fear he would quickly exhaust the market for his music. Had he been an old-style musician like his cousin Bukka, he could have worked as a single whenever he wanted, not worrying about paying a large troupe; had he been a jazz musician, he could have worked the dozens of clubs around Los Angeles varying his sidemen according to the gig, thereby managing to spend a few months a year at home.

But he was neither of these things; he was a modern bluesman. He had carved out a niche for himself in the music world, and he felt he couldn't tamper with the combination that had made that niche without seriously jeopardizing his career. Blues audiences were never big record buyers, and B.B. could stay on top only by direct face-to-face exposure. As a modern bluesman in the early 1960s, he was hostage to the road.

In 1966 his wife divorced him.

THE BIRTH OF ROCK-AND-ROLL

Rock music was born twins: there were two sibling styles, one derived from country and western, one from rhythm and blues. These two sources were distinct and separate corners of the music industry, one white, stemming from Nashville, Tennessee, and Wheeling, West Virginia, the other black, stemming from Chicago, Memphis, Houston, St. Louis, and Kansas City. But, of course, there was overlap between the two styles and their locations, especially since both had wide national followings.

Myriads of factors contributed to the birth of these twin styles, and a description that singles out a few of them is bound to be either partial or an oversimplification. Yet we can single out the few more important ones. As background, consider the national mass markets as dominated by crooners, balladeers, and a few torch singers, mostly white. There was the Godfrey crowd, including Arthur Godfrey himself, Julius La Rosa, Dennis Morgan, the McGuire Sisters, and the Archie Bleyer Orchestra; there were Patti Page, Tony Bennett, Frank Sinatra, Perry Como, Nat "King" Cole, Eddie Fisher, Dean Martin, Billy Eckstine, Frankie Laine, Rosemary Clooney, Vaughn Monroe, and perennials like Bing Crosby, Dinah Shore, and Kate Smith. By contrast, country and western, as well as rhythm and blues were strictly subculture diet, heard only on select stations. The first sign of a breakthrough came in 1954, with the sensational popularity of Bill Haley's hit "Rock Around the Clock," a raucous fusion of swing and rhythm and blues, popularized by the movie *Blackboard Jungle,* for which it was the theme music. The hit rivaled "White Christmas" for its sensational popularity and left the music industry stunned.

Chopping cotton, 1937. *Photo by Dorothea Lange, Farm Security Administration.*

Bear Creek, Kilmichael, Mississippi. *Photo by Charles Sawyer.*

Birthplace of Riley B. King, on the bank of Bear Creek, Kilmichael, Mississippi. *Photo, 1978, by Charles Sawyer.*

"From kin to caint." Clarksdale, Mississippi, 1937. *Photo by Dorothea Lange, Farm Security Administration.*

Planter and black hands, Clarksdale, Mississippi, 1936. *Photo by
Dorothea Lange, Farm Security Administration.*

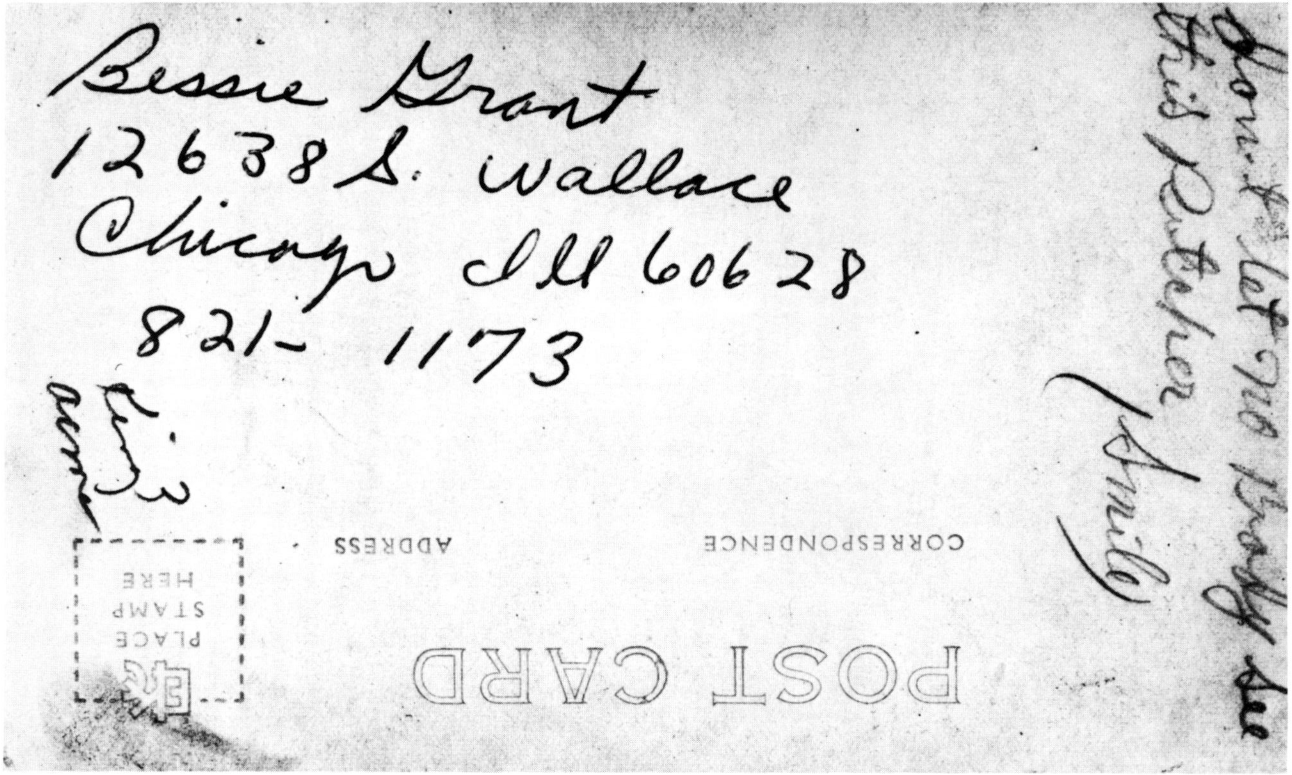

Don't let no Body See
this Pitcher (Smile)

Bessie Grant
1263 8 S. Wallace
Chicago Ill 60628
821-1173

King
acme

POST CARD

CORRESPONDENCE

ADDRESS

PLACE
STAMP
HERE

Reverse side of photo postcard made by Riley King to send to his sweetheart. Message reads: "don't let no Body See this Pitcher (Smile)." The address was added many years later, when Riley's former sweetheart came backstage to return the gift. By then she was a Chicago housewife and he a chitlin circuit star.

Best wishes to miss
Bessie L williams

Riley B. King, age sixteen, the photo on the front of the postcard, taken by a storefront photographer in Indianola, Mississippi.

A Delta cotton field too wet for planting. *Photo by Charles Sawyer.*

Johnson Barrett, plantation owner in Indianola, Mississippi, who employed Riley King as a tractor driver and a sharecropper. *Photo (c. 1955) courtesy of Mrs. Johnson Barrett.*

Photo by Dorothea Lange, Farm Security Administration

Photo by Jack Delano, Farm Security Administration

Photo by Dorothea Lange, Farm Security Administration.

Photo by Russell Lee, Farm Security Administration.

Reverse side of photo postcard made by Riley King for an Indianola girlfriend. Message reads: "Hello Darling Smile this is the Black Singing Boy."

Riley King, age nineteen. Front of the photo postcard by storefront photographer.

Juke joint, Clarksdale, Mississippi, 1939. *Photo by Marion Post Wolcott, Farm Security*

Memphis dance hall, 1939. *Photo by Marion Post Wolcott, Farm Security Administration.*

Marcella Plantation in the Mississippi Delta, 1939. *Photo by Marion Post Wolcott, Farm*

But it was not the major record companies which fathomed the new trend, it was small labels that sold records in the two sub-cultures—labels like Chess Records in Chicago, Specialty Records in Los Angeles, and Sun Records in Memphis. As these small, speculative labels released singles in the new styles, the major labels rushed to issue their own crooning variants, namely sanitized, watered-down, whitewashed versions of the same tunes; the performers took out all the raw gravel of the originals and rounded off all their rough edges. Specialty Records released Little Richard's spellbinder "Tutti Frutti," and Dot Records quickly covered it with Pat Boone's rendition which outsold the original. A sentimental white version of Fats Domino's soulful "Blueberry Hill" did comparably as well. But a polished version of Jerry Lee Lewis' "Whole Lot of Shakin'" did poorly by comparison with the Sun Record original, and no one tried to clean up the later material of Chess Records' new artists Chuck Berry and Bo Diddley. If these facts failed to convince the industry of the futility of remaking works of the new styles in the old ones, all doubt vanished when RCA Victor, a corporate giant in the pop field, bought the contract of Sun Records' hot new property, Elvis Presley. The industry exploded with new sounds full of nervous energy and sexual innuendo; a new market comprised of millions of affluent teen-agers had been discovered.

The midwife to this birth was television. In the past, the music business had occasionally used movies to promote its product, but TV was a new market mechanism. Record companies began to compete for television exposure, and TV programs, in turn, began competing for the chance to show the latest star. Elvis Presley's appearance on the Steve Allen show gave the program an unprecedented boost; Ed Sullivan on the opposite network in the same prime-time slot quickly booked Presley for a series of appearances on his show.

A daily afternoon TV program aired from Philadelphia was devoted entirely to the new music. The program, called "American Bandstand," featured Dick Clark, a boy-faced host who became the first and only national TV-DJ and a powerful force in the new game in play within the music business. Clark openly speculated on the air about the prospects of the new records he played and consulted his teen-age audiences in the studio for their "ratings"; it was a completely new kind of market research that repeatedly informed both the teen-agers and the record moguls watching of the enormous commercial power of the new youth culture. •

While the new releases played, the cameras showed the studio jammed with dancing teen-agers straight from the halls of the public schools in Philadelphia. These teen-agers were untouched by makeup artists and unscreened by any casting director; the older Mouseketeers were replaced by real teen-agers with tight skirts and bouncing breasts, pegged pants and Wildroot Cream Oil hairdos piled up to a high pompadour in front and swept back to a duck's ass in the back. Compared to other fictional portrayals of adolescents in the mass media, the real teen-agers on "American Bandstand" were much easier for the audiences to identify with; beside the idealized characters of Ricky and David Nelson from the "Ozzie and Harriet" TV show, Dick Clark's teen-agers were coarse, acne-faced punks. Compared to Henry Aldrich, the radio character of the 1940s whose comic adventures never went far beyond the time he took his sister to the prom as a substitute for his sick date, the high school kids on "American Bandstand" looked positively sexy.

The birth of rock music broke down one barrier that had kept black entertainers from reaching mass audiences on the grounds that their music was so excessively and explicitly sexual that common decency required that it be kept off the air. Take the lyrics of Little Richard's hit tune, "Long Tall Sally." When Little Richard sang, "I saw Uncle John with Long Tall Sally/He saw Aunt Mary comin' and he ducked back in the alley," everyone who paid attention to the lyrics at all wondered what Uncle John was doing down the alley with that Sally. Wonder turned to incredulity when they heard: "Long Tall Sally she's built for speed/She got everything Uncle John need." Only a few years before Little Richard's whooping and hollering about Sally's anatomy, popular songs were often banned from the air for such innocuous lines as "When we're dancing and you're dangerously near me/I get ideas." Prior to the birth of rock-and-roll, a double standard applied in broadcasting. Stations like WDIA that played rhythm and blues often aired music with strong sexual undercurrents and open references to sex with no repercussions; but stations that directed their programming to white audiences lived in fear that their sponsors would all withdraw and that they would be drowned in public clamor if they broadcast a song like B.B. King's hit, "You Upset Me, Babe," in which he sang, "She's 36 in the bust, 28 in the waist/38 in the hips, she's got real crazy legs/ You upset me baby."

It was not only explicit sex that had frightened broadcasters and record-company executives at first; it was the way rock-and-roll performers looked and acted. Fats Domino with his brocade tuxedo and Little Richard in his zoot suit, pointed shoes and high processed hair violated all white show biz canons; closely shorn Pat Boone in his white bucks or Perry Como in his cardigan were more near the ideal. The same applied to the hillbilly side of rock. Elvis' famous pelvic action, hidden by Ed Sullivan's discreet cameras, was unthinkable before Bill Haley shook the foundation. Jerry Lee Lewis would never have had the chance to breathe hot and heavy or gurgle into the microphone—not to mention the way he stomped on the keyboard with his feet—had it not been for Dick Clark.

With these barriers down, many black entertainers whose music would have been labeled "race music" a few years before could now realistically hope to become stars before mixed and predominantly white audiences. The list of black stars and superstars who cashed in on the new commercial opening is impossible to give accurately and completely, but it surely includes Little Richard, Sam Cooke, Fats Domino, Lloyd Price, Jackie Wilson, James Brown, Chuck Berry, Bo Diddley, the Coasters, the Platters, and the Five Satins.

The new opening made stars of these black performers, but it bypassed B.B. King almost entirely. The dissolution of race music barriers entailed in the emergence of rock-and-roll was less than complete. Race music was drastically shrunken, but there still remained an isolated, cultural island in the mainstream of black American music, and B.B. King was marooned on it. Despite two important career changes around 1960—a change of booking agents and a change of record labels—both of which should have rescued him from the chitlin circuit and helped him make contact with white audiences, B.B. was unable to find his way to the opening through which many lesser black artists had passed.

The move from Buffalo Booking in Houston to Shaw Booking Agency in New York might have done the trick. Shaw did help by getting him bookings as the opening act on national rock tours with artists like Lloyd Price and Sam Cooke. Even as the opening act, B.B. often made more money on these tours than he did as the star attraction on the chitlin circuit. Still, he was getting second money, and his contract often specified that his band would be required to play behind other artists on the tour. His appearances on these tours gave him exposure to young, racially mixed audiences, and they might have bridged the waters around his cultural island. But they didn't. On the contrary, they isolated him further because the audiences were cold, indifferent, at times even hostile toward his music. The young fans, eager to see the stars, were impatient with his slow tempos and mournful lyrics. They wanted the jump and jive, the razzle-dazzle choreography, the chorus of slinky backup vocalists singing the shoop-shoops and doo-wahs. Sometimes he was booed. The heckling came more from black teen-agers than from whites, a fact he attributed to the blues being associated with black Americans' poor origins in this country.

The experience of being booed affected B.B. deeply. To counter the hecklers onstage, he played more up-tempo tunes and cut his commentary between songs entirely; his stage routine became nonstop music. But these measures did nothing to soften the emotional impact of being scorned by the public. It would be unpleasant on any account, but it was a very hard blow for the serious artist that B.B. was, whose whole life was invested in performing.

The move from Kent to ABC Records had looked promising. The new record company had done well with Ray Charles' music and had shown that its interest in B.B. was serious by giving him a $25,000 advance. In principle, he was now free of the race-record mentality that had characterized the marketing procedures of the Biharis. Yet the executives at ABC lacked any understanding of B.B.'s music; they understood the music as little as they understood the economics of the chitlin circuit. Race-record companies may have had their eyes on a narrow market and may have exploited their artists shamelessly in selling their work to that market, but at least they knew how to produce the music without destroying its vitality or diluting its artistic integrity. The producers at ABC decided to showcase B.B. in front of a big orchestra in an effort to make him another Jimmy Rushing or Joe Williams. The result was flat and lifeless; the raw attack that had marked his style up until then was gone from the early ABC recordings. B.B. had managed to jettison the race-record outlook, but in the process he had, for the time being, lost the baby with the bath water.

His private reaction to the frustrations was growing despair. He was an ambitious man, proud of his artistic achievements; standing still was, in the long run, poisonous to his frame of mind. He had watched two musical styles closely allied to his own—jazz and rock-and-roll—gain respectability and win wide audiences of both colors. Before the emergence of rock-and-roll, he had been labeled a "rhythm and blues" artist; when his peers made the crossover from race music, they took the label with them, and he was thereafter known strictly as a blues musician. Not counting his often painful exposure to mixed audiences on tour with rock stars, prior to 1968, he made no more than two appearances before white audiences—both complete fiascos. The first was under a severe handicap: his band was to remain always hidden behind the stage curtain and he, too, was to stay out of sight until the moment he was ready to play. The second was only slightly more favorable. Both experiences only deepened his despair.

Equally painful was the callous attitude of many blacks, who shunned blues music because it was most closely associated with black poverty. By popular views, blues musicians were drunkards and drifters, with a bottle in one pocket and a pistol in the other; likely as not, they died violently and pitifully from shootings, stabbings and beatings, or from the complications of alcoholism and drugs. Jazz musicians, too, scorned blues music. And by the late 1950s, jazz had been accepted on college campuses and absorbed into the music schools; jazz musicians acquired a new status as an elite distinguished by the formal complexity of their music, the technical accomplishments they had achieved in their playing, and the sheer musical knowledge that was minimum entry into their circles. By these standards blues suffered badly for being formally spare and simple, technically rudimentary and intuitive. The musical world is highly stratified. Musicians are gossips of the first order, and much of the gossip concerns the pecking order. Status depends on peer approval and public acclaim, and in that order. Peer approval depends on musical technical skill, musicianship (including knowledge of theory), ability to read complex music on sight, and specific accomplishments. Impromptu jam sessions are usually competitive tests of relative skills and often result in legendary stories about how so-and-so blew so-and-so right off the bandstand.

The hierarchy is acknowledged by an etiquette governing public appearances. Two jazz musicians of roughly equal stature playing in the neighborhood at the same time can be expected to exchange visits, the one of lesser prestige coming first to visit the one of higher prestige; during these visits the musician onstage is expected to honor the visiting musician by introducing him to the audience. Blues musicians followed the etiquette among themselves, but were rarely extended these amenities by jazzmen. Many times B.B. let pass opportunities to hear musicians he much admired rather than risk the embarrassment he would feel if his presence was ignored. In the content of their gossip and in the public gestures by which they acknowledged prestige, the status-conscious subculture of black musicians relegated blues to the cellar.

(This view of jazz musicians as treating bluesmen like shabby, disreputable cousins is B.B.'s own view of the matter and is not shared by at least some other musicians from both sides of the tracks. In this respect, B.B. may be overly sensitive to the status of his genre. Nonetheless it is safe to say that jazzmen generally consider bluesmen less successful—if not less respectable—than themselves.)

Through B.B.'s own eyes, his career looked hopelessly stalled. He gave up hope of reaching Middle American white audiences. From his standpoint, his music was completely unknown to the vast majority of Americans, neglected by his musical peers, treated with indifference or hostility by large segments of black America, and taken for granted by his followers. It seemed that all his energy was consumed in a struggle just to hold his own. It looked as if he had come as far as luck and hard work could take him, and that the only way to go was down, which is exactly where he would go, he reasoned, if he eased off the pace.

By 1960 this attitude had hardened into despair. For the next half dozen years, he continued performing out of grim determination in the belief that he had reached his highest level of achievement in life and that any change in matters would be for the worse. The most dramatic symptom of his hardened despair was the fact that he stopped practicing his guitar. It was burning ambition that had driven him in his quest for self-improvement, and now that his ambition was meeting insuperable obstacles, he tried to stifle it. At the time when he was at the peak of his powers in the years between his mid-thirties and his mid-forties, B.B. King was badly stuck and despondent.

ROCK BOTTOM: 1966

In 1966 B.B. hit rock bottom. The bleak year was anticipated by the disappearance of his second bus in 1965. The trouble began when the Skyliner broke down in Augusta, Georgia. Cato Walker, B.B.'s driver and mechanic, the man who had originally put Big Red on the road, repaired the disabled Skyliner and drove it on to Atlanta, where it broke down again, this time too seriously to improvise repairs. He befriended someone to keep tabs on it, then headed for Memphis to bring back a tow vehicle. When he returned from Memphis to Atlanta, both the bus and its keeper had vanished. He reported the apparent theft to the police and began scouring the city for the missing bus. By chance, he spotted it and went straight to the police for help in recovering it. When he led the cops to the spot where he had seen it, the bus had disappeared, leaving him wondering if the culprits had been tipped off. The bus was never recovered. For years after, Cato watched the highways wherever he traveled looking for the lost Skyliner, like Ahab scanning the sea for Moby Dick. He never saw a trace of it. For B.B., it was a complete write-off. He was not insured for theft.

The theft of the bus was only the beginning of new difficulties. In 1966, in quick succession, the Internal Revenue Service put a $78,000 lien on his income and his wife sued him for divorce. The outlook seemed even dimmer when he realized that other bluesmen were crossing over to Middle American audiences while he remained stuck on the chitlin circuit. The first two problems—his tax troubles and his divorce—were connected, at least superficially: in 1965 B.B. had promised that after twelve months he would cut back his schedule and spend more time at home in Los Angeles. But when the IRS hit him with the $78,000 lien, he felt he could not keep his promise. This did not wash with Sue. She took a generally dim view of B.B.'s financial habits and had tried repeatedly to become involved in the management of his business affairs. She rejected his tendency to run his day-to-day operations like a plantation and offered sound business advice, which he declined, brushing aside all her efforts to get involved. The idea of his young wife running his business possibly offended his sense of manhood and certainly clashed with his idea of what a wife's role should be.

When Sue filed for divorce, B.B. did not contest the proceedings. For his part, he was crushed, and felt betrayed and rejected; in his view it was cruel of her to file for divorce on the heels of his troubles with the IRS. She expressed equivocation and readiness to search for reconciliation. He made his response the keynote of his next record, which became his biggest hit, "The Thrill Is Gone." Sue followed his request and continued her proceedings against him. In 1966, still childless, they were officially divorced, and B.B. King lost what might have been his greatest asset in life: a shrewd and resourceful partner with a mind for business.

VI

The Rise of the Urban Blues

BLUE-EYED BLUESMEN AND THE FOLK CROWD

AROUND 1965, the final barriers that had kept blues as race music began falling. The signs were faint at first, and it would be a few years before B.B. would discover the change and benefit from it. The change, oddly enough, came not through rock channels, nor through any effort by jazz men to popularize a neglected genre; instead new openings were made by the folk-music crowd. Folk musicians and many impresarios already knew about Chicago bluesmen Muddy Waters and Howlin' Wolf. Muddy Waters had already played the Newport Folk Festival in the early 1960s. The change began at the 1965 Newport Folk Festival, which featured an afternoon workshop devoted to blues; the workshop consisted of solo blues musicians from the country-blues tradition, men like Sun House and Mississippi John Hurt. This kind of blues was already known to many young urban whites— especially musicians who considered it as just another form of folk music. For these music lovers, musicians such as Woody Guthrie, Doc Watson, Flatt & Scruggs, Sonny Terry and Brownie McGhee, Lightnin' Hopkins and Bukka White formed a continuous spectrum of styles. It was a spectrum with no place for B.B. King, who had to be relegated to the category of rhythm and blues, a category generally regarded in puritanical folk circles as crassly commercial. In fact the same Newport Folk Festival of 1965 witnessed the public debut of folk-rock music when Bob Dylan appeared onstage with an electric guitar and an amplified backup band; to Dylan's chagrin, the audience responded with boos and shouts telling him to "put that thing away." The festival is remembered today for the Dylan incident rather than the blues session; yet something happened during the blues session that was to have big repercussions for bluesmen, especially B.B.* Performing on the program that afternoon was a group making one of its first appearances before a large white audience outside Chicago, the Paul Butterfield Blues Band. Butterfield and his group played heavily amplified music in their own rendition of blues in the style associated with the ghetto neighborhoods of Chicago's South and West sides. Although Butterfield and three of his five sidemen were white, the music was straight from the mainstream of black urban blues, and it was played with authority and conviction.

The audience did not boo Butterfield, as they booed Dylan; they scorned Dylan because it seemed at first glance that by going electric he was selling out his ideals to commercialism, but Butterfield was entirely new to them, and so was his music. One thing about Butterfield was clear: whatever it was that he was doing, he was the real McCoy. He made easy prey of the audience, and the scores of musicians and impresarios on hand were taken by his virtuosity and stage presence. In their first big gig outside of Chicago, Butterfield and his musicians had made an unqualified triumph and began forming a national following. In the fall of 1965, Elektra Records released the first Butterfield album; over the next few years it gained wide popularity in white Middle America. Butterfield's success was the first mass marketing of authentic amplified blues music—roughly the same kind of music B.B. played, and as such it breached the wall that had confined blues. Through the breach came first a handful of Chicago musi-

* The incident of Dylan's mixed reception and his emotional reaction to the apparent rejection of his new folk-rock style by many listeners in the audience has been told and retold by countless pop historians. Less known are the backstage squabbles that erupted the moment Dylan plugged in his amplifier. These were told for the first time in a book by two intimate participants, Eric von Schmidt and Jim Rooney (*Baby, Let Me Follow You Down,* Doubleday, 1979). So violent was the reaction among some of Dylan's fellow folk artists to his departure from the familiar folk style that Pete Seeger himself, the very symbol of liberal tolerance, seized a fire ax and prepared to cut the cables to the sound system in order to stop the desecration of folk music as he saw it. According to Von Schmidt and Rooney, Theo Bikel stepped in and restrained the vigilant guardian of the tradition. (See my article, "How the Beanie Rebels Dumped the Old Folk Mafia," *The Real Paper,* Boston, June 2, 1979.)

cians and then B.B. King, who was no less dismayed than anyone else to find himself discovered by the mainstream of Americans almost twenty years after making his first recording.

Butterfield's rise and B.B.'s emergence still lay ahead in 1965 at Newport. In the summer of 1965 one could not foresee how Butterfield's success at the festival was the beginning of developments that would lead to B.B.'s arrival in Middle America. That summer Butterfield was just a promising new face, and B.B. was still riding the chitlin circuit. Butterfield himself was a cultural contradiction parallel to Django Reinhardt the Parisian gypsy who became one of the leading jazzmen of the 1930s and 1940s. Both men made impressive achievements in fields of music remote from their own culture. Butterfield's leap took him across races and across town in Chicago. He grew up in a middle-class home in the Hyde Park area of the city; his father was an attorney. As a teen-ager in the 1950s, he heard Chicago-style blues over the local radio; the sounds were sirens calling him to the South Side joints. He immersed himself in blues music and blues culture. Many of the best blues musicians in the country made their headquarters in Chicago, and if you weren't frightened away by tales of ghetto violence, it was an easy matter to go straight to the regular haunts to hear Howlin' Wolf, Muddy Waters, Little Walter, Junior Wells and Buddy Guy.

One musician in particular fascinated Butterfield: mouth harpist Little Walter Jacobs, who played with Muddy Waters and recorded both as sideman to Muddy and as a featured artist on Chess Records. Jacobs was the pioneer among Chicago's mouth harpists, who amplified their instruments by tightly cupping their hands around the harmonica and the microphone—often a cheap radio dispatcher's mike. Going electric this way transformed the harmonica from an accompaniment to a solo instrument, just as plugging in the guitar had changed it over to an instrument with an independent voice. Once amplified, the mouth harp could compete with the electric guitar for sheer volume. Jacobs carried the instrument further than any of his contemporaries. He had a unique tone with a hard rasping edge and biting attack, and he phrased his solos like a horn player.

Butterfield began blowing harp with Little Walter's style in mind. He had a natural gift for the instrument, which he combined with a more conscious concern for amplification techniques than his idol and most other harpists had hitherto given to their playing. He managed to fashion a new sound and a style of playing that was all his own. Butterfield had every bit as much attack as the other harpists, including Jacobs, but his tone had a greater depth and a richness the others lacked, while his phrasing was light and lyrical. In Butterfield's hand, the little two-dollar toy became a new kind of saxophone. But that was not all—he had a powerful, chesty voice to match. As he matured stylistically, his voice and his mouth harp became interchangeable.

Butterfield had personal qualities that gave him star potential. He had a sullen, arrogant manner, reminiscent of film star James Dean, that audiences found appealing. He looked like a character from a Dashiell Hammett thriller: hooded eyes, five o'clock shadow, weak chin, pale skin, long hair slicked back, and a slouch in his walk that capped his tough-guy look perfectly. At a time when rock stars were competing for outlandish dress and for stage antics he wore corduroys and planted himself in a spot onstage, playing from a droll crouch. He always looked slightly degenerate and much older than his years. These may not be qualities we look for in prospective friends, but when it comes to picking heroes, the public often finds them just irresistible.

Butterfield was not the only cross-cultural transplant. Two white guitarists were making the same journey in the same city: one a native Chicagoan, the other from Tulsa, Oklahoma. The more accomplished of the two guitarists was a Chicago Jew named Michael Bloomfield; the other was Elvin Bishop, who had come from Tulsa to the University of Chicago as a National Merit Scholar and dropped out soon after tuning his radio to the Chicago blues stations. Bloomfield and Bishop listened to a great variety of musicians and tried to adapt things they heard to their own playing. But one musician stood in their minds as preeminent when it came to blues guitar, and that was B.B. King. They devoured his recordings, listening for every last nuance, copying all his licks with devotion. When Bloomfield, Butterfield, and Bishop joined together, the music they played owed more to B.B. King than to any other blues artist.

The excitement generated by the Butterfield Band and by Bishop and Bloomfield created new curiosity about the origins of their music. The two guitarists were asked by countless music buffs, critics, journalists from the musical press, and other guitarists, "Where did you learn to play that way?"

Both answered honestly, "By copying B.B.'s licks."

People looked blank. "B.B. who?"

"The real monster," Bloomfield and Bishop would reply. "B.B. King."

Butterfield, Bishop, and Bloomfield helped prepare the way for B.B.'s arrival in Middle America, but how they themselves arrived at a position where they could give a hand to B.B. was a complex process. The story begins in Boston, a few years before the pivotal Newport Folk Festival. For no readily apparent reason, in the early 1960s Boston began drawing talented young musicians—mostly folk-music lovers—and a café society began growing up in Cambridge across the Charles River from downtown Boston. Bob Dylan, Joan Baez, Geoff Muldaur, Maria Muldaur and Eric von Schmidt were all little-known local performers playing Cambridge coffeehouses and taverns. For a short span of less than ten years, Cambridge was a musical hothouse, a city like Paris in the 1920s or Los Angeles in the 1940s or New York in the 1950s, where the leading talent of a generation gathers and feeds on its own sheer vitality. The leading café—the focal point of this new wave—was Club 47. The music scene was not limited to performers alone but also included nascent impresarios and record producers, one of whom, Paul Rothchild, is central to the rise of the urban blues. Rothchild wanted to break into the business as a record producer. He began by recording local artists on portable equipment in improvised studios. A few of his crude sessions were actually released under the Club 47's own label, "Mt. Auburn." His first job for a major label was with Prestige, a jazz label run by Bob Weinstock. Rothchild had a nose for talent and a clairvoyant sense for fresh markets and coming trends. Jac Holzman, president of Elektra, a small struggling folk label that featured artists like Theodore Bikel and Oscar Brand, lured Rothchild to his company. Rothchild's first recording for the new label was the music of the Even Dozen Jug Band, featuring John Sebastian (later of the Lovin' Spoonful) and Maria D'Amato (later Maria Muldaur).

Soon Rothchild brought Tom Rush into Holzman's stable and organized a recording featuring young white single artists performing old-fashioned country blues; a record whose title, *The Blues Project,* was later adopted by a new group roughly in the style of Butterfield. The album, a loose collection of shallow imitations of classic rural blues, generated some excitement and talk of a blues revival. The very idea of reviving blues that harkened back to the music of Sun House and Robert Johnson completely bypassed the contemporary thriving blues tradition of B.B. King, Bobby Bland, and Junior Parker. Fortunately, Rothchild was not too preoccupied with bygone days to miss entirely the living blues being played on the chitlin circuit. Part of Rothchild's knack for spotting new talent came from paying close attention to the gossip of Fritz Richmond, washtub bassist in the Jim Kweskin Jug Band, a wacky Cambridge bunch featuring the quavering voice of Geoff Muldaur.

Rothchild knew that when Richmond talked about a new musician, he should listen carefully. On New Year's Eve, 1964, Richmond called Rothchild from Chicago and told him to take an early plane to Chicago to hear a new group, the Paul Butterfield Blues Band. Rothchild had met Butterfield once on the West Coast and the young, white mouth-harpist had not made any particular impression on him. Regardless of that fact, when Richmond recommended Butterfield, Rothchild came quickly. This second encounter with Butterfield impressed Rothchild deeply and when he also heard the guitar playing of Mike Bloomfield, who had his own band at the time, he persuaded the two to join forces and brought them to New York to record.

In the spring of 1965, Elektra released a sampler of bluesy tunes called *What's Shakin'.* The album featured Butterfield with Bloomfield, a few cuts by Tom Rush, some tunes by John Sebastian, and one or two by keyboardist Al Kooper. The sampler sold very briskly—over 200,000 copies in the first few weeks. Jac Holzman, president of Elektra Records, was bewildered by the sensational sales, but Rothchild was confident that the sudden popularity was all over the Butterfield cuts.

Rothchild had no easy task recording Butterfield. The band was new, and its style was novel. No one had ever recorded blues quite like Butterfield's, though countless tiny studios in Memphis, Houston, and Chicago had recorded the music of the black blues artists who inspired the Butterfield style. Moreover, Rothchild was accustomed to recording the quiet, delicate music of folk musicians, not the churning, amplified sounds of an electric band. Together the Butterfield band and producer Rothchild learned their new craft of recording electric blues. When the first version of the album was complete—packaged and waiting at the pressing plant ready for distribution—Rothchild pronounced the product unworthy of the group and proposed to his boss, Holzman, that they rerecord the entire album, save for one good cut, "Born in Chicago." Holzman agreed to let Rothchild record Butterfield live at the upcoming Cafe Au Go Go date in New York, an expensive proposition at the very least, especially for a small label like Elektra.

When it was over and Rothchild had miles of fresh tape in the can, he told Holzman there was not an inch worth saving—that it was either back to the studio or return to the original inferior version. Holzman was apoplectic, according to Cambridge folk gurus Eric von Schmidt and Jim Rooney. (See their *Baby, Let Me Follow You Down,* Doubleday, 1979.) After Holzman calmed down, he agreed to let the producer of the Butterfield group take the band back into the studio for another try. On the third time around, both the musicians and the producer knew what they wanted. The results were extraordinary.

From the dozens of new takes, Rothchild, who had an uncanny sense of how to patch together tiny segments, made a smooth, apparently seamless recording that by his own reckoning contained 263 mid-song splices. From the cover photo to the programming of the cuts, the resulting album, called simply *The Paul Butterfield Blues Band,* is a model of well-conceived, impeccably executed recording. Every instrument is clearly articulated, and the mix is near perfection. Even those passages of Bloomfield's guitar that are tinged with reverb are not lost in the clamor of the other instruments. The quality of the mix is such that every instrument sounds as if it is poised just behind the speaker cloth. The album, released in the fall of 1965, was not a hit in the standard sense of dominating the charts, but in the long run it sold steadily; years after the average hit would have dropped from sight, it still had brisk sales and remains in print today, still available in many shops.

In retrospect, it is difficult to appreciate how novel was the sound of the first Butterfield album when it appeared; but to listeners who had never heard B.B. King play his guitar, or Little

Walter blow his amplified mouth harp, Butterfield, Bishop, and Bloomfield sounded like musical revolutionaries. Bloomfield had all the raw power of rock guitarists, and the rhythm section churned with the same unrelenting momentum that rock music enthusiasts were demanding; but the Butterfield musicians were technically far advanced over rock musicians of the time, who were, by and large, primitives in comparison. *The Paul Butterfield Blues Band* had the rhythm and texture of the best rock groups of the time, plus a fine sense of melody and embellishment. Bloomfield's swoops and slides and his elaborate figures up and down the blues scale played at full volume were a revelation to listeners, accustomed to hearing rock guitarists repeat the same three-note figure for eight out of twelve bars of their solos. And Butterfield's electric mouth harp was a sound so novel that many new listeners could not identify the instrument.

Besides producing Butterfield's first recording, Rothchild helped the Chicago musician with another important move in his career, when he arranged for Albert Grossman to become Butterfield's personal manager. Grossman was already directing Bob Dylan's move from musical guru of the socially conscious protest-minded college set to superstar of intellectuals and teenyboppers alike. The public does not often see such characters as impresarios and personal managers, but Richard Pennebaker's documentary film, *Don't Look Back,* about Dylan's rise to stardom, gives a glimpse of Grossman in action. He is the man with gray hair tied back in a knot, speaking on the phone in a voice just above a whisper, telling a concert producer that unless he gets exactly what he has stipulated his star will not appear, contract or no contract. Grossman was a good judge of star quality. A few years after taking on Butterfield, he took over management of a promising young female vocalist, Janis Joplin, who had made a big impression on West Coast audiences during her regular appearances at the Avalon Ballroom.

The rapid rise of the Butterfield Blues Band came partly through the sensation stirred by Mike Bloomfield, and his acclaim was part of a new trend of making culture heroes of guitarists. The instrumentalist as culture hero was nothing new. Charlie Parker, Benny Goodman, and the early Satchmo had been worshipped; but since the birth of rock-and-roll, pop stars like Elvis were not idolized for their musicianship or their virtuosity with a particular instrument.

Now came a new kind of star: the guitar maestro. The fascination with this figure was as much with the instrument as with the hero. From the beginning, the electric guitar was the basic instrument of rock-and-roll, though in the genre of black rock-and-roll (the side of rock music emerging from rhythm and blues) it shared the limelight with the saxophone (e.g., Little Richard, Junior Walker and the Allstars, Bill Doggett). It is an instrument ideal for representing the culture that embraced it. It is primitive in the extreme: six strings stretched on a board, hand picked and hand fretted; no moving parts; more rudimentary than a harpsichord; an ancient instrument. But, the instrument is also high technology: electromagnetic signals, generated by tiny magnets beneath the strings, amplified by electronics and fed to a bank of speaker cones. The sound it makes is full of urban clash and clang and has more percussion in it than the piano and vibraphone combined. It requires extreme dexterity and precision to play well. The electric guitar is the mediation between the two poles: the primitive hand-held harp and the highly technological synthesizer. The electric guitarist is both a conjurer who manipulates the strings with tiny movements of his fingertips, and a sound engineer who chooses his electronics and programs them. He is part violinist, part (stringed) harpist, part pool shark, and part engineer.

Bloomfield played the role to its limit. He was infected with an irrepressible boyish enthusiasm; every new wave of sound from his own speaker seemed to move him to new heights of ecstasy, driving him on to even greater heights of inspiration. He was the thoroughly self-indulgent hedonist. His playing was full of brilliant flourishes and long, pulsating sustains; he used his amplifier to make the notes sound bowed, rather than plucked, and in this way gave the instrument a hornlike voice. By the time he left the Butterfield Band in 1968, Mike Bloomfield was better known than Butterfield himself. His new group, The Electric Flag, with drummer Buddy Miles, was the first "supergroup" composed of stars from other groups. [Later supergroups included Blind Faith, Cream, and Crosby, Stills and Nash.]

Bloomfield was not the only guitarist to play this new role, nor

was the role confined to blues: Eric Clapton, Gerry Garcia of the
Grateful Dead, Jimi Hendrix, all these rock-n-rollers achieved the
same status, not to mention bluesmen Johnny Winter and Elvin
Bishop. Together they prepared the way for the maestro of the
maestros, B.B. King. Clapton must be mentioned separately and
put together with his English peers, vocalist Eric Burden of the
Animals, vocalist/mouth harpist John Mayall, and guitarist Peter
Greene, who all studied black American blues and reimported it
to the United States after digesting it.

Deciphering how a career as topsy-turvy as B.B.'s evolves in
any particular way is inevitably an occult art in which a crystal
ball is an extremely useful tool. Yet it is not too farfetched to say
that Butterfield's emergence as a pop star, thereby setting the
stage for B.B., was nearly quashed in the very moment Butterfield
got his decisive break at the 1965 Newport Folk Festival. And if
Butterfield had never made it, then quite possibly blues today
would still be strictly a ghetto commodity and B.B. would still be
riding the chitlin circuit. It happened this way.

Butterfield was scheduled to perform at the afternoon workshop devoted to blues. The first half of the program consisted entirely of old-style solo bluesmen, all of them black. The emcee
was Alan Lomax, the famous American folklorist and musicologist, who had discovered many blues musicians and been midwife to their music with portable recording equipment. He had a
great reverence for these old craftsmen and a high degree of scep-
ticism toward young upstarts who would presume to follow in
their tracks. Folklorists are preservationists and tend to be
purists, a natural attitude for those who spend their lives searching for *the real thing* in order to preserve it for future generations.
It was a purist sentiment Lomax expressed when he came to the
microphone to announce the Butterfield Band after a long delay
while the formidable tiers of amplifiers and speakers were set up
onstage. First, he reminded the audience that they had already
heard the best bluesmen in the world during the first half of the
workshop. Then, he reflected that in a bygone age people fashioned their own instruments and made their blues music in the
shade of a tree, where nowadays people seem to need mountains
of fancy hardware to make even a toot or a squeak. Finally, he
introduced the Butterfield Band, saying, in effect, that now the

truth would be out: the world would see if these smart alecks can really play blues. When Lomax went backstage, he came face to face with Albert Grossman, who demanded to know what kind of introduction Lomax intended to give if he didn't mean to put the kibosh on Grossman's new property. The two had words, and in a flash they were on each other, rolling in the dirt.

This story reveals how sensitive attitudes were toward change in musical fashions in general and toward electric amplification in particular. As matters worked out, nothing Lomax said affected the audience reaction to Butterfield either way. But if the audience had howled at Butterfield as they did the next night, when Dylan plugged in, perhaps things would have stood very differently. And perhaps when a good thing is blocked for long yet keeps knocking at the door, any opportunity will do, and any minor event may start the avalanche.

A TREND-SETTING CLUB AND A PIVOTAL BOOK

The first bluesmen to benefit from the new awareness of urban blues were the Chicago stalwarts, musicians like James Cotton, onetime mouth harpist from the Muddy Waters' band, Junior Wells, Buddy Guy, and Otis Rush. James Cotton, who had schooled Butterfield in harp techniques, quit Muddy's band, formed his own group, and put his career in the skilled hands of Albert Grossman, who booked him in coffeehouses that catered to folk-music audiences. Chicago groups were the natural early beneficiaries because Butterfield was from Chicago and because the first opportunities for bookings before white audiences came from small folk cabarets which could not comfortably accommodate large bands like those of B.B. King and Bobby Bland.

The Club 47 in Cambridge was instrumental in establishing the market appeal of urban blues in Middle America. Shortly before Butterfield's triumph at the Newport Festival, the Club 47 changed hands and came under the management of Jim Rooney, a Cambridge folk musician whose tastes were eclectic. Rooney grew up in Boston at a time when the Boston Navy Base brought in thousands of sailors from the South, putting country music and rhythm and blues in big demand; during his teens, he heard Symphony Sid broadcasting over Boston's WBMS before the famous disc jockey went to New York and became one of the best known DJs in America. Rooney listened to all kinds of music and visited George Wien's Storyville where he heard Duke Ellington, but at first it was country music that excited him most. When Cambridge became a mecca for musicians in the 1960s, Rooney was in his natural element.

Soon after he heard the Butterfield band at Newport, Rooney booked them into his tiny Cambridge coffeehouse at 47 Palmer Street and followed with a steady parade of urban bluesmen. Muddy Waters, Howlin' Wolf, Junior Wells, and Buddy Guy, Otis Rush, J. B. Hutto and blues-oriented jazzmen like Mose Allison and George Benson all played Rooney's Club 47. The response was tumultuous. Cambridge music fans, hitherto always romantic purists devoted to the transparent sounds of folk music, lined Palmer Street down to the Brattle and around the corner toward Harvard Square waiting for one of the 150 seats in the cracker-box club. The impact was swift in other cities as word spread on the cabaret and coffeehouse circuits that young white Middle Americans were craving urban blues.

WHEN THE BUTTERFIELD BLUES BAND began storming the country, Middle America was completely ignorant of the modern blues tradition. Only ghetto record shops stocked records by artists like Little Walter and B.B. King. There was an ample literature on the older solo blues artists of the Deep South, but none on the younger contemporary black artists who played amplified blues in the urban centers.

(I met Percy Heath, bassist in the Modern Jazz Quartet, sometime in the late 1960s. Heath had grown up in the part of Philadelphia called "South Filthy" and had often heard Muddy Waters play in the taverns around his neighborhood. After expressing great affection for Muddy, Heath asked me if I could explain how it was possible that white Americans heard the Rolling Stones and other British groups perform Muddy Waters' music and yet had never heard of the original. He apparently suspected that a white conspiracy was keeping the black origins of pop music a secret. My answer left him befuddled. "Because when we look for the composer's name in parentheses after the song title on the record label, we see the name 'Morganfield,'" I said.

He looked at me blankly, as if this was no proper explanation. "Who's 'Morganfield'?" he asked.

"McKinley Morganfield is Muddy Waters' real name!" Now, one decade later, white fans know that McKinley Morganfield is Muddy Waters, that Chester Burnett is Howlin' Wolf, that Walter Jacobs is Little Walter, and Walter Horten is Big Walter or Shaky Walter. You have to know these things in order to find the records: the real names are a kind of key to enter the world of blues through records. It is slightly ironic that black musicians took on good catchy monikers in order to project an image and spread their reputations, and years later white blues fans struggled to decipher this code by scouring liner notes and jazz encyclopedias for their real names. The real names of these artists are probably still unknown today among black blues fans, who need no entry to the genre or the culture—least of all through records.)

The mysterious cloud that obscured urban blues from the sight of Middle Americans was blown away by the publication of a thorough study of the genre in 1967. The book, titled *The Urban Blues*, was written by Charles Keil, a white graduate student at the University of Chicago, who had been reared in one of the most notorious enclaves of the white upper-middle class: Darien, Connecticut. Like Elvin Bishop of the Butterfield Blues Band, Charles Keil was a cultural transplant, a white who came to Chicago to study and was lured by the ghetto siren sounds. *The Urban Blues* was a rare combination of sensitive, hip, savvy discussion with exhaustive scholarship. According to Keil, it was no accident that nothing had been written on this subject: the music of urban bluesmen, he wrote, had been systematically neglected by scholars, historians, music journalists, critics, and folklorists (most, if not all, white) out of priggish snobbery; the musical literati had previously channeled the little attention they paid to blues exclusively toward the older generation of solo blues artists from the rural South—and this out of a patronizing attitude. The historians relished the discovery of old, near-forgotten bluesmen (and Dixiemen), many of them presumed dead, and the older, more infirm, the greater their delight. Nothing would please the patronizer so much as finding a senile, arthritic, toothless alcoholic who cut ten sides for Vocalion Race Records in 1930 and disappeared immediately thereafter; if he could still get his stiffened fingers around the neck of a guitar and if his name was something like "Slackjaw Willie" or "Hamhock Jones," all the better. The careful attention to this fading category contrasted to the stony silence concerning the living, thriving tradition of contemporary blues which evolved from the older styles through migration from the rural South to the urban North. Keil wrote his book, he explained, to fill the vacuum and right the balance.

Keil tried, with overall success, to supply in one volume the entire missing literature on urban blues, the history of its evolution, the elaborate interconnections among musicians, and an analysis of the cultural connection between the music and its social milieu.† Keil devoted an entire chapter of his book to B.B. King. His sensitive portrait of B.B. as an artist was B.B.'s first in depth pen portrait outside the black press. By this time white audiences had begun accepting Muddy Waters and Howlin' Wolf, but B.B. remained buried. As Keil put it:

> I doubt that more than a few thousand white Americans outside the Deep South have ever heard B.B. King's music. If one first-class citizen in a thousand could identify his name, I'd be very much surprised. All this adds up to a lack of future for our hypothetical bluesman: his potential market is certainly there; but it is not very big and, more important, it is sharply circumscribed.

Keil held out hope that things would change for B.B.:

> B.B. King, though he rejects the possibility, may find that his blues style will in time win for him a substantial white as well as Negro audience.

This prophecy was, in part, self-fulfilling. The long range impact of *The Urban Blues* greatly widened the breach in the color lines opened by the white emulators of black blues. The book went through nine printings and can still be found on bookshop shelves. Most libraries have the book, and it is used in countless college courses in black culture, in sociology, and even in musicology. By educating the public about the neglected genre of urban blues, Charles Keil helped prepare Middle America for the arrival of B.B. King.

† In addition to calling attention to the historical importance of this book and praising it for its literate style and thorough scholarship I wish to add my personal gratitude to its author. I hope I have learned much from Keil's book and I hold myself in his debt.

WAITING FOR B.B.

The arrival of B.B. King was a complex process. In retrospect, now that he is a celebrity with whites and blacks alike, his twenty years of obscurity seems bizarre. But prior to his emergence, it looked improbable—at the very least—that he would ever play the casinos of Las Vegas, the jazz clubs of New York, the luxury hotels of Miami, or the Ed Sullivan show. How did he get from the chitlin circuit to the prestige entertainment rooms of Middle America?

B.B. King's success was not an isolated phenomenon; he rode to the top on the crest of a wave of sudden popularity for his genre. The way was well prepared for him by other blues artists, both black and white. As the late bloomer of the new trend and yet its pre-eminent artist, he came as a climax to the new wave that was three years in building. The exact details are many, and each is rather small: the net result was the outcome of an intricate interplay between concert promoters, tavern owners, radio station program directors (AM and FM), the musical press, record-company publicity agents, record shop owners, and, as ever, the most important and least predictable factor, the public itself. As I. C. Jarvie, the noted historian of cinema, has observed, when it comes to mass media no one knows how the interplay works, even when it works to great advantage; no one can predict what will be the final verdict of the public.‡ The rise of the urban blues gives only the barest outline, which can be concluded by observing that two years after white Americans got hip to the urban blues, they still had not met B.B. King. Yet when he arrived on the scene, he came to a throne as the true heir whose identity is finally revealed.

‡ I. C. Jarvie, *Movies and Society* (New York: Basic Books, 1970).

VII

The Arrival of B.B. King

CINDERELLA AND THE ACCOUNTANT

IN 1968, the Black Horatio Alger story of B.B. King takes on a Cinderella tone as the Delta-plowboy-made-good becomes the pre-eminent artist of a neglected genre, who finally receives his just desserts when he is recognized as the reigning master of his craft. The new twist is complete with a dramatic appearance before an adoring crowd of white youths at the Fillmore West in San Francisco, his first appearance in front of a white audience since the disastrous and humiliating performance years before when the band was required to play from behind a curtain in order to keep a discreet buffer between the white patrons and the black musicians.

The Fillmore appearance took B.B. by surprise. He was unprepared for the sea of white faces that confronted him, bewildered as he listened from the wings to the long, laudatory introduction by Fillmore director Bill Graham, and overwhelmed by the standing ovation he received when he made his entry. Graham then booked B.B. for the Fillmore East. His performance there was opened by Mike Bloomfield, who introduced B.B. as the greatest living blues guitarist. The transition from obscurity to fame among the whites was accentuated for B.B. by sharing the bill with Johnny Winter, an albino Texan. B.B. recognized Winter as the slender, cross-eyed kid who had entered an all-black Texas roadhouse years before and asked to sit in with the band. Looking at his silvery hair and nearly transparent skin, B.B. had decided, against his musical judgment, to let him play, rather than let himself open to charges of reverse discrimination. The black Texans were flabbergasted at the credible blues played by the gangly alabaster guitarist, and they awarded him a standing ovation; pleased as B.B. was, he was also hurt: it was a compliment no black audience had ever given B.B. King. Now, years later, an all-white audience gave B.B. the same honor before he had even played a single note. Two years after Middle America got hip to the blues, B.B. finally made his debut.

The lag between the rise of urban blues in Middle America and B.B.'s dramatic emergence worked decidedly in his favor. An air of anticipation preceded his arrival, and he was able to start his own climb from the crest of the wave at its very peak. Two new elements in his career converged at this splendid moment when all the world seemed ripe for a love affair with him: a hit record —his biggest yet—to give him a powerful booster on takeoff, and a new manager. The two combined to make his new status more like a comet in a long orbit than a shooting star that burns brightly, but briefly, before flickering out. The hit record was "The Thrill Is Gone," an adaptation of a Roy Hawkins song which B.B. had been carrying in his head for years, uncertain of how to shape it in his own style, and it could not have come at a more opportune time. The new manager was Sidney A. Seidenberg, a New York show-business accountant, who had been keeping B.B.'s books.

In 1968, B.B. had a falling out with his current manager, Lou Zito, himself a former musician who had played drums with the Charlie Spivak band. When B.B. left Buffalo Booking in Houston, Texas, in the early 1960s, he lost contact with Don Robey (the nominal head of Buffalo Booking as well as president and founder of two record labels—Duke and Peacock). He also dropped the talented young woman who was Robey's right hand, Evelyn Johnson, the strategist who had guided B.B.'s path on the chitlin circuit. By her own admission, his switch to Zito left her a trifle bitter. But Zito promised a tour abroad. B.B. was satisfied with Zito's early efforts on his behalf, especially his success in arranging B.B.'s foreign tour. It was long overdue: B.B. first traveled abroad years after other blues artists had been appreciatively received by hordes of European blues aficionados.

Later, things changed. Zito handled large quantities of B.B.'s cash and was authorized to spend it at his own discretion; eventually, as had happened before and was to happen again, B.B. lost trust in the man who was accountable only to him in handling his money. There was a dispute over the use of credit cards, and B.B. felt abused when he learned that Zito had given authority to his own nephew to sign for expenses without ever consulting B.B. He resolved to have it out with Zito, and the two agreed that they would abide by the final verdict of Sidney Seidenberg, the accountant in charge of the books, who also kept books for the Dorsey Brothers and Tom Jones. When Seidenberg gave his final accounting, he ruled that B.B. owed Zito a modest sum—less than $10,000, according to B.B. The experience left B.B. with a sour taste in his mouth, and, after paying Zito, he broke off with him. Yet B.B. was impressed with the impartiality Seidenberg, a white man, had seemed to show in working to resolve a dispute between a white and a black man.

While he handled his own affairs, B.B. consulted Seidenberg on day-to-day problems. Sooner or later, B.B. prevailed on Seidenberg to take official charge of his career. Seidenberg had given him better advice off the cuff than the other big shots who had taken their rightful cut (and more, too, maybe) and it seemed right that Seidenberg should be his official manager. Seidenberg agreed and told B.B. he intended to make a bundle off him. "For every million you make, I'll get a hundred grand," he said.

In recruiting Seidenberg as his full-time personal manager, B.B. was falling back on a pattern which had been a standard success formula in the entertainment business from the Borscht Belt to the chitlin circuit and from Broadway to Bourbon Street: the aggressive management of an ambitious Jew and the gifted artistry of a talented black. The prototype of this combination was Satchmo and Joe Glaser. Long after Armstrong had achieved world renown he was still fond of telling how he was disposed to look for such an arrangement.

"Just before I left [New Orleans to join King Oliver's band] old Slippers, the bouncer at the honky-tonk where I played, came up to me and said, '. . . Always keep a white man behind you that'll put his hand on you and say, "That's my nigger." ' Years later I told that to Joe Glaser, my ofay manager, and he said, 'You're nuts.' "*

For Satchmo, Joe Glaser was that white man. The partnership

* *Louis Armstrong—a self-portrait,* The interview by Richard Meryman (New York: The Eakins Press, 1966), pp. 27–28.

made Satchmo into the greatest jazz superstar of the age and Glaser into a powerhouse in the entertainment business. Glaser's Associated Booking became the premier booking agency in show business.

Now B.B. was following the pattern set by Satchmo, and, appropriately, one of his new manager's first moves to upgrade the artist's stature was to install him in Glaser's stable as one of Associated Booking's stars. Then he renegotiated B.B.'s contract with ABC Records and obtained a commitment for more energetic promotion of B.B.'s records—not simply as a specialty artist with appeal to a reliable but narrow following, but instead as an artist with both breadth and depth of appeal. His minimum guarantee per performance was substantially increased over the paltry sum—well below $1,000—to which he had grown accustomed. The choice bookings began rolling in.

It is impossible to assess with any precision what was Seidenberg's contribution to B.B.'s steady rise from the time of his big hit in 1968. There is a show-business mystique attached to managers. Satchmo had his Glaser, Elvis his Colonel Parker, Dylan and Joplin their Albert Grossman, and the Beatles their Brian Epstein. In the glittery world of entertainment where stardom descends on an artist quite miraculously and without apparent rhyme or reason, the success of stars such as B.B. King or Joan Baez is often attributed to behind-the-scenes wizards who know the password that opens every door and the alchemy of image making. Moreover, when performers do become stars, they are very much in demand and then the managers call the shots, thereby enhancing the mystique of the manager as the wizard— perhaps rightly, perhaps not.

No one knows how to bestow stardom; most of the ingredients that go into the chemistry of stardom, whatever they are, must be volatile (talent and artistry are never sufficient to assure stardom, and in some cases they can be liabilities), and even the shrewdest managers have little control over matters. It is naturally in their interest to have people believe they have much control; and since no one knows for sure and since stars glitter, the manager can and often does share the glitter. There are no wizards in show business, perhaps, but surely some managers look like ones.

All the same, most artists cannot do without managers to manage their affairs. If B.B.'s career is any measure, then any kind of management is better than self-management since no matter how poor his management has been from time to time, whenever he has managed his own affairs, his career has declined. For strictly technical reasons, it is not practical at all to be both performer and manager.

Once Seidenberg switched from the role of accountant to that of manager, he threw himself into the new job of manager with abandon. He hired a large publicity staff and added other performers to his list of artists. A film crew was recruited, and shooting began for a documentary on B.B. under Seidenberg's direction. As B.B. prospered, Seidenberg acquired a reputation as a show-biz wizard. Among the artists who clamored to join the "SAS Family of Stars" was a rising group from Georgia fronted by a dynamic female vocalist named Gladys Knight. Seidenberg added Gladys Knight and the Pips to his list of performers; soon this group's popularity exceeded even B.B.'s. Another rabbit had popped from the wizard's hat.

For a time, Seidenberg seemed unstoppable. Yet show business is a game of chutes and ladders, and after a while his wizard's touch went cold. The first sign of trouble was grumbling from B.B., who felt that Seidenberg was neglecting him in favor of Gladys. His grumbling turned into a formal protest in late 1973. When several months passed with no reply, B.B. King officially dissolved his partnership with Seidenberg and became his own manager once again. Seidenberg later denied ever having seen B.B.'s letter of protest. Then came trouble with Gladys when she married, became pregnant, and fell out with the Pips. The chemistry within the group and between the artists and their manager had gone sour; Gladys announced her intention to become a single and dump Seidenberg. Now Seidenberg needed B.B., and, truth to tell, B.B. needed a manager badly. In 1977 they were reconciled.

Wizard or no wizard, Seidenberg was experienced. As an accountant to entertainers, he had doubtless acquired intimate knowledge of the infrastructure in the business, and his ham-fisted approach fits the conventional wisdom as to how things get done there. However, this conventional wisdom is viable because it is widespread; otherwise, its adherents are bound to be more fumblers than deft technicians. Seidenberg's handling of the documentary film about B.B. is a case in point. Rather than hire an experienced director, he chose to supervise the filming himself. The end result was that after shooting hours of footage and spending tens of thousands of dollars, less than five minutes' footage was worth saving. B.B. had given his man carte blanche in matters of promotion, of course; he could do nothing but complain, and he was too much of a gentleman for that.

In the eighteen months following the peak popularity of "The Thrill Is Gone," B.B.'s itinerary changed completely: the chitlin circuit gave way to a combination of jazz clubs (New York's Village Gate and Lennie's on the Turnpike in Boston) and rock palaces (the Fillmores East and West and the Boston Tea Party). The new market for B.B.'s music expanded steadily to include college concerts and the dining rooms of luxury resort hotels. An important plank in the foundation of his new career was laid down when he appeared at a showcase performance before an audience of social chairmen representing student bodies on campuses around the entire country. The showcase engagement, held at the Peabody Hotel in Memphis on February 3, 1969, was a kind of marathon audition at which several artists gave a special performance free of charge, with the prospective buyers flown in, all expenses paid. [Together with Blues Boy King escaping the chitlin circuit was also the country and western clown prince Roy Clark, escaping the honkytonk circuit.] B.B. was a solid success with the campus representatives, and college concerts became a staple in his schedule. More than any other facet of his changed routine, with the possible exception of television appearances, B.B.'s regular stints in college gymnasiums from Boise to Chapel Hill solidified his new career by exposing him night after night to the young affluent whites that comprise the broad base of America's middle class. A few days after the showcase at the Peabody, B.B. made his first network TV appearance on "The Tonight Show," a lucky break provided by Flip Wilson, who was substituting for Johnny Carson. Other TV dates followed on the Mike Douglas, David Frost, and Merv Griffin shows, as well as return spots on the Johnny Carson show proper.

CINDERELLA AND THE WOODEN RINGMASTER

There were several benchmarks on the way of B.B.'s climb: a ten-day tour with the Rolling Stones in 1970, tours to Europe and

Australia in 1971, a forty-five-day world tour in 1972 that established B.B.'s global appeal, an African tour sponsored by the State Department, numerous European excursions, and success even in Israel, where the legendary Ella Fitzgerald had not succeeded. And then there were bookings at various theaters in the round—the Circle Star in San Carlos, California, the Westbury Music Theater on Long Island, the Front Row Theater in Cleveland, Ohio—where Middle Americans, many of them middle-aged, attended monthly concerts by subscription series, plus a stint at the posh Royal Box in Manhattan's Americana Hotel. There was also a Grammy Award, and Las Vegas dates at Caesar's Palace, where he shared billing with Frank Sinatra, and at the Dunes, before he signed a three-year contract with the Las Vegas Hilton.

In 1978 representatives of the Russian government came to Lake Tahoe, where B.B. was playing an extended engagement in order to preview his show for audiences in their country. Months of delicate negotiations followed. Copies of the lyrics to every song in his act were submitted in triplicate to the Soviet embassy. Finally an official invitation was issued for a concert tour that spanned the Soviet Union from Georgia to Moscow and deep into the heart of Asia.

Yet, of all these triumphs, the one with the most symbolic significance for B.B. was his appearance on the Ed Sullivan show in 1971. Ever since Elvis Presley first appeared before Sullivan's cameras, playing the Sullivan show had been a sign that a rising new performer had arrived with the American public. Sullivan, a former sports columnist who began his variety show in 1949, when it was called "The Toast of the Town," became a royal arbiter of mass appeal. In fact, Presley's case demonstrated that fact, because although Elvis had already appeared before a national television audience, on the Steve Allen show, which ran opposite Sullivan, it was only after playing for Sullivan that the mass audience deemed him acceptable. Steve Allen was considered a zany, intellectually oriented comic and jazz pianist, so his approval counted far less than puritanical Sullivan's. In later years, the public came to think of Elvis' appearance on the Sullivan show as his debut, precisely because Sullivan held the imprimatur for public recognition.

Not all the performers appearing on the Sullivan show were

celebrities; every program included a handful of nonentities to provide the show with a carnival air. The vaudeville performers and circus acts that rounded out the bill had the effect of bringing the level of entertainment down to the recognized lowest common denominator of mass taste; it was a crucial part of Sullivan's success that his show looked conspicuously lowbrow. When viewers tuned in on Sunday evenings at 8:00 P.M., they saw a show very much like the stage shows at county fairs between the harness races and the hell drivers in the last days of summer. The vaudeville atmosphere was enhanced by the fact that Sullivan was a holdout to the idea that videotaping robbed a show of its spark; when all other major network shows were taped, the Sullivan show went on the air live.

On October 8, 1970, when B.B. played the Ed Sullivan show, the program included a list of performers that reflected both the character of B.B.'s new surroundings and the breadth of his new audience. There was another musical act, The Carpenters, to sing their latest hit, "We've Only Just Begun." There were two top Borscht Belt comedians who did their durable routines: George Burns, for the Serutan set, and Robert Klein, for the go-go people. And there were two county-fair stage acts to round out the bill: a man who made shadow figures with his hands, and the winners of the Harvest Moon Ball Dance Contest (one couple from each category, including a pair of old-fashioned jitterbug artists—blacks, of course). The finale was provided by crooner Tony Bennett who sang behind a fifteen-piece band onstage.

An account of how the Ed Sullivan show was produced and how B.B. reacted to the situation, personally, will show how far he had come and yet how much he still clung to his old self for reassurance.

When B.B. was admitted to the stage door at the Ed Sullivan Theater by the Pinkerton Guard at 9:00 A.M. that Sunday morning, only fatigue hid his fear. In spite of his unfailing stage presence, B.B. is still intensely afraid of new audiences in unfamiliar surroundings. But now he was more tired than frightened. He had played at the Fillmore East the night before and had not finished the last set until around 4:00 A.M. Now he had to do a run-through in the morning, a dress rehearsal with tape running before a live audience in the early afternoon, followed by possible additional rehearsals to make adjustments after previewing the tape prior to the real 8:00 P.M. performance in front of live cameras.

Before his turn came for the first run-through, he sat in the second row watching The Carpenters rehearsing their lip-synch number as the technicians checked all the details of camera movements. Although the stage was quite small, the cameras saw the scene in keyhole shots through cardboard frames covered with pastel flowers so that the monitors around the studio showed angelic faces floating in a spacious sea of soft-focus petals. When the stage manager called for "the King group," a set appeared in less time than it took B.B. and his band to find their marks on-stage. Colored bands arched across the backdrop with a legend "B.B. King," imitating the cover from his current album. Usually musicians on the program would sing two numbers, one in each half of the show, but B.B. was allowed a lucky break when the producer gave him one uninterrupted six-minute slot in which he could do a medley. B.B. was pleased because the single extended spot would give him more effective exposure, and a medley projects the image of an established star with a string of hits behind him.

The run-through was brief and routine; B.B. asked the band to repeat the modulation of keys that provided the transition from one song to the next. After twenty minutes, the stage manager, speaking into the mike on his headset, announced, "That's it. Mark it and strike it." His voice boomed over the loudspeakers around the stage. The set disappeared as quickly and soundlessly as it had gone up. This was the mark of how a live variety show was produced: the division of labor is microscopic, and every component is precisely coordinated; in the span of a sixty-second commercial, a herd of dancing bears and all their paraphernalia could be replaced onstage by a fifteen-piece orchestra complete with multi-tiered bandstand. Throughout all the preparations, Sullivan himself was nowhere in sight, though the senior members of the production crew invoked his authority occasionally by saying, "Mr. Sullivan likes it this way."

During the two-hour wait until dress rehearsal, B.B. distracted himself from the tension of anticipation by conducting a monologue on life in Mississippi and cotton farming. Addressing the half dozen guests hanging about his dressing room he explained that on the Barrett plantation they worked every day "from kin to cain't"—that is, from dawn, when you can first barely see, until the last light of day faded, and you can't see at all. He recalled that one year during World War II, truckloads of German POWs were brought to the fields from a nearby compound to work alongside the plantation hands—initially under heavy guard, but later with only token security. When the trucks arrived from the compound in the morning, the regular field hands had already been working a few hours; and in the evening, when the trucks returned the foreign prisoners to their barracks a few hours before sundown, the regular laborers stayed on working until darkness fell.

"This got to me sometimes," B.B. said. "It wasn't that I thought the POWs should be treated more harshly, but the fact that we led a harder life than captured enemy soldiers seemed unfair to me."

He described the details of harvesting cotton, complete with elaborate physical demonstrations, using improvised props, and told about the violent rainstorms that sent blinding sheets of water sweeping across the unobstructed open fields of cotton. "You wouldn't believe it," he said, "but sometimes after such a storm, we'd find little fishes, 'bout half the size of your little finger, wiggling around in the puddles."

It was odd and moving to listen to him while he stood on the threshold of his greatest triumph, explaining to a rapt audience of urbanites how to raise cotton. It seemed as if he was trying to find firm ground to stand on as he floated in an electronic fantasy world. He capped his lecture with a startling confession that although he had watched all those aspects of cotton farming and performed many of them himself, he didn't consider that he actually *knew* them until years later, when he read them in an encyclopedia. It was several minutes before it dawned on me what was the significance of his final confession—that it demonstrated the utter depth of his conviction that as a black plantation hand, he must necessarily be ignorant of all that surrounded him, and it underscored his belief in the absolute primacy of book learning.

The cassette recorder on the makeup table softly played an old blues with the unmistakable thump of a Chicago band. The music filled the lull that followed B.B.'s lecture. "That's Little Walter [Jacobs] playing," B.B. said finally. "He really had something

going for him—a sound all his own—and he might really have
gone someplace if he hadn't been so crazy. Every time he'd get a
little money in his pocket—three or four thousand dollars, say—
he'd go off on a spree, drinking and gambling, missing his gigs.
It's a pity he ended up the way he did. He really had something."
B.B. was referring to the fact that Walter Jacobs died from the
effects of a beating.

Dress rehearsal was approaching and the guests began filing
out. B.B. and Seidenberg conferred on one remaining important
detail. Sullivan might beckon B.B. to join him at his side just as
he finished performing to give a final shoulder-to-shoulder wave
to the audience in the style of triumphant political candidates.
This last kudo was an important status symbol and was only
accorded to select performers. There would be no advance word
if Sullivan would award him the final touch, and B.B. must
remain alert for a signal from the reigning emcee.

Sullivan dress rehearsals were full-fledged shows before a full
house. The audience this time was a typical mixture of tourists,
Cub Scout Packs and little old ladies in cloth caps who make the
weekly rounds of TV game shows and variety programs. The orchestra, situated in another studio entirely, struck the theme on
cue, and the control-room engineers blended canned applause
with the rough and irregular sound of the real studio audience
clapping. The tape rolled, and Ed Sullivan stepped from the
wings.

In person, Sullivan seemed a caricature of his TV image. He
was every bit as wooden as the nightclub impressionists who imi-
tated him. His Cro-Magnon jaw, hunched shoulders, slicked-
down hair with the Simonize shine, and his odd, stilted way of
speaking were every bit as stylized and peculiar as the humorists
portrayed them. Gesturing toward the tiny balcony with a grand
sweep and speaking like a carnival barker, he announced the line-
up for the evening's "really big show," including a special
surprise, which turned out to be baseball stars from the recent
World Series. From the moment the orchestra struck the theme
until the credits rolled to close the show, the whole production
ran as one well-tuned machine, and most impressive of all was
the fact that nothing that appeared on the screen—not even the
shots of the baseball stars standing up at their seats in the
audience—betrayed the fact that the show was produced in a tiny

TV studio that only gave the air of a mammoth theater like the Roxy or Radio City Music Hall. With Sullivan, the wooden ringmaster, barking in-between acts, The Carpenters sang their treacle, George Burns flashed his pearly whites and gestured with his cigar, the shadow man did his parlor tricks, the Harvest Moon contestants strutted their stuff, and B.B. sang his heart out for six minutes. The hoped-for summons to rub shoulders with Sullivan never came. Credits rolled, Sullivan vanished, and the theater emptied.

The tape was run almost immediately after closing the rehearsal; B.B. watched it on a monitor in the dressing room together with his entourage. They ogled the tight shots of B.B.'s hands picking the guitar and the long, lingering shots of his face. They watched the noticeably classier production on crooner Tony Bennett's numbers with a touch of envy they made no effort to hide, and rendered the verdict: "That's the treatment you get when you're a regular." Satisfied that he had done all he could for the moment B.B. stretched out on the couch and fell instantly into a deep sleep. When he awoke a few hours later, the theater four floors below was already full. At 8:00 P.M., EST, the sign above the stage glowed ON THE AIR and the orchestra struck the theme. Another live broadcast of the Ed Sullivan show had just begun. Shortly before the midpoint of the show, Ed Sullivan announced B.B. by proclaiming, "And now, from Indianola, Mississippi, the great blues singer, B. . . . B. . . . King!" In the six minutes that he played and sang, 50 million Americans heard B.B. King belt out the lyrics he had sung in every performance for the past twenty years:

> I've been downhearted baby,
> Ever since the day we met.
> Our love is nothing but the blues.
> Baby, how blue can you get.

Part Three

Looking Through the Kaleidoscope

VIII

The Once and Future King

THE STORY of B.B. King is three stories knit into one. The first is the development of a personality, the second is the growth of an artist, and the third is the making of a career. These three facets of the man—his character, his art, and his career—are so closely woven together that each can be more fully understood by taking the other two into account. This chapter begins with an analysis of B.B.'s character and continues with a discussion of how his character projects onto his career; the next chapter will use the character analysis that follows here to better understand his music.

IT IS NOT easy to dissect a man in print, even less so when he is living, and all the more difficult when he is a friend. There may be something slightly indecent in probing a man's soul in public; yet this is part of the biographer's job. I hope that my analysis will show that B.B. is an extremely sensitive man; hence some of the views expressed in the pages immediately following may be unpleasant to him. But the same analysis will show that he is capable of enormous self-detachment; at times he looks upon himself with the same cool detachment as if he were looking at a total stranger. There are rare artists who come into their own almost full-blown from the start; they seem to need no training, nor even any period of growth. Robert Johnson, the early Delta bluesman and one of the founders of the Delta blues guitar style, seems to have been one such artist. The slang expression describing such artists is the descriptive term "a natural." Most artists, B.B. no less than the average, require training and discipline—particularly hard when self-administered—and these require a degree of self-detachment, too. B.B. has it.

When amateur musicians listen to themselves on tape for the first time, they sound to themselves like strangers. "Is that really me?" is the standard comment of the novice. But professionals, also, listen to their own recordings at least with one ear, as if they were hearing someone not themselves—that is to say, with critical detachment, ready to judge the results impartially. B.B. King read the galley proofs of this book with eyes as cool as his ears when he listens to the playback in the studio. He seemed to have grasped the fact that this chapter, in particular, is my tribute to him, warts and all.

The three facets of man, artist, and star, form a pyramid. The artist is the child of the personality, and the star was born from both. Or, to put it another way, and carry the interplay further, B.B. King's art is a solution to a deep personal problem of self-respect; and his career is a solution to a new problem, the problem of gaining recognition, which was generated when he solved the first problem by becoming an artist.

CHARACTER DEVELOPMENT

The development of B.B.'s character is a reaction to his harsh childhood. Riley King had all the hardships that came with being born black in Mississippi during the 1920s, and the incumbent psychological burdens that go along with them: poverty and the tendency to see the social order that inflicted that poverty on black people as permanently fixed and sometimes even God-given. To his good fortune, he was endowed with sufficient innate strength of character to emphatically reject the idea preached by his black elders that some people were put on this earth to be of service to other—presumably superior—people. Still, as a boy, the earth ended at the Mississippi state line, or perhaps even two counties within those borders, and nothing in sight could give him much hope of occupying any social rank except the very lowest. In Mississippi every black child of that day, including Riley, was educated daily in the complicated etiquette by which those at the bottom of the social hierarchy acknowledged the superior position of their betters. Always call a white man "sir" and a white woman "ma'am," never question white honesty, always give way to whites on the sidewalk, never question white authority, and so on. Black children were raised on a medieval idea of justice: there was no recourse in the law to seek redress for injustice inflicted from above; even murder, in the form of lynching, was not outlawed per se. It is too much to expect from anyone to have grown up black in Old Mississippi without at least the suspicion of one's own inferiority, and B.B. King is no exception.

Added to the great difficulties of growing up black in that place and time, Riley had to contend with being, for all intents and purposes, an orphan and an only child. From the age of five, when his parents separated, he barely knew his father, lived with his mother only infrequently, and seems to have formed little attachment to his grandmother, with whom he lived most of the time during the nine-year period between his parents' separation and his grandmother's death when he was fourteen. No high-flown discussion about the absence of role models and sibling relations is necessary to realize that he had a rough lot in life; common sense alone is sufficient to show that a child growing up in dire poverty as a kind of cast-off among people who were little more than medieval serfs would have great difficulty believing in his own basic worth.

B.B. never speaks about his childhood in bitter terms, and he seems to bear no malice toward anyone from that time in his life; nevertheless the pain of his early years still manifests itself—for example in his confusion about the details. He placed the death of his grandmother a full four years prior to the date confirmed by state records, and he stretched one happy interlude when he lived with the Cartledge family from one year to four. Other important details were out of sequence, too. His childhood is a blur in his adult mind except for individual episodes and shining figures which he recalls with vivid clarity and beautiful imagery. Yet the most convincing evidence of his deep-seated self-doubt, and also the most moving sign that one part of him wanted to shrink from the world is the fact that in his youth—I cannot specify details (!)— Riley King stammered. But let me speak of the rare positive moments in his youth.

Young Riley had many positive experiences to compensate for

the harshness of those years. He was treated with unusual kindness by many people, both black and white, who went out of their way to help him in any manner compatible with the social order. The white families who were his landlords when he was a boy sharecropping, his black schoolteacher, and later the plantation owner who employed him driving a tractor all took a genuine personal interest in his welfare. The whites among these people were neither revolutionaries nor even social reformers but for the time and place their ideas about race were decidedly enlightened. Most notable among these was Flake Cartledge, the white farmer who took him in when he was a penniless kid of sixteen who had nothing but the rags he stood in. Of course, by all accounts, Riley was an extremely likable fellow, and it was easy for Cartledge and others to take to him.

These compensating experiences must have had the effect of rescuing Riley from despair about his lot in life and his inherent worth. The most important contribution to saving him from the feeling of low self-esteem was his schoolteacher, Luther Henson. If there is any hero in the story of the life of B.B. King, it is Henson, who made his break from Mississippi where he stood in constant fear, and escaped to Oklahoma, but soon returned—partly out of a sense of duty to help black children learn survival and self-improvement. All his life, B.B. has been addicted to self-improvement, a trait he learned from Henson. Whether it is learning to read music or fly an airplane, part of his attention is always devoted to finding ways of bettering himself. Many of these programs are mere tokens, like learning a few words of a few foreign languages. Nonetheless, both the serious and the token improvements speak to some deep need in him, which surely is fundamental to securing his self-esteem. Henson worked quite deliberately to instill this habit in his youngsters. With great anguish he saw how the poverty of their families numbed them and eroded their health, and how the Jim Crow culture damaged their self-respect; to combat the first he taught hygiene and nutrition, to counter the second he held up the achievements of black artists as models of respect, and showed his pupils black men and women whom they could emulate.

Today B.B. regularly makes time in his frantic schedule to browse bookshops, and he cannot pass a "How To" book without at least looking inside its covers. In conversation he displays a hypersensitivity about literacy and often hints that his own literacy is somehow most regrettably marginal. His insecurity about being fully literate has no objective basis, and this, together with the fact that at one time in his adult years he diligently practiced his penmanship, points to a fear that people would label him an ignorant, illiterate nigger. After all, in the grossest sense, literacy always has been the great divide between the educated and the uneducated. At first this fear struck me as wholly irrational in this day and age; then I met one of his schoolmates who said, with a dash of pride, "I can write my name pretty good," and later I met another who wrote out an address for me with painstaking care, one letter at a time, two or three separate strokes to the letter. Obviously, then, B.B. has just barely escaped illiteracy, and though now it may be neurotic for him to worry that he'll be labeled an ignorant nigger, his concern about appearing illiterate is not so crazy after all.

Nowhere did B.B.'s passion for self-improvement find greater expression than in his music. By the same token, the self-doubt that is the ever-present goad to his artistic efforts is also the ever-present underminer of self-appraisal as an artist. Since he began his career as a musician, his life has been that of a workaholic. At times this mania has been channeled into practicing his instrument, at other times into learning composition and music theory by the Schillinger system, and lately into his devotion to his massive record collection. He immerses himself in music, his cassette player is never far out of reach, and much of his time off at home is consumed in recording music to carry on his next time out on the road. The music soothes him, bathes his soul; its familiarity reassures him. Always it offers the prospect that his ear will be improved, and so it is subliminal work.

Yet all his musical achievements and the steady acclaim he meets are insufficient to put aside his insecurity about his musical ability. He is intelligent and thus never spurns the constant extravagant compliments he receives; he accepts them graciously, while believing that the public is naïve and overgenerous, and that he is merely a very accomplished performer, not even an especially skilled musician, and hence can manage to hypnotize or seduce his audiences until they fall into a spell under which they lose their sense of proportion. The great subtlety of his music notwithstanding, he insists emphatically that he is musically un-

sophisticated and that his knowledge of music is slight compared
to what many jazz musicians know. He often says things like "I'm
a real dummy when it comes to music."

So much for his schoolteacher, Henson, who taught him and
gave him the abstract sense that learning is self-improvement,
thus pointing the way to self-esteem. Of the other shining figures
against the blurred background of his childhood memories, next
comes, doubtlessly, his benefactor, the farmer Cartledge, who—
he still remembers—never said "nigger" and never called him
"boy" and thus became his idea of a decent and just man; next,
his employer, the plantation owner, Barrett, who represented for
young Riley the image of a true gentleman—the successful patriarchal employer; and then comes the preacher Fair, who by the
use of music delivered his flock from the depths of despair and
gave them cathartic ecstasy; he still represents the paradigm performer. Finally his mother, Nora Ella King, the ideal, the gentle,
the warmhearted. No one looms so large in his childhood as his
mother, a woman he knew only in his very early years, and even
then no more than intermittently.

Two memories of his mother stand out strongest in B.B.'s adult
mind. In the first he is huddled with her in a corner of their cabin
after she had left his father, Albert King—for another man, Albert said. A storm is pounding the cabin and the wind has just
torn the roof off. The rain falls on them. She protects him. . . .
The other most vivid recollection is the scene at her deathbed.
She tells Riley, "If you are always kind to people, your kindness
will be repaid, one way or another. And you will be happy in
your life." And I think B.B. is both kind and happy.

He was just a boy of nine, called to her bedside from the yard
where he was playing with his kittens; she died that afternoon,
and by sundown she was laid out on the cooling board in the next
room.

At his mother's death, Riley lost the main buttress in his life
against the terrible storm outside and the major source of his
sense of worth, in addition to the usual orphan's painful loss of
motherly affection. As a compensation for his loss, she left him a
moral prescription to seek refuge in the milk of human kindness,
and today he clings to that morality perhaps as a last, fragile link
to his mother. Indeed, the need to lead a moral life is one of the
most basic features of his adult character. His moral code is not

particularly complex and seems to have no special religious basis. It consists of truthfulness, a sense of responsibility for the consequences of one's actions, willingness always to give the benefit of doubt, generosity whenever one can afford it, and a determination never to go back on one's word, to keep every promise unless released from it by the other party—all of which may be summed up by the Golden Rule.

More important than the specifics of his morality is his basic need to see himself as a moral man. This need which can be traced to his mother's fleeting but profound influence, is a counterbalance to his ambition and is an unusual trait for someone in a profession full of unscrupulous hustlers, charlatans, and ruthlessly ambitious people. He strives for the success of a just man, as if winning success at any price would defeat his purpose of proving himself a worthy man. This last point makes him truly autonomous—moral not only by a simple code, but also by the highest and most sophisticated philosophical criteria available to date.

The contrast between B.B.'s personal morality and the morality of his profession is too important to let pass with only casual mention. After thirty years as an entertainer, there are few people he has known who bear him any ill will, hardly a soul who has any complaint against him, real or imaginary, and not the faintest trace of scandal in his life. B.B. King is immaculately clean—a claim few people in public life can make. The occasional complaint I heard in the course of my research was remarkably venial. For instance, in Memphis his old friend, Andrew "Sunbeam" Mitchell, told me, "I'm mad at B. He did me wrong." He explained that he had recently cancelled B.B.'s appearance at Club Paradise, Mitchell's huge nightclub in downtown Memphis, because B.B. had violated the terms of his contract by making another appearance in Memphis just two weeks before his scheduled date at the Paradise. This sounds very uncomplimentary to the star, except that the other appearance was a $50-a-plate benefit for the NAACP, where the star played for free and without his own band. Sunbeam knew all this; he told me with pleading eyes that he had his business to consider and he couldn't risk taking a loss, so he had to cancel B.B.'s date, however reluctantly. Club owner and star discussed the matter by phone, and Sunbeam asked B.B., "How can you do this to me?" Yes, Sunbeam still bears him a grudge. Yet after his lengthy, righteous explanation of his gripe, he changed tone abruptly and said, "But I still love him. He's a wonderful guy."

B.B. BECOMES A SOCIAL CLIMBER

After his mother's death, 9-year-old Riley stood in an emotional vacuum. His closest kin was his grandmother; he had no brothers and no sisters and no idea of his father's whereabouts. He was starving for emotional contact with other people; his dire emotional need was most filled in church, where the Sanctified preacher, Archie Fair, stirred the congregation with his electric guitar. Riley had an unusually strong voice and as it developed, he became a mainstay of the worship service, a collaborator with the Sanctified preacher Fair. After church let out, when Fair visited his sister, who was married to Riley's uncle, the boy singer experimented with the singing preacher's guitar; eventually Fair allowed young Riley to play his instrument during the service.

For this emotionally starved boy, the playing of a leading role in generating the ecstatic emotional communion that filled the room when the faithful received the Spirit must have had a profound effect. He was hooked on music. It became the staple of his meager emotional diet. When he began playing to blues audiences in his early twenties, he took for his own Archie Fair's formula for group catharsis, and he never made more than minor modifications on it. Forty years later, he often performs a symbolic sermon on his guitar, with the band acting as the congregation, answering almost instantaneously every shout of his instrument verbatim. It is a conjuring trick of stunning ingenuity, one of the most inspired musical ideas of B.B.'s fertile imagination.

Music offered B.B. deliverance from his emotional vacuum and a way to secure his self-respect. In his late teens he discovered a new benefit to be gained: money. When he found that he could make more over a short weekend singing on street corners than he made all week driving a tractor on Johnson Barrett's plantation, and that the coins jingled for his blues tunes but not for the gospel songs he sang, he was set on a course that took him much farther than anyone could have imagined then. He began to realize that he might have a way to escape the poverty of his life as a sharecropper and plantation hand, that possibly he had a profession. In spite of his devotion to spiritual music, he seems never to have been inclined to become a preacher himself. It was the emotional power of the music that excited him, not the religious conviction it expressed. The switch to blues was inevitable.

As B.B. became successful, first in Memphis, then on the national chitlin circuit, his quest for self-esteem took on a new social dimension in addition to the more private, psychological process by which his steady improvement as an artist boosted his appraisal of his own basic worth. From childhood he had struggled not to fall victim to the idea that he was just an ignorant, illiterate, dirt-farming nigger without rights, a boy good for nothing more than chopping weeds out of the cotton rows. Now, with money flowing and requests rolling in from around the country, success offered him new ego support. His quest broadened to include the pursuit of social respectability. B.B. King became a social climber.

The word "climber" has a bad connotation in our society, an odd fact in a country where upward mobility is preached as a kind of national theology. Why this negative tone should be attached to the word is hard to fathom, and why anyone should begrudge a person's ambition to rise above the lowest niche in the social ladder is equally puzzling. Of course, climbing for blacks in the Old South was defiance of Jim Crow, and Jim Crow is Uncle Sam's southern cousin; it is no mystery why southern whites thought poorly then of any nigger trying out his luck: it threatened the very social order. For this reason, Luther Henson, B.B.'s teacher at the Elkhorn School, lived in constant fear that someone would take a notion to teach that uppity nigger a lesson for putting crazy notions in the burry little heads of those nigger kids. But climb they tried. Walter Doris, Jr., a classmate of B.B. in Henson's school, stayed in Kilmichael, Mississippi, and successfully climbed his way up to deputy sheriff of the county—a notch on the social ladder unthinkable for a black man to hold when Junior Doris was a boy. And Riley King became the world-renowned blues singer. A digression on the subject of social climbing may make it easier to understand B.B.'s case.

In the bottom half of the social scale, money matters less than education; the difference between manual labor and mental labor in determining a person's social status is very large. Our colleges and universities are full of the sons and daughters of successful Americans who are determined that their kids will find greater respectability than they themselves did because they never went to college; a union leader may look enviously at the vice-president of a small corporation simply because the union job is associated with manual labor and the position of corporate executive is considered brain work. These silly ideas are the stuff many an American movie is made of. They are popular mythology.

The situation for black Americans has never been good and was especially bleak until the last two decades. Prevented by law and social convention from exercising existing means of moving up they had to invent novel ones. One classic innovation is the invention of a new slot in the social ladder: jazz musician. Even before the civil rights movement killed Jim Crow, the slot of jazz musician was recognized around the country, including the Deep South, as was the slot of black college football players in the Midwest: on the condition of compliance with the rules of segregation of course. As if to endow the new slot with more official status, a mock-nobility was established, with a Duke (Ellington), a Count (Basie), and a King (Cole) reigning. The important thing about this social slot was its connection with the mainstream of American life; it was much more than a level in the pecking order among blacks, but rather it was recognized by whites as having its own prestige. Jazz and football were respectable. Jazz musicians held the stage at Carnegie Hall; the leading jazzmen played the concert halls of European capitals. Satchmo gave a concert for the King of England and made the slot official by conferring honorary membership on the King when he dedicated a song to him and said, "You can dig this one, can't you, Rex!"

(College football was a different matter, and kid stuff by comparison. Hence, ex-college-footballers had to go back to the steel mill or join the ranks of the civil rights movement.)

How does B.B. King fit into this scheme? He doesn't. The social respectability of jazz did not extend to blues; the new slot of jazzmen was closed to bluesmen because blues was for blacks only. It did not matter that blues and jazz were closely related musical styles or that bluesmen and jazzmen borrowed heavily from each other. While jazzmen played Carnegie, bluesmen rode the chitlin circuit. Blues music, born in the Mississippi Delta, re-

Riley B. King, age twenty.

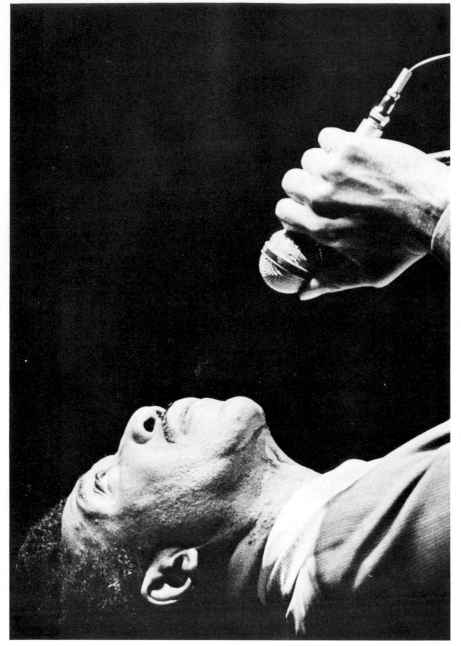

McKinley Morganfield Photo by Charles Sawyer

Booker T. "Bukka" White, B.B. King's second cousin. *Photo by Charles Sawyer.*

Juke-joint jitterbugs strut their stuff for the crowd in Clarksdale, Mississippi, 1939. *Photo by Marion Post Wolcott. Farm Security Administration.*

A game of "Georgia skin." Such games, featured at "Gamblers' Balls," often ran for days on end, making the chitlin circuit a lively, sometimes violent place for entertainment. *Photo by Marion Post Wolcott, Farm Security Administration.*

Robert Henry, with hat, leaning on the counter at his Beale Street record shop and shoeshine

Robert Henry, Memphis impresario, the first to manage Blues Boy King. *Photo (c. 1935) courtesy Mrs. Robert Henry.*

In the North, the chitlin circuit was dominated by the Howard Theater in Washington, D.C., the Royal in Baltimore, the Apollo in New York, and the Regal in Chicago (shown here in 1941). *Photo by Russell Lee, Farm Security Administration.*

B. B. King with his first road band and "Big Red," the jalopy bus, in front of the Club Handy on Beale Street, Memphis, c. 1955. Left to right: B.B. King, James "Shinny" Walker; female vocalist Benita, Earl Forest, Evelyn "Mama Nuts" Young, Cato Walker, "Sleepy," Jerry Smith, Ted Curry Millard "Mother" Lee, Ployd Newman, Kenny Sands, Calvin Owens, Richard Lillie, Lawrence Birdeye, Paul Pinkman, Frank Brown. *Photo courtesy Andrew "Sunbeam" Mitchell.*

Little Richard. *Photo by Charles Sawyer.*

The Arrival of B.B. King, Boston Arena, 1970. *Photo by Charles Sawyer.*

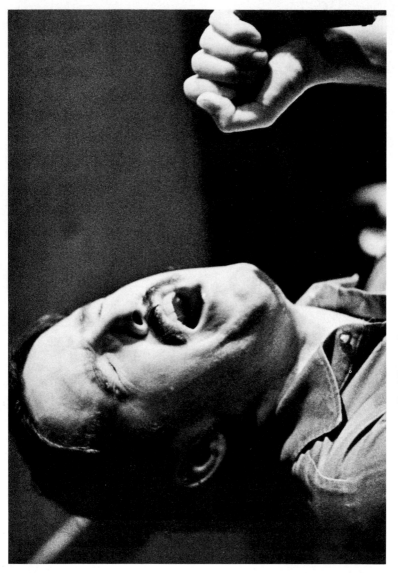

Paul Butterfield. *Photo by Charles Sawyer.*

Elvin Bishop at the Fillmore East. *Photo by Charles Sawyer.*

Sidney Seidenberg in his office in New York City. *Photo by Charles Sawyer.*

And old coalition. *Photo by Charles Sawyer.*

Ed Sullivan Theater, New York, October 1971. *Photo by Charles Sawyer.*

Dr. Riley B. King with Kingman Brewster, Yale president, at the occasion of B.B.'s receiving an Honorary Doctor of Music from Yale University. *Photo by William Ferris, courtesy The Center for Southern Folklore, Memphis, Tennessee.*

mained associated with the poorest aspects of black culture; it was the music of the juke joint and the brothel. The musical distinction between blues and jazz might be very fine, but the social distinction was enormous. Jazz was the unique American art form, certified clean, all-American entertainment fit for the senior prom; but blues was lowdown, dirty nigger music.

This left B.B. in a tough spot. He had raised himself up from the poverty of sharecropping in the Delta only to find himself stuck on the chitlin circuit. Economically speaking, bluesmen were the sharecroppers of the music industry: marginal and ever in debt. Just as planter Barrett took half the proceeds from the cotton B.B. had to keep raising on the man's land, now the Bihari brothers, who ran Modern Records, took half and more of the composer's royalties on every song which B.B. both wrote and recorded on their labels. Socially, blues was scorned even by many middle-class blacks who were eager not to be reminded of their humbler roots, and also by young black urbanites determined to be hip and cool, qualities they rarely attributed to this traditional down-home music. Until the sixties, of all black Americans, few were quite unaware of blues, but many were ashamed of it.

(The view that blues was regarded with shame by some black Americans, particularly middle-class blacks, is an opinion disputed by some black musicians I have consulted; the opinion is B.B.'s and may reflect his ambivalent attitude toward himself as much as it reflects the social status of blues. However it can be safely assumed that a vast majority of the blues audience was, until the late 1960s, poor and lower-class, and that middle-class blacks freely patronized jazz, but by and large, steered away from blues. The situation, incidentally, is not peculiar to black Americans alone: many cultural traits of simple folks the world over are rejected by snobbish social climbers.)

So B.B., whose grasp on his self-respect had always been shaky, was stymied. He might have changed by switching to jazz, but that solution seemed to him phony; the self-image as B.B. King the blues singer required respectability for that person, not for some hypothetical musician he might have been if he became something he wasn't. Besides, he was devoted to blues music, and he couldn't bear the thought of betraying his love And if he was ever seriously tempted to switch to jazz, his doubts about his musicianship could stop him too. The doubts about his musicianship were merely his doubts about his basic, personal worth, though translated to artistic language; but he didn't understand that fact then, and may still not fully appreciate it. The only solution was to make blues respectable. There was nothing left but to stick it out and do what he could to give blues a better name. His own personal identity was grounded in his music; for better or worse, he was stuck with the blues. And so long as blues was race music, he was stuck. Plain stuck.

B.B. did what he could: He made blues respectable. Deliberately and studiously he became a gentleman; he was chivalrous with women and magnanimous with men and women alike; he always dressed well and conservatively—no zoot suits or gold lamé tuxes and when he went fishing on his rare day off, he wore a $200 suit because he owned nothing less elegant; he avoided scandal. He made a heroic effort to break his career free of the race-music pattern by hiring a white manager and signing with a major record label. Alas, it was not these measures that won a wider audience for blues music, it was broader social forces. Yet when the barriers that had confined blues throughout the first twenty years of his career were finally broken, B.B. was there, ready to be received as King of the Blues by the great mass of Americans, all self-confidence, all of a part, the king who is too superior to behave differently, whether popular or not.

DURABILITY: THE INGREDIENT ESSENTIAL TO SUCCESS

The statistics of B.B.'s durability are staggering. He has survived sixteen auto accidents; in the year 1956 he played *342 one-night engagements;* he has played an annual average of 300 performances in recent years; in thirty years he has taken a total of only two months' vacation. The components of such durability are both physical and mental. On the physical side, it is mostly a matter of genes. He has a high resistance to disease—since 1950 he has had no major illnesses—and he has remarkable recuperative powers over minor illnesses. But even his physical capacities are much a matter of self-discipline and lengthy training. He is a dynamo of energy with enormous reserves but also with a finely tuned sense of how to stretch them to the maximum and stop just short of physical collapse. (He did collapse once from physical exhaustion on a stage in Sydney, Australia, but he lost only one day's work as a result.)

His awareness of his own capacities is very sharp and shows itself in many subtle ways like the fact that he hardly ever asks the hotel switchboard to hold his calls—only when he is on the verge of collapse. And there is his ability, mentioned earlier, to wake from a deep sleep, to answer the phone, conduct important business in a fully lucid state, then go directly back to a deep sleep—this ability he has learned. And on the rare occasions when he is utterly fatigued, nothing which would fail to raise the Witch of Endor will waken him: this, too, is a matter of training. On the more purely mental side there is his high moral standard and concern for his reputation that drive him on to make the next gig.

In the worst of his auto accidents (around 1961), B.B. was thrown through the windshield and received a cut on his upper arm that exposed the bone and partially severed his triceps; he was rushed to a hospital where the cut was closed with a few dozen stitches, and then he drove on to play his gig. (It was his right arm that was injured; what playing he managed on his guitar was done without picking, using only the fingers of his left hand to strike the strings by hammering down hard on them as he fretted the notes.) This feat of durability is typical in that it had both a physical side (the fact that his injury did not put him in shock) and a mental side (the fact of his determination to play despite an injury which anyone else would have considered severe enough to release him from any obligation).

The mental side has deeper levels than mere determination: on the middle level is B.B.'s feeling that he is a hostage to the road, that the bulwark of his career has been his personal appearances, not radio air play, nor record sales, and that his fixed overhead demands his high productivity; on the same level is his high standard of work acquired in his teens working in Mississippi. On the deepest level operates the driving force of his ambition, and this, in turn, is a by-product of the campaign to secure his feeling of basic worth: no matter how often he performs, he must do his best and all the time progress.

B.B.'S CAPACITY for survival and his determination will be better appreciated if we compare his career with the careers of two other musicians who fell victim to the attrition of the road:

Johnny Ace and Greasy Simmons. Johnny Ace was B.B.'s first piano player who went on to become a star justly rivaling B.B. in popularity for a few brief years before he died with a bullet from his own pistol lodged in his brain. Greasy Simmons was a slight acquaintance of B.B. from the time of their late teens, when they both lived in Mississippi. Simmons never made a record and, after ten years' scuffling and knocking about taverns and nightclubs in the Deep South, he gave up his career as a musician to be a better family man. Now he lives in Chicago.

Johnny Ace: Blues Balladeer

John Marshall Alexander, Jr., was born and raised in Memphis, Tennessee. The son of a minister, he graduated from Booker T. Washington High School and entered the Navy in World War II, though he was underage. When he returned to Memphis in 1946, at the age of seventeen, he began playing piano in local joints and hanging out in a Beale Street pool hall. From his high school days he was known as an affable, happy-go-lucky kid. He was rowdy with boys and shy with girls, despite his evident sex appeal. In 1949 he joined up with B.B. who, though four years older, was less wise to city ways; but B.B. had the jump on Johnny as a rising local entertainer because he had his own radio show over station WDIA, the new black sound of the Middle South. When B.B. left Memphis to begin his career as a national star after "Three O'Clock Blues" hit the top of the R&B charts, he turned the band over to Johnny, who then repeated B.B.'s pattern of mutually reinforcing local performances and radio appearances over WDIA. Like the other DIA personalities and B.B. before him, he acquired a show-biz nickname: "Johnny Ace."

In 1952 Johnny Ace signed with the Texas R&B label, Duke Records, owned by the Houston empire builder, Don Robey. Robey was a black of extremely light complexion, who became a kind of godfather of the race-music industry in the late 1940s and 1950s. He began his recording business when he cut five sides with Clarence "Gatemouth" Brown, the headliner at Robey's Houston nightclub, The Bronze Peacock. Robey named his new label "Peacock" after his club, and acquired Johnny Ace when he bought Duke, the fledgling Memphis record label, from James Mattis, a WDIA disc jockey. During his years as a race-record mogul, Robey recorded Johnny Ace, Bobby "Blue" Bland, Little

Junior Parker, Willie Mae "Big Mama" Thornton, The Dixie Hummingbirds, Little Richard, and even B.B. King, though his 1953 recording of B.B., cut in Covington, Tennessee, was never released, presumably because of conflicting contracts with Modern Records. When Robey sold his recording and publishing interests to ABC Dunhill Records for a reported $1 million, his empire included four record labels: Peacock, Duke, Songbird, and Backbeat.

Soon after signing with Robey, Johnny Ace had a hit with his tune, "My Song," which went to the top of the R&B charts in 1952. In the eighteen months that followed, Johnny was on the charts more or less continuously with a string of hits. He had a boyish charm that women found irresistible when he sang his maudlin ballads; decades after his death, musicians who knew him still compare him with Nat "King" Cole and Lou Rawls. While his songs were on the R&B charts, Johnny was in constant demand for personal appearances; not only were black audiences clamoring to hear him, but whites began buying his records, too. He was among the very first R&B artists to show a potential for "crossover." Johnny Ace began a meteoric rise toward the stratosphere of stardom.

Estimates of Johnny's character vary. Milton Hopkins, guitarist in the band that backed Johnny Ace onstage at the time of his death, remembers him as a prankster, full of irrepressible energy and benign mischief. "He'd tackle guys in the band, two or three at a time; he didn't know his own strength," says Hopkins, who, incidentally, played with B.B.'s road band from 1970 until 1978. According to Hopkins, Johnny's idea of fun was driving his Oldsmobile 90 miles per hour, his pistol in hand, shooting out the zeros on roadside speed-limit signs. Hopkins was on the stage at the Civic Auditorium in Houston, Texas, Christmas Eve 1954, when Johnny killed himself in his dressing room. By contrast, bandleader Johnny Board, who later spent a few years on the road with B.B., playing tenor saxophone, remembers Johnny Ace as reserved and soft-spoken, but not prone to brooding. Earl Forrest, one of B.B.'s early drummers, remembers Johnny Ace best for one hair-raising ride in Johnny's Olds from Houston to Beaumont, Texas; not even the speeding ticket and stern lecture he got enroute from the Texas Highway Patrol slowed Johnny down. Evelyn Johnson, who managed Johnny's performance schedule from the Buffalo Booking Agency in Don Robey's Texas empire, remembers Johnny's stage fright, which kept him glued to his keyboard showing only his profile to the audience, never looking his fans in the face; only after he had been out on the road long after most musicians would have become seasoned performers did Johnny screw up the courage to squarely face his listeners.

Details about the events leading up to Johnny's violent death are sketchy. B.B. saw him a month or two before the fatal shooting on Christmas Eve, and noticed that he seemed to be bearing up poorly under the strain of his newly achieved peak of fame. Earl Forrest recalls that Johnny bought a small .22 caliber revolver in Tampa sometime in November 1954 and that not long thereafter the two of them had a friendly scuffling match that was over almost before it began, in which Forrest, a small, delicate man, managed to take the pistol away from Johnny. When spirits calmed down, Forrest handed the pistol back to Johnny. A few days later, Forrest again wrestled the gun from Johnny, this time with the help of a character he remembers only as "Big Frank" (probably Frank Brown, B.B.'s driver). Again he gave the gun back to Johnny when the fracas was over.

A few weeks later, a separate incident took place in Don Robey's Houston office, which was the nerve center of Robey's record companies. There in Robey's office Johnny nearly succeeded to give up his weapon for more than a few passing minutes. According to Evelyn Johnson, who witnessed the scene, Johnny walked into Robey's office and spotted another of Don Robey's singers, Gatemouth Brown. Johnny, in jest, pulled his pistol on Gatemouth, but the singer responded by pulling a knife. They pretended to start a fight, but then they put away their weapons. Johnny gave his pistol to Robey to have the plastic grip replaced by a pearl handle. Robey took the pistol but returned it later that afternoon, telling Johnny he couldn't have the pearl handle applied during the weekend; Johnny could give it back the following week.

Gatemouth Brown's version of the incident in Robey's office is at variance with the one given by Evelyn Johnson. According to Gatemouth, Johnny did in fact pull the pistol on him, but he denies drawing a knife on Johnny. "I never drew a knife on a man in my life," said Brown nearly thirty years later. "He made me mad doing a thing like that, and I told him, 'Johnny, if you want to point that thing at someone, point it at yourself.' Then a few days later I got a call and someone told me that he'd— well I call what he did 'suicide.' "

According to two reports, the day before he died, Johnny repeatedly fired the gun out a window, thus provoking several complaints about the noise.

At least a few versions are told concerning exactly what happened in Johnny Ace's dressing room the night he died. His death is usually ascribed to Russian roulette, since the gun was a revolver. Yet the authoritative version of the story which is probably fairly close to the exact truth is the one told by Willie Mae "Big Mama" Thornton who was in the dressing room when the gun discharged. Early that night, she took the gun from Johnny; whether she took it by persuasion or by force she did not mention, but Big Mama was capable of force, and she was afraid he was going to hurt someone. She removed the lone bullet and pocketed both revolver and bullet. Later that night, Johnny was in a relaxed mood with his girlfriend Olivia and Big Mama. He laid some sweet talk on Big Mama, making her return the gun with a promise that he wouldn't repeat his horseplay. But no sooner did he get it than he pointed it at Big Mama herself and teased her.

They were still in the dressing room—Big Mama, Johnny and Olivia. "Don't you snap [point] that on me," Big Mama said angrily.

Then Johnny turned the gun toward Olivia, who was sitting on his lap. This angered Big Mama even more, and she barked at him, "Stop that, Johnny! You're going to get someone killed!"

"There's nothing to worry about," he replied coolly. "Look, I'll show you!" He put the gun to his temple, pulled the trigger, and that was that.

Olivia screamed. Word spread quickly to the backstage area In a moment the emcee, "King Bee," a local DJ, came out to stop the Johnny Board Band and make the chilling announcement The show stopped dead. Some patrons threw debris on the stage in disgust and disbelief.

News of Johnny Ace's death spread like lightning around the whole country. A few days later, when he was buried in Memphis, a throng filled the church and then followed the coffin to the cemetery in reverent silence.

The circumstances of Johnny Ace's death raise so many questions and answer so few. Perhaps the most perplexing is this: Why should a talented young man with the world opening up to him die in such an unnecessary and patently foolish way? There is no plainly obvious answer that will banish the futility of Johnny Ace's death, but B.B. pointed the way toward an explanation when he commented on the last time he saw Johnny shortly before the tragedy.

"I think the pressure was beginning to get to Johnny," he said. "You can't imagine how it is, out here. You spend three nights in one hotel and learn that the door to the right goes to the toilet and the one on the left goes out into the corridor. Then you change cities, and the first night in the new hotel, you wake up standing in the corridor, not sure where you are or how you got there. As it turns out, you turned right heading for the toilet, more asleep than awake, and the directions in this hotel are reversed."

He expanded further by saying, "People come at you all the time: people with propositions, people asking favors, people telling you that you promised to do this or pay them such and such, and you don't remember any such thing." All this is not to mention the psychological pressures which go with public adulation and loss of privacy—the unhappy lot of every celebrity.

Gatemouth Brown had his own assessment of why Johnny should have done what he described as suicide: "Some people just can't handle success."

One explanation of Johnny Ace's death, often heard these days in the various dressing rooms across the country, is the summary dismissal contained in the quip: "He was just a crazy kid." This is comforting because it raises no subtle problems; it places his death in the same category with the accidental death of a child who locks himself in an abandoned refrigerator and of a teenager who is killed when he dives from a great height on a dare. Yet if this comforting dismissal were satisfying to any measure, the topic would have died many years ago; twenty-five years is a long time for gossip to survive.

But Johnny Ace was no kid when he shot himself; he was a grown man and very similar in character, occupation, and circumstance to those who keep musing about him. Even B.B. still remembers the case all too vividly. And, indeed, Johnny Ace's behavior prior to his death is too subtle to be written off as no more than "just crazy." He gave up the pistol to friends at least four times in the preceding days, and this, together with his constant playing with the weapon, which people around him described as a "fascination," suggest that he had an emotionally charged attraction/repulsion toward the pistol. From this standpoint, Johnny's behavior looks as if he was working up to something, or perhaps trying to resolve some conflict in his life one way or another.

There is another marginal episode, and one that may point to his being in a self-consciously self-destructive mood that Christmas Eve, which clashes with the picture he projected, of an unreflective and carefree person. It happened on the road to Houston a day or two before Christmas Eve, with Johnny Ace and his band in his Olds. Johnny was at the wheel. According to bandleader Johnny Board, Ace ran through a red light and sideswiped a curb. Then he pulled over and stopped the car. Turning to Board, he said, "I don't know what's wrong with me. I shouldn't be driving. Take over the wheel, will you?"

It is impossible to know Johnny Ace's frame of mind when he died but the sketchy evidence supports the following conclusions concerning his death: (1) It was not a case of Russian roulette; he did not spin the pistol cylinder, and it was no game he was playing; (2) It was not suicide in the standard sense: he did not deliberately shoot himself; and (3) It was not an accident in the normal sense of the word: Johnny Ace was leading up to a violent death. What then is left? There are no words to properly describe his actions, and those that come to mind are bizarre: "deliberate accident," "accidental suicide," "semi-deliberate self-destruction," and even "semi-suicide."

Johnny Ace's life and death illustrate a simple point: the ways in which life on the road can claim an entertainer are subtle and unforgiving. Other entertainers from B.B.'s circle have also died of violence inflicted by human hands. Before B B 's time, there were Delta blues founder Robert Johnson, who was poisoned by a jealous woman, and Delta guitarist Charlie Patton, who was stabbed to death by his lover. During B.B.'s career, harmonica players Little Walter Jacobs and Sonny Boy Williamson both died of beatings, and singer Sam Cooke was shot to death by an angry motelkeeper. The media report many an entertainer killing himself with booze and drugs and senseless brawls. They are not that senseless, I think; they may express despair.

B.B. is different. He avoids guns and violence. I once witnessed a minor episode that impressed this point on me with vivid clarity. It was late one night in his hotel room after a performance in Boston. With us was José Perez, a local crony who once served briefly as B.B.'s valet; now, when B.B. comes to Boston, José dogs his heels and falls into the role of valet and bodyguard. He is completely devoted to B.B. and behaves toward his adopted hero in a way that is both protective and servile. In short, José is B.B.'s Sancho Panza. This particular night, José had just finished washing out B.B.'s socks, a task he had undertaken entirely on his own initiative. B.B. was sitting on the bed, making small talk with me. José approached B.B. and announced that he had a treasure to show. He took a leather holster from his back pocket and pulled from it a small chrome-plated pistol, which he plopped down on the bedding beside B.B.

"Isn't she a honey, B.?" Perez asked.

B.B. recoiled from the gun as if it were a snake poised to strike. "I—I—don't like guns," he stammered.

Perez plucked the gun from the spot where it lay on the sheets and murmured that ever since he drove a cab in the city, he never went about the streets without old Bessie in his pocket.

Leslie "Greasy" Simmons: Blues Journeyman

I met Simmons in 1978 in B.B.'s dressing room at The Burning Spear in Chicago. His short, slight build contrasted with B.B.'s taller, much stouter frame, though in age and background they shared many traits. He mentioned that when they were teen-agers in Mississippi, he and B.B. had played music together occasionally. I showed interest and he responded eagerly, telling electrifying yarns without ever dropping his down-in-the-mouth style of speech. In the course of the evening, he told me in bits and pieces the story of his career as a musician—a career that he eventually folded. Now he works as an administrator for the Chicago Housing Authority, and lives with his family on the South Side.

Les Simmons grew up in Chicago and Mississippi. He lived with his father and stepmother, a devout Catholic, who raised her son in the church. At intervals, he lived with relatives, including an uncle who owned a large farm in Missouri.

"My uncle was quite a man," Simmons began his tale. "One of his field hands killed a man in a fight. It was around the time to bring the crop in, so when the sheriff put one of my uncle's men in jail, it deprived him of a valuable hand. That was hard on my uncle, so he went to the judge and worked out a deal. My uncle built a little prison, complete with bars and a toilet, made out of cinder blocks, right in front of the farm on his own land. The judge released the man into my uncle's custody, and when the guy wasn't actually out in the fields working, he stayed locked up in that jail. The guy was finally acquitted as a justifiable homicide, but the little jail is still there."

Simmons attended high school in Greenville, Mississippi, and for a brief eight-month period as a teen-ager, he attended a nearby Catholic seminary (integrated), where he began studying for the priesthood. His one-word explanation for leaving the seminary: "girls."

He came from a musical family and learned to read music without any formal instruction. In high school he traveled around Mississippi with his own band. While playing in Indianola, Mississippi, he met Riley King. Young Riley, about the same age as Leslie, asked to join Simmons' band, but Simmons turned him down, he said, because he couldn't read music. (B.B. later learned to read by the Schillinger method.)

In 1944, after graduating from high school, Simmons enlisted in the army when word reached him from Chicago that the FBI was looking for him for failing to register with his Chicago draft board. He was trained as a dental technician, but finagled a transfer to a musical unit. When he returned from Europe with $7,000 in his pocket from a scam involving cigarettes and cameras, he went AWOL to take three saxophone lessons from his idol, Earle Bostick, in New York.

After his discharge from the service, Simmons went to work for an uncle who had a dental practice in Clarksdale, Mississippi His job was installing heart-shaped gold crowns—often with a diamond inset—a popular fad of the time. ("You didn't buy your girlfriend a gold ring in those days—you bought her a gold tooth, whether she needed it or not.") He worked there only a short time until he enrolled at nearby Tougaloo College, where he took teaching courses. ("After I graduated, I had trouble getting a teaching job in Mississippi—not so much because I was black, but more because I was Catholic.") At Tougaloo he formed a new band and weekends went out on the road. He also acquired his nickname in college when one of his Mississippi classmates commented on his citified Chicago ways: "That nigger ain't no slick city boy, he's just a greasy motherfucker." The term stuck, and among his Mississippi peers he became "Greasy."

Although Simmons had several bands over the years, he never billed himself as bandleader after an incident in which a young woman, who had seen his name and face on a poster advertising his group, accused him of getting her pregnant. He finally escaped suspicion because the sheriff's cook's husband was Greasy's chauffeur, and he could account for all of Simmons' time during the days when she claimed the injustice had been done her.

Among the places Simmons played with his Tougaloo band was a club owned by an infamous hustler, whom I shall call Leo "Jack" Jackson. Jackson's club, which I shall call "Jumpin' Jack's," was located on a strip of bars and nightclubs known as the Gold Coast, about ten miles outside of the city, where gambling was common though not strictly legal. As he tells it, Greasy was sitting at the bar in Jumpin' Jack's one slow afternoon in the summer of 1948 when a law enforcement officer (white, naturally), walked in and asked for Jack. It was the middle of the day, and the club was nearly empty.

"Jack, did you kill Mr. So-and-so?" asked the officer, referring to a recently murdered white man.

"Uh-huh. I did," Jackson replied.

"Was it because you been seeing his wife, Jack?"

"That's right."

"How long you been doin' that, Jack?"

"Three and a half years."

"Jesus Christ, Jack. . . . How much cash you got in the joint?"

"Seven thousand dollars from last night's till, plus the contents of the slot machines."

"That's enough for starters. I'll give you eight hours' head start before I set the dogs on you. Don't go to Alabama and don't go to Arkansas. When you get situated, take a post office box and get in touch with me. I'll send you more money then."

The lawman then walked out of Jumpin' Jack's as casually as any customer would.

According to Simmons, Jackson wound up shining shoes in Chicago, Jumpin' Jack's closed soon after Jackson's disappearance, and Jackson died some years later in utter poverty.

From this story of a white Mississippi lawman allowing his black friend, a self-confessed murderer of a white man, to escape, Simmons draws the following morals: no inviolable laws or social conventions governed life in Mississippi in those days; and, in some cases, friendship could cut through all other constraints.

After college, Greasy Simmons went to New York City to make his fortune as a musician. It was his big move. He laid out money on an apartment and began rehearsing a new band. Then he made what he now regards as the fatal blunder of his career as a musician.

"I was dumb," he recalled with a shrug. "I hadn't been reading the trade newspapers, and I didn't know that 78 rpm records were on the way out. I let a guy sell me a $3,000 recording machine for making 78s. . . . Thought I was so smart . . . Thought I got such a good buy . . . I paid $1,800 for the goddamn thing. It was the last 78 rpm recording machine manufactured in the United States. When I realized what I'd done, I said, 'This is it. This is the end.'" Despondent about his blunder, Greasy Simmons lost heart on his bid for big-time success in New York and headed for Chicago.

En route to Chicago, he met his Tougaloo sweetheart in Detroit. With rekindled love, and moral pressure from his family in Chicago to settle down both bearing down on him, Simmons married and moved back to Mississippi. Before very long, he was working at three different jobs and playing saxophone with a new band. A sympathetic nightclub owner with a paternal attitude toward Greasy financed the purchase of a large house for Simmons and his new family. Two children were born. Greasy was overworked but fairly prosperous. Music was still a central part of his life although his ambitions were considerably more modest now than they had been when he left Mississippi bound for New York.

One thing about his new musical career as a Mississippi musician stuck in his craw: Negroes were barred from the local musicians' union. During a Christmas visit to Chicago, he called on

James C. ("C" for Cesare) Petrillo, the baronial head of The American Federation of Musicians, who ran the organization for decades. He told Petrillo that Mississippi locals barred colored musicians, yet, nonetheless, the all-white locals took the standard cut from the wages of unionized colored bands from the North whenever they played in Mississippi.

Petrillo told Simmons, "Go back to Mississippi and reapply to your local. If you are still refused, call me."

Simmons followed Petrillo's advice and phoned him when his second attempt to join the local met with no more success than his first. Within a few hours, two officials of the local appeared at Simmons' house and offered him membership.

"*I* don't want to join your union," he told them. "I want my *whole band* to join the union." Simmons and his band were admitted to the local, and the color bar against black musicians in Mississippi was broken. The year was 1957 or 1958—he can't recall exactly.

By 1960, racial tension was steadily rising in the Delta. When a shotgun blast tore through the kitchen of his Hattiesburg home one evening while he and his family were out, Simmons decided to move back to Chicago. For the next several years, Mississippi was an inhospitable place. One return visit in 1964 is fixed in his mind. In that year, Simmons came back to Mississippi to attend the funeral of Vernon Dahmer, local secretary of the NAACP, who was killed when his house was fire-bombed. As Simmons crossed the state line into Mississippi, he noticed a car fall in behind him. Fearing for his family's safety, he pulled into a filling station. The trailing car followed, and out stepped two FBI agents who called him by name and announced that they would be accompanying Simmons throughout his stay in the state.

As he wound up his rambling yarn, Greasy Simmons stroked his brow and asked rhetorically, "What I want to know is how the hell the FBI had any idea that I was coming to Mississippi. I guess I'll never know."

Now Les Simmons works for the Chicago Housing Authority, managing apartment buildings. He handles a steady stream of banal tenant problems: leaky pipes, domestic quarrels, teen-age gang terror, etc. Occasionally he plays his saxophone in his living room along with his son, who studied music at Roosevelt University.

Why did Greasy Simmons drop out and B.B. become a star? The question is not altogether fair to Greasy, unless we allow for the role of luck in determining an entertainer's prospects. It is no slur on B.B.'s greatness to point out that he was lucky to arrive in Memphis at a time when conditions favored his rise. A few years sooner or later, he might not have had the same opportunities offered just then, and just to him. This is not to claim that B.B. was just plain lucky: he suffered many setbacks much more disastrous and depressing than the disappointment Greasy Simmons suffered when he was swindled in New York.

The difference lies exactly here: unlike Greasy Simmons, B.B. carried on with hardly any concession that such setbacks cost him dearly just as they had cost Greasy. Also there is B.B.'s towering talent to take into account; without it, B.B. would not have achieved his success or fame. On the other hand, it should be clear that all other things being equal, perhaps if Greasy Simmons had had B.B.'s talent as a kid, he might still be managing apartments in Chicago today, his fortunes and determination being what they were then. Indeed, he may have had all of B.B.'s talent and more; perhaps the only relevant differences in determining their lives was the fact that on the threshold of manhood, Simmons was a city slicker in a land of bumpkins, already a big shot with a reputation of being a greasy motherfucker, whereas B.B. was an orphaned sharecropper with a red Stella guitar and a stammer. Maybe the difference that gave Riley King the edge was his great doubt that he mattered at all in this world.

THE FUTURE KING

For the past five or six years, B.B.'s career has been on a plateau, due in part to the three years' suspension of his mutual interests with manager Sidney Seidenberg. There is still a wide gulf in status that separates his career from that of any superstar such as Bob Dylan, Frank Sinatra, Ella Fitzgerald, Nat "King" Cole, Elvis, or Bing Crosby. What, then, are his prospects to gain this level of popularity and become a permanent fixture on the American scene, even after he is gone? He is strong, healthy, and still relatively young; he remains ambitious and energetic and, though it might be accurate to describe him as mellow, still his appetite for success remains high. Seidenberg is now wholly committed to making a big score with B.B. In his heart of hearts, Seidenberg dreams that B.B. will become the next Satchmo—a kind of American institution on display for the world, a symbol of our culture, loved and admired the world over.

What are Seidenberg's chances to see B.B. as another Satchmo? First, we must assume a given background, including some specific details about both the world and B.B. Assume that the world remains more or less the same for the next twenty years— we are not stricken by some national or global catastrophe, especially, a general economic collapse, and that B.B. himself remains intact, physically and mentally. Assume also that there is no sudden lucky fluke that propells him into the strongest limelight possible, something like the election of a black vice-president who befriends him and determines to make him a national symbol. How then do the chances for such things stand? A closer and more technical comparison of Satchmo and B.B. may give us a clue.

Satchmo began his rise on the wave of popularity for the new art form, jazz. As time went on, he was able to stand in the public eye for a new, uniquely American musical tradition, so much a part of an era that we call it The Jazz Age. As jazz conquered the world, Satchmo reaped the profits in personal popularity. Not Duke Ellington, the great composer and bandleader, not Count Basie, the superb suave showman and pianist, but the older, more earthy, Satchmo, the more folksy, New Orleans waif, and protégé of King Oliver, the mythical primeval New Orleans master.

Where do jazz and blues differ so? Blues is not the new wave; quite to the contrary, it is even more primitive than the simplest jazz which, if anything, is a sophisticated derivative of blues. Perhaps blues is more of a folk art. But then blues has never acquired the wide, popular devotion of American folk—country and western music. From this standpoint, Charlie Pride, the black country and western singer, is in a position superior to that of B.B. Nor is blues pop music proper; quite to the contrary, if anything, it is a sophisticated forerunner of rock-and-roll. Yet American folk music never evolved to something more sophisticated. And precisely because blues music is the foundation of jazz, it stands closer to the center of American culture than either of the other two forms, and its musical subtlety and flexibility make it a better, more versatile vehicle for expressing popular sentiments and thereby reaching people in their hearts. In short, B.B. has exhausted the surge of popular fashion that put him where he is now; the rest of his climb will have to be solely a matter of personal popularity. In this respect, he is fortunate to be the most accomplished artist in a highly appealing musical genre.

To drive the point home, consider the place of the ballad in folk art and its appearance in diverse musical genres—European folk music, calypso, the music of Bob Dylan and other folksingers, and, to return to our point, blues, country and western, and jazz. Jazz is least suitable for the ballad; the other forms favor long, drawn-out ballads. B.B., on the other hand, has a two-liner ballad:

> Nobody loves me but my mother,
> And she could be jivin', too.

Satchmo sang "Hello, Dolly" like no one before or after, making a piece from a musical into jazz. His "Mack the Knife" is a similar feat and is even a ballad of sorts. But not quite: it does not express popular sentiment, as Joan Baez and B.B. do in their music.

But there are other factors. A musician can make it without a home base, as did Bob Dylan and Woody Guthrie, but it helps to have one. Satchmo had advantages B.B. misses. Satchmo had Bourbon Street; B.B. has only poor old Beale. Throughout his career, Satchmo's popularity was supported by a national awareness of his music, New Orleans jazz, maintained by the symbols of New Orleans, the city, and Bourbon, the street. In comparison, B.B. has Memphis, a racially divided city whose Chamber of Commerce declared insolvency, and Beale Street, which after urban renewal looks like London after the blitz. The difference is enormous. Many vacationers and foreign tourists include New Orleans on their itinerary in order to hear jazz, or Nashville to visit the Grand Ole Opry, but few would think to include Memphis to hear blues. There are efforts under way in Memphis to raise the city to the level of Nashville and New Orleans, but great obstacles remain like racial tension and competition between two powerful white families which dominate public affairs in the city. Alas! If B.B. is to become a superstar like Satchmo, he will have to do it *sui generis*—solo!

True, Bob Dylan has no home base either; he had to capitalize on Woody Guthrie. Woody was an Okie; like B.B., he was *sui generis,* too. Plainly, as Dylan and Guthrie demonstrate, a home base is not a prerequisite to superstardom, but it helped Satchmo in a big way, and this is one advantage B.B. doesn't share with Satchmo. (There is always the possibility that B.B. could make Memphis and then in turn Memphis make B.B., but neither B.B. nor Seidenberg is inclined to pull off a coup.)

Satchmo had tremendous personal appeal. His charm and sense of personal style would have made him popular even if he had been a juggler. Satchmo radiated excitement whether he stood on a stage before thousands in a vast hall or before the close-up lenses of Hollywood cameras. He sparkled. Does B.B. have any quality like this? As a performer he does, but in strictly personal terms he is handicapped by a slow, methodical style of personal contact. His forte is his seriousness, his taking seriously even the personal troubles of his listeners while he plays and sings to comfort them, making himself like the preacher whom in childhood he adopted as a model. Yet when the music stops and he sits with the talk show host, he is somewhat plodding and intentionally lacks luster—again in the poise of the local country preacher. The glitter of a star onstage is genuine, and B.B. has cultivated it; in other places, even in the dressing room, it may sound phony, and B.B. shuns it with equal persistence.

One advantage Satchmo had and B.B. shares is good management. Satchmo's career was managed by Joe Glaser, who built a show business empire with his Associated Booking, the biggest in the business. Satchmo always credited much of his success to Glaser and often said that the best advice he ever got was from a New Orleans bouncer who told him the night before he left to join King Oliver's band, "Always keep a white man behind you that'll put his hand on you and say, 'That's *my* nigger!'"

Times have changed. Show business is no longer so fraught with racism as it was in Satchmo's early days. Yet there is still no substitute for good management. An artist needs someone running interference for him or her, someone who is dedicated to moving the artist through the swamps of the entertainment industry. It's not enough to have a recording contract with a major label and a contract with the major booking agency because these organizations have far more artists under contract than they can energetically promote; so long as B.B. is making money for them, the agency and record-company executives would be content to leave him just where he is, languishing on his plateau, bringing in reliable dough. It's Seidenberg's job to cajole these companies into marshaling their promotional machinery behind B.B., and this is Seidenberg's forte. Most important for B.B.'s prospects is Seidenberg's preference for long-range goals over middle-range and short-range profits. He does not hesitate to send B.B. on money-losing tours, if he believes they have long-range advantages for raising B.B.'s general popularity; one thing Sid Seidenberg does with great aplomb is spend money, and in a speculative business like entertainment, there is no room for the miserly.

Yet all this is mere musing on the question at hand. The biggest hazard to B.B. possibly rising to the show-biz stratosphere is his own mixed feelings about success. He craves it because it soothes his self-doubt and rescues him from the brink of poor self-esteem. But he also shuns too much of it because it may rescue him enough to let him relax his efforts. He refuses to let success banish his self-doubt and hence it generates a new kind of self-doubt: Am I worthy of this success? The standard response to this last kind of self-doubt is to dissociate oneself from the success. Show business is littered with the ruined careers of entertainers—and this applies to other professionals, even scientists—who fall into this trap of comparing their own intrinsic worth with the worth of their product and with their fame. It is a natural trap to be caught in since people often strive to achieve in the hopes of thereby boosting their own self-appraisal. The trap is insidious: among the people who would take such a comparison seriously, only the megalomaniac can emerge with his or her self-esteem intact. People who are dedicated to their work would be well advised to keep the following rule in mind: *If people scramble for the mere chance to touch your hand, don't ask, "Am I worthy?"* The penalty for falling into the trap is self-destruction. The burden gets too heavy; the suspense grows as the star worries: "Will the public find me out, will they discover that I'm masquerading as a great person?" The standard way of breaking the suspense is self-ruin.

B.B. expresses his mixed feelings toward success and curbs it somewhat by gambling. Like most people who gamble heavily, he has had some very big scores which only feed his fever. But his gambling didn't begin then; he has gambled all his adult life from the time before he left Mississippi. The opinions he expresses about his gambling are the standard gambler's rationalizations. He writes off his losses as mad money spent in entertaining himself. His winnings are no more real to him than his losses, but rather a gift from Lady Luck; such manna from heaven had better be shared and spent freely. When he loses, he shrugs and reaches for another ticket; when he wins a thousand dollars he beams, tips the keno runner fifty or a hundred, and reaches for two tickets. He believes that to win big you've got to play steadily, apparently oblivious to the fact that the long-run player always loses. Quite offhandedly he professes theories on gambling quite beneath the intelligence he shows in other matters, theories such as: to win in keno, you have to follow the trail of the numbers, just like you stalk a deer in the forest.

B.B.'s gambling may be a technique for dissociating himself from the fruit of his success, money, and, in turn, from success itself. If, after all these years at the tables he lands up filthy rich, it will be Lady Luck's work, not his. And if he is broke, well, he never had anything to begin with so he'll be no worse off than when he started. As long as he loses at the tables, he will be forced to keep up his brutal schedule of appearances. In this sense, gambling is his way of driving himself in quest of ever-higher success, of dragging out the campaign to prove himself to himself and thus put off the final reckoning in which he might be found unworthy of his success.

The idea that his gambling and his deepest, most fundamental ideas about his own basic worth are connected in some fundamental way is not mine alone; B.B. himself openly links his gambling losses and his root emotional insecurity, from the stage of the casino cabaret. When he plays Harrah's Casino in Lake Tahoe, Nevada, he tells his audiences, "Like everybody else that comes here, before I leave, Harrah's has got what I came with and a little more besides. So I know what it's like when you're playing twenty-one—we don't like to call it *black*jack, you understand—and the dealer shows a nine and you're holding sixteen. You look at her—I say 'her' because I prefer to play with the lady dealers—you know it gives you something nice to look at while you're losing all that money—so you look at her with a real funny look on your face like you're pleading with her and you say, 'Hit me,' and she hits you with a six. Busted! That's when you feel like singing,

> 'Nobody loves me but my mother,
> And she could be jivin', too!' "

So the story is simple. Riley B. King could be busted when he lost just one dollar; to revive the same feeling nowadays, B.B. must lose a few thousand! With everything else in his favor, B.B. could blow it at the tables in Nevada. If Satchmo's mantle comes within reach, B.B. may be unable to stretch out and grasp it and may instead choose to plunge headlong into self-ruin. Possibly. More likely, though, if the opportunity presents itself, he will find ways of prolonging the delicate balancing act he has been carrying on throughout his whole career. After all, with all his losses, gambling and otherwise, B.B. did manage to prolong a very delicate balance, a very long time. Nagging self-doubt is the companion of most great figures, from Billie Holiday to Lyndon Johnson, and those who were really free of it, like Harry S Truman and Satchmo, are the exceptions, not the rule. So far, gambling has been a safety valve for B.B., not a cancer; and though it is probably in large part responsible for the fact that he has never become wealthy, it has, thus far, never threatened him with complete ruin. Moreover, B.B. now has a stabilizing influence in Sid Seidenberg, whom he credits with helping to minimize his losses in recent years.

All things considered, barring disasters and flukes, Seidenberg stands a decent chance of seeing B.B. to the stratosphere where only demigods tread. The divine right of kings may be his.

IX

The Music Alone

IT IS OFTEN NOTED by cultural historians and musicologists
that the musical styles forged by black Americans are the nearest
to a unique indigenous American art form. Certainly blues is at
least one of the chief musical genres in that sphere, and B.B. is its
grand master. Consequently, B.B. King, the pre-eminent bluesman, must be acknowledged as a major musical figure of our
time, even by those more ready to visit a concert hall than a tavern or a nightclub.

To come to grips with B.B.'s musical achievement it is important to understand how he has managed to be innovative and
original while remaining within the narrow confines of the blues
form, a form too spare and restricting to accommodate the avant
garde and too rigid to permit a breakthrough.

Everyone concerned with the arts will admit when comparing a
ballad with a novel, a sketch with an oil canvas, a violin solo with
a Wagnerian opera, that art is the struggle with limitations; yet
they fail to apply this to blues—out of a mixture of prejudice and
ignorance, as usual in such cases.

BEGINNINGS AND GROWTH

The musical biography of B.B. King—the story of his musical
growth from the time of his childhood when he was a stalwart of
the congregation in the Holiness Church until his adult years as
the pre-eminent blues singer and guitarist of our time—is the

story of a loner, immensely sensitive to the influence of the greats of gospel, blues and jazz. With the possible exception of Bukka White, B.B. never had a music teacher and never served an apprenticeship under a fully developed artist from any musical genre. Throughout his musical growth, he has remained highly studious and yet he is almost entirely self-taught. Many important artists have grown up in musical families and many, like jazzman Louis Armstrong, who played with King Oliver in his youth, and bluesman James Cotton, who lived, traveled and played with Sonny Boy Williamson when he was still a boy, have served a period of tutelage under an older, experienced artist. These are advantages B.B. never enjoyed. From the time he left Mississippi, B.B. has always performed as the featured artist, and ever since 1955, he has carried his own band with him on the road.

His interest in music dates from early childhood when church music stirred his soul and he was enthralled by the sounds he heard on his aunt's wind-up Victrola. After he and his kin moved up to Kilmichael in the hilly region of Mississippi, his aunt Mimy's Victrola became an ever-more-important antidote to loneliness and insecurity. Jemima Stells, his maternal aunt, had a great sense of propriety and her console Victrola, along with her pedal organ, was one of her prize possessions. On that Victrola her nephew listened to Blind Lemon Jefferson, Jimmie Rodgers, Charlie Patton and Lonnie Johnson, plus many gospel singers, like Reverend Gates. And there was Preacher Fair who left his guitar on the bed when he visited his sister (married to one of B.B.'s uncles); that guitar was the first instrument B.B. played.

B.B.'s urge to make his own music must have been strong because he made a primitive one-stringed instrument using the side of his sharecropper's cabin for a sounding board and a piece of wire from a discarded broom, stretched between two nails. His landlord, Edwayne Henderson, still recalls seeing him lying on the porch on his back, plucking the wire with his bare toe. He made melodic sounds by sliding a bottle neck or a kitchen knife along the wire to vary its effective length. It was a kind of one-stringed, vertical steel guitar with his house as the sound box— not very portable.

B.B. was sixteen before he could afford his own guitar, but by then he had already learned a few basics on Reverend Archie's electric guitar well enough to play on occasion at the Sanctified preacher's services. His only source of systematic instruction was the Nick Manaloft instruction books which he bought by mail order through the Sears Roebuck catalog. From these he learned basic musical notation and a few fundamentals, but the songs they offered, songs like "Clementine," "You Are My Sunshine," "Green Eyes," and "Dancing in the Dark," were not the music that he yearned to play well, and the style of single-note runs he aspired to play was not found in these books, which used chord fragments instead of straight melodic passages. The musical traditions of blues and gospel, which he was struggling to absorb, were oral and recorded traditions, not literate traditions.

During his Kilmichael years, he devoted most of his musical efforts to gospel music and concentrated on playing his instrument to support the singing group he had formed with cousin Birkett Davis and schoolmate Walter Doris. His musical development began in earnest at age seventeen, when he moved to Indianola in the Delta in search of better working conditions and the prospect of forming a new singing group with cousin Birkett, who had already moved down there.

Indianola opened a new musical world for B.B. He saw the top jazz and blues musicians who passed through town to play in the local gin mill, Jones' Night Spot. He befriended many local musicians and some of the itinerant ones as well. Records were much more accessible in the Delta than they had been in Kilmichael, and B.B. began hitchhiking to other Delta towns to meet musicians and work the street corners. His new gospel group with cousin Birkett and three others was in constant demand in middle-Delta churches and they sang on the radio in nearby Greenwood, Mississippi.

During the mid-1940s, in his formative years, B.B. acquired distinct musical tastes, and those have stayed with him his life long. To the two favorites of his early teens, guitarists Blind Lemon Jefferson and Lonnie Johnson, he added an abiding feeling for the sounds of vocalist/bandleader Louis Jordan, and saxophonist Lester Young. In 1944 he first heard the music of a guitarist who influenced nearly every jazz and blues guitarist to follow and who had a profound, though subtle, influence on B.B.'s playing: Charlie Christian. The exact circumstance of his first exposure to Christian's music was a curious one. A local joint had a coin-operated moviola which played four- or five-minute selections by popular musicians like Louis Jordan, Count Basie, Duke Ellington, Harry James, and the Mills Brothers while a sound-synched screen showed movies of them. This machine, a primitive forerunner of television, offered the customer no choice of selection; the songs played in strict sequence, and only barroom regulars who learned the order might know which song and artist a quarter would fetch up. One selection featured Benny Goodman with Teddy Wilson on piano, Lionel Hampton on vibes and Charlie Christian on guitar, playing two tunes, "Seven Come Eleven," and "Solo Flight." Christian's impact was not instantaneous: the young tyro had to warm up to the new, sophisticated sound, but after a while he found himself eagerly anticipating the Benny Goodman sequence to come around on the moviola program, so he could hear Christian's new style. Christian had revolutionized jazz guitar by making the instrument an independent voice in the jazz combo. Prior to Christian, the guitar had been to jazz what the banjo was to Dixieland: a rhythm instrument with harmonic color, managing only very simple melodic statements by using rapid chord sequences. As a solo instrument, until then it had been a decidedly inferior member of the jazz band. However, Christian was extremely adept at the old-fashioned business of using harmonic support to the solo instruments. Indeed, young King learned from Christian's recordings how much harmonic variety he could inject into his blues by using different chord inversions and sprinkling into otherwise standard blues progressions augmented chords and an added sixth with major triad chords. It was Christian's music that opened his ears to the possibilities of diminished chords.

But Christian's main contribution was in making the guitar a solo instrument. Listening to Charlie Christian, young King came to think of his instrument as being on a par with the primary voice in the modern jazz band, the saxophone. It thus encouraged him to listen to saxophonists to learn the complicated, largely intuitive and extremely subtle art of melodic phrasing.

Much is said and written about melodic phrasing, but it is rarely defined. It may help to digress momentarily to describe what it is about the way someone plays that is called phrasing. Phrasing is a matter of nuance comprised mostly—but not entirely—of the musician's timing. When people speak about a

comic's timing or an actor's delivery, they are describing the same
quality as melodic phrasing, only identifying it in another artistic
medium. An actor's delivery is what the actor brings to the
spoken lines that does not appear in the script. Similarly, a musician's phrasing is the nuance he gives to the notes he plays by the
precise timing of his execution of those notes—by the way he
runs notes together or plays them distinctly, and by the way he
hesitates or anticipates certain notes.

Phrasing also consists of the way different melodic phrases are
tied together throughout a given melodic line. Most of the characteristics that make up the way in which a musician phrases his
music are not to be found in the musical score; some of them are
too subtle to appear in a score, and others are deliberate departures from the written score. In sum, phrasing comprises much
of what is idiomatic in music in general, and in jazz and blues in
particular. It is this fact, as much as any other purely technical
obstacle, that stands in the way of collaboration between jazz and
classical musicians, for what the jazzman takes as intuitively
obvious in the way that a particular passage should be executed
may completely escape the other musician. An example may help
to illustrate.

Among jazz groups who have performed with traditional classical musicians is the Modern Jazz Quartet, which, during its long
life as a successful jazz ensemble, received several invitations to
play with symphony orchestras. During rehearsals, MJQ leader/
composer/pianist John Lewis found himself unable to induce the
symphony musicians to hesitate at key places in the score before
playing the first note of certain phrases. No amount of coaxing or
demonstrating on the keyboard would persuade the orchestra to
phrase the notes the way Lewis intended them to be played. Then
he got a brainstorm: he told the classical musicians to replace the
opening eighth notes with a sixteenth rest and a sixteenth note in
their copies of the score. Suddenly the symphony was swinging
where before they had played the same passages stiffly and without feeling.

Our young bluesman learned some of his phrasing from this
source, and some from that, some he invented; but of the many
sources one stands out above the rest: the French gypsy guitarist,
Django Reinhardt. King discovered Django in a curious way. Although his recordings were available in some American record

shops, his music had not made it to backwater places like the
Delta in the mid-1940s. So it came as a complete surprise when
Willie Dotson, an Indianola friend, brought King several of
Django's recordings which he had bought in Paris on leave from
the army during World War II. Dotson was musical, and he and
King had swapped musical gossip and traded licks many times before Dotson was drafted; when he heard Django's music in Paris,
he knew how much Riley King would appreciate the new sounds
and perhaps profit from them as well. Dotson carried the fragile
78 rpm acetate records back from France to Indianola, Mississippi, to an eager Riley King, who learned from them three
things: an appreciation of harmonies, an understanding of phrasing, and a knowledge of scales. As to harmonics, Django, like the
other musicians he played with in the Hot Club in Paris, employed the full range of the twelve-tone scale. Naturally, there
were harmonic combinations he favored, but he scampered up
and down the customary jazz scale, ducking into nooks and cran-
nies where bluesmen rarely strayed, hitting flatted sixths and
natural sevenths with unfettered ease. There is little or nothing
specific in B.B.'s mature harmonies to identify as borrowed from
or inspired by Django, though in private moments when he is
playing for his own enjoyment or as exercise, he can sometimes
sound remarkably like the gypsy jazz master, whom he never met
in person. Nonetheless, B.B.'s debt to Django is very large and
should not be underestimated.

Django's phrasing was both precise and fluid. He used a smattering of "bent notes" (notes that slide up to pitch from a quarter
or half tone below), a technique which delays the anticipated
note and enhances it. Bending of notes became a hallmark of
B.B.'s mature style. Django's free interchange of various modes of
the scale, from Mixolydian to Phrygian impressed on B.B. the
need for versatility on his fingerboard, and encouraged him to mix
modes of the scale, too.

Two other influences stand out in B.B.'s progression to musical
maturity; these are the period of tutelage he spent with his cousin
Bukka White, and the many hours he spent listening to the first
bluesman to demonstrate the potential of the electric guitar in
blues music, T-Bone Walker. The style of B.B. owes to both
Bukka and T-Bone the determination to develop innovative techniques of playing the electric guitar.

The two older bluesmen had very different techniques, but they both built their styles on achieving characteristic sounds by handling their instruments in certain very specific, highly technical ways. Bukka handled his hollow, metal-bodied six-string National steel guitar one way, and T-Bone handled his wooden, hollow-bodied, electric guitar in quite another way. Very early in his development, probably as far back as the days when he sat in Reverend Archie's Holiness Church, young Riley appreciated the fact that the technique used in playing the instrument determines the voice of the instrument and different techniques can give the same instrument voices as different as any two human voices. He also grasped very early that the voice of an instrument is its pathos.

At the age of twenty, he lived with cousin Bukka during his first ten-month period in Memphis. They played together evenings, and Bukka is the closest thing he ever had to a teacher. What most impressed him about his older cousin's playing was the vibrato sound he made with the piece of metal pipe Bukka wore on the little finger of his left hand by dragging it over the strings in a trembling motion. The technique was common to most Delta blues guitarists and is sometimes called "slide guitar" or "bottleneck." Because the sliding metal pipe varies the effective length of the vibrating strings continuously, the pitch varies continuously, too—glissando is the technical term—like the way the pitch of a violin or of a slide trombone can change, rather than in steps, like the pitch of a piano must change or the pitch of the guitar string varies from fret to fret when it is played the conventional way. The slide device turned the guitar into a fully chromatic instrument, capable of giving all shades of tone— quarter tones and eighth tones included. It thus made the guitar panchromatic.

Using the slide on his finger, Bukka could make the instrument cry like a human voice or sigh like the wind. B.B. describes it now by saying, "The sound seemed to pierce my flesh." He tried to use the slide, but his broad palms and stocky fingers couldn't control it smoothly. To compensate, he abandoned the slide altogether and turned to a technique he had seen others use to achieve minute shadings of tone. This technique consisted of stretching the strings by sliding them sideways across the neck, almost like pulling the string on a crossbow. The resulting increase in tension in the string causes the pitch of the vibrating string to rise, just as if the tension was increased by tightening the tuning peg.

What B.B. lacked in control of the slide, he possessed with this technique. He found he could not only slur up to a given note from a half-tone below, in the technique of "bending notes," but he could apply and release the tension in rapid oscillation to create the vibrato sound Bukka got with his metal slide. This method of slurring pitch by stretching the strings is not entirely B.B.'s invention; T-Bone Walker and other electric blues guitarists used it around the time he was first experimenting with it. However, he did invent a novel way of stretching the strings to achieve vibrato, which remains his unique device even today. Other electric guitarists take a tight grip on the neck and stretch the strings with the muscles of their fingers. B.B. uses the muscles of his forearm to stretch the strings, moving his whole hand in a fanning motion generated by swiveling his forearm from the wrist. He barely grips the neck at all while making vibrato; rather, he sometimes cradles the neck lightly in the arch between his thumb and index finger, and sometimes only the finger actually pressing down on the vibrating string is in contact with the neck. This technique, completely novel to B.B., is an important factor in making the rich, fluid quality to his vibrato sound. It seems to give him much better control over both the speed and depth of the oscillation of pitch which makes up the vibrato quality.

It was during the time of his stay with Bukka that B.B. bought his first electric guitar—a Gibson—and an amplifier, both purchased with money borrowed from Bukka. Starting with that first amplified Gibson, he transformed the electric guitar into a new instrument for blues, building on the fundamentals laid down by T-Bone Walker. Initially, electric amplification was simply a device for giving the guitar a louder, stronger voice, one that would be heard amid other instruments and over the din of noisy taverns. It was originally seen as an improvement over other devices for projecting the instrument, the metal pan attached to wooden-bodied guitars and the all-metal National steel guitar But King soon recognized, playing his first amplified guitar and listening to T-Bone, that amplification made the guitar a different instrument He set out deliberately and methodically to exploit the unique character of the electric guitar to fashion a distinctive voice for his instrument.

Once he had developed the voice of his instrument and acquired a great diversity of technical devices, he then drew from a rich variety of sources, including many vocalists and horn players, in shaping his own style of improvising; once he had acquired the means to say something, his eclectic view of music endowed him with stylistic elements of great power and emotive force. He has a view of playing that completely transcends his instrument and allows him to grasp the fact that he is striving for the same thing in his playing that jazz singer Ella Fitzgerald and saxophonist Lester Young reach for in their music (just to mention two major artists who have inspired him).

Lester Young is of more than incidental importance because he has influenced B.B.'s style at least as much as any guitarist. Tenor saxophonist Lester Young, known as "Pres" (short for "The President") was one of the most influential jazzmen ever. In fact, during the latter part of his career, he so captured the imagination of other tenormen that he felt haunted by hearing his own sound coming from others' horns. By the time B.B. had access to a broad selection of records, Young had made several recordings. In the forties, Charlie Parker and Dizzy Gillespie invented cool jazz, or bebop, which is dazzling in its complexity. Lester Young, who had already played for years with Count Basie and Fletcher Henderson, still played with a crystalline simplicity; his tone was sweet and gentle and he played his solos in a dreamy, laconic way using evenly spaced eighth notes played legato (smoothly). Young's great affinity for vocalists influenced B.B.; indeed Young's own listening was concentrated on singers more than other saxophonists. Some of Lester Young's best solos were recorded as instrumental accompaniment to singer Billie Holiday. B.B.'s belief in the aesthetic unity of all good music shows in his effort to bring his guitar playing and his singing close to the playing of a saxophonist, who, in turn, tries to approach the sound and delivery of the human voice. B.B. plays his guitar like a saxophone—not like the emerging sax of Charlie Parker but like the old-style singing sax of Lester Young. B.B. manages to combine a very deep familiarity with all the peculiarities of his instrument—all the possible idiosyncracies the instrument possesses—with a view of music that is thoroughly transcendent of any particular instrument. It will remain one of his greatest achievements for the rest of his career.

BIOGRAPHIES of musicians usually give highly detailed accounts of the artist's development from earliest to very latest recordings, complete with precise comparisons of solos and intricate cross-references that cite the session men at recording sessions and the names of musicians who shared the bandstand at renowned jam sessions. In B.B.'s case, this approach makes little sense because he has always been a loner and he is largely self-taught. Moreover, B.B.'s decision to remain within the blues framework is a self-imposed limitation that allowed for development only along the lines discussed above.

It is evident that the blues is a narrow format; hence one cannot play blues and be avant garde. B.B.'s development has therefore been confined to expanding the expressive range of his instrument by means of his technical innovations and learning to play with increasingly deeper subtlety. Anyone who compares his very earliest recordings of the late 1940s (available on a reissue by Kent, titled *Anthology of the Blues/B.B. King, 1949–1950,* KST 9011) with those of his mature years will hear the evolution of a raw, unrefined talent into an artist of formidable skill and rare powers of expression. (His better-known recordings of the 1950s and early 1960s are collected in a two-record set, *From the Beginning,* Kent: KST-533; his performances from the mid-1960s are well represented on two live albums—*Live at the Regal,* ABC: ABCS-509 and *Blues Is King,* Bluesway: BLS-509.)

Yet B.B.'s determination to make blues music socially respectable and his deep love of the most basic blues styles have kept him close to the fundamental form of the blues. He put himself in a position that obliged him to be content with adding harmonic color and gentle rhythmic variations, stopping short of the extensive use of polyrhythms and polytonality. Of his strictly musical innovations, the boldest was his shift of emphasis in the blues scale to elevate the sixth degree of the scale to a new level of importance, an innovation worthy of a careful look in later sections of this chapter.

Once the composition of his audience began to change with his arrival in Middle America in 1968, B.B. allowed himself occasional departures from the blues form. He began performing and recording material that went beyond the traditional harmonic pattern (tonic, dominant, subdominant, I, IV, V) used in blues. He added diversity to his repertoire with the elegant composition "Hummingbird" (1970) by rock superstar Leon Russell, and a few ballads like "Guess Who" and "It Takes A Young Girl" (1973). *Midnight Believer,* his 1978 album recorded with the Jazz Crusaders, is a fusion of soul and blues not found in any of his previous music or in the records of any other artist, bluesman or soul singer. His biggest hit, "The Thrill Is Gone" used strings for the first time in blues recording, a device he used freely thereafter. Nonetheless, all these impressive additions cannot be appreciated unless seen as refinements designed to add elegance and polish to the music without thereby changing its basic character. B.B.'s development has never been aimed at making a breakthrough, unless one thinks of it as a breakthrough to further distill the grapes of blues from wine to cognac.

By the same token, it must be said that in devoting himself to blues, B.B. chose a musical form which defies expansion and that before his career was completed, he had exhausted the form—or so it seems. At this point, it looks very unlikely that B.B. will have a musical heir—but there is no telling what may happen with innovations, artistic or otherwise, and genius may find liberation at the end of a blind alley.

B.B. has been connected with virtually all the major rhythm and blues artists who were contemporary with him. One of the earliest piano players to record with B.B. was Ike Turner, then barely sixteen and working as a talent scout for Modern Records in Memphis and the Deep South. B.B. has appeared on the same bill with rock stars from the heyday of early rock-and-roll—Lloyd Price, Fats Domino, Jackie Wilson, and Sam Cooke, among others. His earliest recordings were made for Modern Records by Sam Phillips, the mastermind of Sun Records (the original label that first recorded Elvis Presley, Johnny Cash, Carl Perkins, and Jerry Lee Lewis). In addition, B.B. had, at one time, a close association with blues singer, Bobby "Blue" Bland, but if there is any influence of one musician on the other here it is surely B.B , the older, more mature of the two, who influenced Bobby

Of all the musicians B.B. knew and played with, only his cousin Bukka and Memphis bandleader Bill Harvey, who fronted

B.B.'s first road band, influenced his musical development in a profound manner. Harvey's contribution to B.B.'s growth was not in any particular stylistic direction; it was rather to impress on B.B. the tremendous importance of listening to other musicians in his effort to develop his own style. He was to B.B. what brother Theo was to Vincent van Gogh. In his thirty-year career, B.B. has had only one real collaborator—an obscure musician named Ferdinand Washington, known to other bluesmen as "Fats"—whose role as B.B.'s collaborator was confined to composing lyrics. From time to time when B.B. was composing and had in mind a particular sentiment he wanted to express and felt blocked, he would telephone Fats Washington and together they would work out the idiomatic expression; in this way B.B. came to crystallize key phrases like "If you can't do any better, I'd better get me somebody else that will," and titles like "Waitin' on You," and "Get Off My Back, Woman." The other names that frequently appear as co-composers of many of B.B.'s early songs—"Josea," "Taub," and "Ling"—are not collaborators at all. They are cryptonyms used by the record-company people who registered the copyrights to the material in order to allow the company to keep half the composer's royalties due B.B.

In early 1979 B.B. King hired Calvin Owens as arranger and musical director for his band. Owens is a contemporary of B.B., a protégé of Bill Harvey, the seminal R&B band leader from Memphis. Hiring Owens, who played in his first road band, was a return to his musical roots for B.B. He gave his new band leader full authority to form a new band and rewrite any old arrangements that Owens might feel needed refurbishing. A tall, assertive, self-confident man with graying temples, Owens replaced all but one of B.B.'s former road musicians, keeping only drummer Calep Emphrey, who knew B.B.'s routine and has always had inexhaustible reserves of physical strength, an important trait for the one musician most responsible for stoking the boiler onstage. (Emphrey, who comes from Greenville, Mississippi, near B.B.'s hometown of Indianola, began as drummer for bluesman Freddy King; his sheer physical capacity is indicated by the ease with which he once stood in for Bobby Bland's missing drummer when Bobby and B.B. were playing a double bill, an assignment that required him to play back-to-back double sets.)

Owens arrived at the first engagement with a suitcase full of charts and a newly recruited band, larger, louder and brassier than any ensemble to play behind B.B. in at least a decade. He is tireless in his effort to achieve a sound true to the basics he learned from Harvey in the early 1950s at the Club Handy on Beale Street. Most arrangements have been rewritten many times and over the months since he took charge Owens has replaced several musicians who have proved not exactly to his taste or unworthy of his standards. He records performances regularly and studies the results for flaws to be corrected at the frequent and arduous rehearsals which he calls.

The change from a medium-sized ensemble, lacking a strong leader and relying on intuition to follow B.B. onstage, to a large, highly disciplined, power-packed band under the tight control of a bluesman straight from Beale Street injected new life into B.B.'s performance. Ever since he reduced the size of his band around 1960 he had missed the feeling of a mighty engine behind him; he yearned to have a reserve of musical power he could call on when he wanted to pull out all stops. Now he has it. When audiences listen to B.B. King playing today with Calvin Owens' band backing him, they can hear the fire of a Beale Street that exists only in the collective memory of a handful of musicians now still active.

This ends the account of B.B.'s growth as a musician, save one item: his singing. Everything that has already been said here about B.B.'s musical progress, which does not specifically concern his guitar playing, applies to his singing as well because he hears music with an aesthetic unity. He believes that the qualities that make good music transcend the peculiarities of any one instrument, including the human voice, and hence he strives toward the same goal—whether he is singing or playing his guitar. Indeed, he claims to hear himself singing while he is playing. Unlike his playing, which matured through years of systematic effort, the only practice he has ever given his voice has been on the bandstand, singing his heart out.

As a singer, B.B. is completely natural and has never trained his voice. His vocal style is straightforward, chesty, and open-throated, with a heavy dose of gospel sound, unlike some blues singers who sing with a somewhat nasal tone. He often skirts the border between the sung and the spoken word and sometimes crosses over to deliberate speech, but he is generally too sonorous to be compared to the blues shouters. He makes free and easy use of melisma, the technique common in gospel music of singing the same syllable over several notes, and often he interjects falsetto notes, a habit he claims to have picked up from old-style blues singer Dr. Clayton, also known as "Neckbones."

JAM STYLE VS. CONCERT STYLE

The commonly accepted framework that divides the world of music into classical vs. popular obscures some other extremely important distinctions in the way music is composed and performed. The first of these distinctions is between music with a high degree of improvisation and music which is mostly or entirely prescribed by the composer (or by tradition). Because much pop music is performed in strict accord with the specifications of the composer and arranger, and also because more and more so-called classical music is written to allow the performer considerable liberty, the old distinction of classical vs. pop is at best a partial picture of what gives special character to different kinds of music. When Frank Sinatra or Tom Jones take the stage, they perform with a carefully rehearsed orchestra playing thoroughly prepared scores, and hence they share more in common with the musicians in symphony orchestras or chamber ensembles than with other popular musicians like, say, Miles Davis or Eric Clapton. Or when the Boston Pops plays the Beatles, there can be no getting around the fact that the music is transformed from the original version. On the other hand, concert-hall musicians performing the works of contemporary composers John Cage and Robert Cogan will find the score impossible to execute unless they improvise in accord with the composers' very general directions; they have more in common with jazz and blues performers than with traditional symphony musicians. The opportunity for improvisation is a unifying element of enormous power as witnessed by the quick and fluid cross-cultural exchange between Western rock musicians and Indian raga players.

The unifying force of improvisation is too often neglected, so much so that we lack a term to designate the class of music that relies on improvisation regardless of whatever other stylistic characteristics the music might possess such as cool vs. hot or folk vs. rock. Hence we need to coin a new term that will designate all music from Cage and Cogan to King and Shankar, which is improvisational in character. Perhaps "jam style" will do as well as any.

Improvisation in Western music is not a strictly twentieth-century phenomenon and is not limited to nonclassical styles. In the eighteenth century, classical composers took it for granted that performers would add their own embellishments in the form of trills, grace notes, and the like. Some composers, like Bach, who were against even this much improvisation, wrote in the embellishments of the melodic line themselves in order to co-opt the performer's liberty. The concerto was usually scored with fermata (long pauses) for the orchestra—at least between the movements and codas, in order to let the soloist improvise a cadenza.

Basso continuo, which went out of fashion in the late eighteenth century, gave the bass player a free rein with the bass part; there was only a framework in the score. Always there is the inherent limitation of any written score to specify exactly how the music is to be performed; much is necessarily left to the performer. The improvisational element is present to some degree in nearly all Western music—especially in phrasing, which can scarcely be specified. However, with the appearance of jazz and blues in America, around the turn of this century, came a style which was predominantly improvisational in character—"jam style" music—and this was something decidedly new.

What are the relative advantages and disadvantages of improvisational jam-style music and highly prescribed concert-style music?

Jam style offers the musician tremendous freedom within a specified, more or less narrow framework. Without the framework, jam-style musicians would have no format within which to collaborate, so the framework must be given; yet, once given, anything goes, so long as it is compatible with the framework. The payoff comes in spontaneity. Any idea that comes the way of the inspired performer can be developed on the spot, so long as it doesn't violate the framework.

By contrast, concert style allows the composer complete liberty to alter the framework, while requiring the performer to stick to the score. What is lost in spontaneity is gained in precision, clarity, and the overall design. With the quest for clarity and precision comes the need to eliminate all spurious sounds which the instruments may make: sounds like unpleasant overtones, or the scraping of bow on string. In short, concert-style music must be exceedingly clean. Even this convention in favor of clarity over murkiness is violated by avant-garde composers like Charles Ives, who made textures, including the murkiest, paramount in his style.

No instrument is perfect; even a Stradivarius violin or a Haynes flute will have its quirks, and the same goes for the most accomplished performers who each have their idiosyncracies. A few concert-style musicians, Casals and Segovia principally, have managed to ignore the spurious sounds of their instruments while boldly reaching new heights of expression. Yet most performers exert tremendous effort to suppress the extraneous in search of purity.

The clarity and precision of concert-style music makes possible an integration of the individual voices of the orchestra or choir into—ideally—a single voice. Of course, the quest for absolute purity and total integration is bound to fall short of perfection, and even coming close to achieving it may kill the life force in the music.

For jam-style music, the situation is much different. The free-wheeling character of this kind of music maximizes the individuality of every instrument, and dwarfs the small imperfections of performance, which are the bane of concert-style musicians. Almost no excess of individuality will, in and of itself, spoil jam-style music; and murky, muddy textures obtained by muting the strings, rasping the reeds, or any other technique to give a harsh edge to the voices of the instruments are often exploited as major stylistic devices.

By any standard, blues is jam-style music. The significance of the foregoing discussion for understanding B.B. King's music is twofold: first, all his guitar playing is improvisational within a very narrow framework; second, in fashioning a distinctive voice for his instrument, he has capitalized on precisely those characteristics of the electric guitar that concert-style acoustic guitarists would regard as impurities to be suppressed.

NEW TECHNIQUES

How King has managed to achieve the unique sound of his guitar is a purely technical matter. The sound of an electric guitar is generated in a different way from the sound of an unamplified acoustic guitar, though both employ vibrating strings. The magnetic pickups that generate the sound of an electric guitar are not simple microphones of the sort used to amplify the human voice, and consequently the quality of the voice the instrument produces is not a simple replica of the unamplified voice of the instrument. The electric guitar sounds different from an acoustic guitar and, equally important to the musician, plays differently, too.

The voice of an electric guitar originates in the magnetic pickup positioned just below the strings. The pickup contains small permanent magnets wrapped with a continuous coil of fine copper wire. The vibrating metal guitar string nearby causes the magnetic forces reaching out from the magnets to oscillate, and these fluctuations cause oscillating electric currents in the copper coil surrounding the magnet. It is these tiny oscillating electric currents set up in the copper coil that are carried to the amplifier, where they are greatly boosted and then used to drive the speaker, which actually makes the sound one hears. The key feature of a magnetic pickup which makes it qualitatively different from an ordinary microphone is the fact that the magnetic pickup responds directly to the metal string, without the intervening medium of the air.

The physical factors which influence the particular, characteristic voices of electric guitars and acoustic guitars are very different. With an acoustic guitar, the design and construction of the body are important factors, whereas the sound of an electric guitar is not appreciably affected by these factors. With an electric guitar, the design and placement of the pickups as well as the metallic composition of both pickups and strings is important in determining the character of the sound. An acoustic guitar has no pickups at all, and *may* have nonmetallic strings. Even more important in making a comparison of the two instruments is the fact that an electric guitar is really a system composed of guitar, amplifier, and speaker, and how the musician employs these other two components—amplifier and speaker—influences the final product.

As young Riley experimented with his new instrument and compared his sound with the sound he heard on T-Bone Walker's records in those early formative days, he discovered how very sensitive the electric guitar is to different techniques of handling the strings. For one thing, the pickups are very sensitive to percussive contact with the strings; the exact way the pick is drawn across the strings changes the attack of the sound. Also, the way in which the strings are pressed down on the fretboard matters greatly. If they are pressed down hard and held firmly, the tone is clear and sustained; if they are pressed down loosely and released quickly, an instant after being plucked, the resulting sound is highly percussive, choppy, and almost immediately deadened, like the sound of a banjo. Moreover, if in pressing the strings down on the neck they are hammered down very hard against the fretboard, the resulting blow to the strings is sufficient, because of the sensitivity of the pickups to weak vibrations, to make the notes sound loud and clear without plucking the strings with the pick at all, a technique called "hammering on" the note.

Hammered-on notes have a different attack than picked notes; and hammering on, as a substitute for picking, may increase speed and fluidity of playing. B.B. discovered that if he pressed the string down just behind the fret, the note was sustained longer by pressing down more firmly as the note began to fade. This discovery enabled him to capitalize on the great advantage of the instrument to sustain the volume of notes, which T-Bone was the first to employ. This capacity for sustain overcame the great limitation of the acoustic guitar for playing single-string runs or melodic passages; on acoustic guitars such runs lack the dynamic range from loud to soft required for them to be effective and they tend to die in mid-course. More than any other electric blues guitarist, T-Bone established single-string runs as the main form of expression for the electric guitar in blues music. B.B. took the form of expression and developed it to dramatic new heights.

As his technical command of the guitar grew, B.B. extended the expressive range and diversity of the instrument. To achieve indefinite sustain of certain notes he learned to employ acoustic feedback. Acoustic feedback occurs when the sound waves from the speaker meet the vibrating string in such a precise, synchronous way so as to make them resonate, i e , so as to reinforce the vibrations of the string—which originally caused the sound waves to issue from the speaker—and maintain the oscillations of the string undiminished. The system of guitar, amplifier, and speaker thus forms a closed chain—the string driving the speaker (via the amplifier), driving the string, at a constant level. Such feedback is very tricky to produce because it relies on combining resonances in the instrument and the electronics and so only certain notes will give feedback; it depends also on the exact distance between the guitar and the speakers in so delicate a way that the feedback may appear and disappear as the guitarist turns even slightly toward or away from the speakers.

On this point of acoustic feedback, King's innovation shows most dramatically the difference between jam-style and concert-style musicians. Electric guitarists were aware of feedback long before anyone thought to exploit it, but at first it was regarded as one of those spurious sounds to be suppressed, rather than a weapon in the stylist's arsenal.

Over many years, B.B. experimented with all of these technical factors—picking and fretting techniques, feedback, hollow-bodied guitars, solid-bodied guitars, electronic reverberation devices, amplifiers of all different makes—and he listened with dogged persistence to T-Bone's records, fiddling with the controls on his own equipment, varying his playing techniques, in an effort initially to get a faithful copy of T-Bone's sound and, later, to shape a unique voice for his own guitar style. After more than a decade of experimentation, he had succeeded to give his guitar a voice of its own, as unique and easily recognizable as any human voice. The combination of equipment he settled for employs a slender, Gibson hollow-bodied stereo guitar, Model Number ES355, strung with light-gauge Fender "Rock and Roll" strings. He prefers an SG amplifier once manufactured by Gibson, now discontinued, but often uses a Fender "Super-Reverb" or Fender "Twin Reverb" amplifier. All three of these amplifiers are powerful units which can achieve formidable volume, yet they are much less powerful than the monsters commonly used by rock musicians who often use two or more Marshal or Sunn amplifiers in tandem. The way B.B. uses the combination of hardware, especially the stereo feature of his guitar, is an important part of his style, and this is the last remaining nuts-and-bolts aspect that needs attention before we turn to less dry and strictly technical matters.

Most electric guitars are equipped with a pair of pickups—one near the tail, close to the bridge, and one close to the midpoint of the strings near the place where the neck is attached to the body.

There are separate volume and tone controls for each pickup located on the guitar body. The first pickup, near the bridge, emphasizes the high-frequency overtones which make the treble part of every sound; these high frequencies give the piercing highs of the overall sound. Without them a note will have an edgeless, flutelike sound; with lots of them it will have a trumpetlike or a stringlike brilliance. The other pickup near the midpoint of the strings tends to emphasize the lower-frequency overtones, the ones that give body and bass to the sound. The conventional guitar is wired with a single line to the amplifier, and it is equipped with a three-position toggle switch which connects either pickup to the line separately, or both pickups together. The stereo guitar which B.B. uses has a two-channel line running to the amplifier, and the cord connecting his instrument to the input sockets on the amplifier divides into two plugs at the amplifier end; thus the standard two-channel amplifier can separately process the electrical impulses transmitted from the two pickups. With this system, B.B. has greater discretion in mixing his sound.

B.B. sets the tone and volume controls on both channels of his amplifier to maximum setting and mixes the sound entirely from the controls on the guitar. He sets the stereo balance control in the middle and never changes it. He adjusts tone and volume controls for each pickup to suit his taste. In a single sweeping motion, he can turn the volume control with his little finger and the tone control with the heel of his hand. He has maximum control over the whole frequency range within quick reach of his right hand. While he is playing, he can boost one end of the spectrum and suppress the other; and then, in the next phrase, change the voice of his guitar by flattening the spectrum or switching emphasis to the other end. And he is able to modulate his overall volume level from full power to a mere whisper. While he plays, he steadily remixes his sound. Picking usually near the middle of the strings where the middle and low parts of the frequency spectrum are strongest, using an oblique motion not strictly perpendicular to the string, which gives a rough edge to the attack, he adjusts and readjusts the guitar controls to make the sound now full-bodied, now lean; now percussive, now sonorous; now loud and strident, now soft and plaintive; sometimes rough and guttural, but always clear and distinct.

B.B. AS A STYLIST

It is time now to analyze B.B.'s style of guitar playing. The analysis will avoid deep technicalities, but for those with eyes and ears for fine points and patience for complexities, a thorough analysis of one B.B. King solo is given in Appendix IV. From his guitar playing, we will extend the discussion to his style as a vocalist and lyricist and conclude the with a characterization of his method of performance. First to the specifics of his playing.

B.B. King's guitar playing is deceptively simple, in the sense that what looks like harmonic complexity is no more than clever variations of the most rudimentary harmonic patterns and what looks like speed is really agility. First, he has a musical signature —a five-note figure with which he begins most of his slow blues songs; this signature, together with a second figure, is the basis for most of his improvised melodic fragments. The two figures are the cornerstones of his playing, and variations of them, used in combination, comprise a musical grammar which has been absorbed by virtually all other blues guitarists. The signature begins and ends on the fifth degree of the scale. ("Degree of the scale" denotes simply which of the eight sequential notes in a regular eight-note scale is singled out for attention. Thus the "fifth degree of the scale" is the note called "sol" in the scale sung as "do, re, mi . . .") There is a basic tension intrinsic to the fifth and first degrees of the scale, in the sense that the fifth degree seems to beg resolution by a return to the first; so the figure which is B.B.'s musical signature imparts a feeling of delicate tension. Written out, the signature looks like this:

The fourth note of the figure, which falls on the first beat of the second measure (E as shown above in the key of C), is slurred from a half tone below (by stretching the string), and the last note, ending on the fifth degree of the scale, is usually played with heavy vibrato.

B.B.'s other basic figure relies heavily on the sixth degree of the scale, and herein lies one of B.B.'s main innovations: the elevation of the sixth note in the eight-tone scale ("la" in the sung scale) to a level of major importance in blues (it originates in jazz). The sixth note in the scale in combination with the root note is harmonically an extremely elegant sound. The reason why this should be so is somewhat complicated and difficult to explain, but briefly and very roughly the reason is the following.

If the eight notes of the regular scale are played in succession starting not on the first degree of the scale but rather on the sixth degree and ending on the sixth in the octave above, we get a minor scale played in another key. This is called the Aeolian mode. Hence the sixth note has an air of ambiguity between major and minor. Perhaps it can be considered plain bitonality; that is, if the ambiguity between the two scales can be kept both harmonically and melodically between two occurrences of the same major chord with the added sixth, a musicologist would be hard pressed to say that it is not using two scales at once. B.B. is extremely sparse and simple with polyrhythms, so we would expect him to be extremely sparse and simple with polytonality as well.

The second basic figure begins on the sixth and hits the sixth again on the first beat of the measure; both sixths are usually played as bent notes approached from a half tone below. A great many improvised figures in B.B.'s solos are variations on these two basic forms.

A few more technical devices comprise B.B.'s working elements of style. He freely employs quarter tones, especially the quarter tone just below the fifth degree of the scale and the one between the sixth and flatted seventh, a place of unique ambivalence that carries both the elegance of the sixth and the mellowness of the flatted seventh (the flatted seventh, it may be recalled, is the mainspring of all blues melodies). Besides the technique of bending notes a half or whole tone, he also makes liberal use of *glissando* or the technique of sliding the fingers along the strings. He rarely strums chords in the midst of solo improvisations but he sometimes plays quickly rolled cascades of three or four notes together.

How do all these stylistic devices sound when he puts them together? *Like boy Riley fighting his stammer in an effort to express himself.* His melodic statements juxtapose long, plaintive notes with bursts of eighth notes, followed by long silences. The effect is like speech, when we hem and haw in frustration, searching for the right words. When they come, just before we give in to desperation, we blurt them out in a sigh of relief.

At other times, B.B. resolves accumulated tension with a series of precisely placed staccato notes that step gingerly and ever so deliberately over the otherwise rolling rhythm with the result that the statement seems to break through with resounding clarity. He separates successive statements with long pauses, as if to gather his thoughts; very often he leaves the second and third beats of four-beat measures to silence, and uses small melodic fragments to arch over the fourth and first beats of successive measures. He rarely plays very long passages of uninterrupted eighth notes and never strings together more than a few sixteenth notes. All in all, his playing is a supreme effort at clarity, marked by agonizing doubt that he will succeed to make himself fully understood.

In his struggle to find self-expression, B.B. combines several factors to bring his playing close to the spoken human voice. He has very consciously shaped the voice of his guitar to sound like the human voice; his neatly dovetailed melodic figures which answer one another give his solos the character of a dialogue; and his intermittent tendency to confine his figures to a narrow range of notes give the tight melodic fragments more the aspect of inflected speech than the melody of song—much in the style of speech-song used by Arnold Schoenberg in his *Pierrot Lunaire* and *Ode to Napoleon*. The similarity between his improvisation and ordinary speech is so close that during the long pauses between melodic statements people from the audience sometimes call out, "I know what you're saying, B.B.," or "Make her talk to you," and, of course, "Tell it like it is, B.B." Undoubtedly his feat at bringing song and the spoken word so close together in his music goes back to his youth in church, where the preacher roused the congregation with words half-spoken, half-sung, sometimes chanted, sometimes shouted, and whether or not he had it deliberately in mind to do so, he has fashioned a style of playing that is closely parallel to the phenomenon among Pentecostalists called "speaking in tongues."

In his handling of lyrics, B.B. manages to carry further his introduction of the spoken word beyond the effect he achieves by speaking with his guitar. It was a habit of freewheeling Delta bluesmen, including his cousin Bukka, to add a measure or a half measure here and there to the standard twelve-bar blues. For solo artists with no sidemen to coax along, it was no problem; but when B.B. began playing with other musicians in Memphis, they found it unruly that he would stretch some lyrics over two bars where one was customary. However, B.B. made a virtue of this habit, with the result that his lyrics are not tied tightly to the melody and in their independence they begin to approach speech.

Take for instance, the lyrics to B.B.'s 1960 recording "And Like That":

> If your love is so doggone true,
> And you want me to love you too.
> You don't have to swim in the sea,
> But all things in life ain't free.
> Put the ring on your hand,
> And I'll get the preacher man.
> And like that.

The rhythm of the first four lines is straightforward; each line falls naturally into two groups of three syllables with the emphasis on the last syllable, followed by two syllables, with the emphasis on the second. Thus the second line is sung (And you *want*) (me to *love*) (you *too*). In the fourth line, the word "all" must be stretched to two syllables, to make it conform with the first three. The fifth and sixth lines are shorter than the previous four lines and of uneven length: line 5 has six syllables and line 6 has seven syllables. Everything up to this point is more or less straightforward, considering that the odd syllable in line 6 can be absorbed by compressing the two-syllable word "preacher" into a single syllable. Ordinarily, these two lines would be phrased as follows, conforming to the pattern of the first four lines:

> (put the *ring*) (on your *hand*)
> (And I'll *get*) (the preacher *man*)

But B.B. chose to phrase the sixth line this way:

(And I-*I'll*) (get the *preacher* man)

This abrupt irregularity, caused by stretching the syllable "I'll" into two syllables runs this next-to-last line of lyrics into the measure reserved for the seventh and final line, with the result that the final line—"And like that"—appears out of rhythmic context and takes on the character of speech. The fact that the last line conforms to no rhyme scheme further enhances its independence.

Phrasing is not the only device by which B.B. detaches his lyrics from the melodic and rhythmic structure to make the words sound half-sung, half-spoken. In some places he stretches the lyrics out for a whole measure, so that the standard eight- and twelve-bar blues becomes nine or thirteen bars of music. Listen, for example, to "Payin' the Cost to Be the Boss," where his use of melisma (repeated syllables) so delays the onset of the chorus that an extra measure is required to accommodate the title line.

In sum, then, the infusion of speech into B.B.'s music is reflected in his playing, both in his super-deliberate phrasing which, by his own account, is a musical representation of the life-long struggle against his old stammer, and in his style of "speaking in tongues" with his instrument; and it is to be found in his tendency to divorce the lyrics from the melody, so that they sound half-spoken. This characteristic is much more than a stylistic device confined to his music. It is part of the larger picture of his conception of the blues performance.

B.B. AS A PERFORMER

Now we have arrived at the final aspect of B.B.'s music, the one he personally feels is the most important, his craft of performing before a live audience. There is no necessary connection between performance craft and musical craft. A performer of very limited musical craft might nonetheless be extremely skilled at thrilling audiences; conversely, the most skilled and inspired musician might be unable to light the faintest spark in his listeners for lack of skill at establishing a rapport with his audience. From the start, B.B. has seen performance craft as more important than musical craft. He has thus tried to pattern himself after bandleader/saxophonist/singer Louis Jordan. During his long, successful career, Jordan was never regarded as a musical heavy, yet he was extremely popular with a wide audience both black and white, and recorded duets with Bing Crosby, Ella Fitzgerald, and Louis Armstrong in the 1940s; musicians respected him for his craft as a performer.

B.B.'s craft as a performer is taken straight from the Holiness Church. His earliest musical experiences were in the congregation of Sanctified preacher Archie Fair and at that time they filled a big yawning void in him left by his mother's death. Reverend Archie's electrified services left a permanent mark on him, but religion had little to do with the experience; it was a matter of saving his soul in the here-and-now, not for some distant rendezvous with his Maker, and not from a sense of guilt but of despair. So B.B. secularized the service and made it the basis of his career.

The craft he borrowed from Reverend Archie is based on two principles: maintaining the entire performance, singing, playing and talking between songs in a conversational mode, and repeating a dramatic cycle of mounting tension, climax and release, in ever-increasing swings.

Let's consider the latter first. He has at his disposal to generate tension the following musical elements: the volume at which he sings and plays, the tempo of the songs he chooses and the lyrical content of his songs. When he goes onstage, the audience is already at the first peak of excitement, created by the anticipation of his arrival, and he always maintains it for the first few minutes with a loud up-tempo number; for years his opener was a jumpy rendition of "Every Day I Have the Blues." Lately he uses either "Caldonia," the Cab Calloway favorite, or "Let The Good Times Roll," the Louis Jordan standard, to open.

He invariably breaks the initial tension in the second number: a slow blues that starts softly and builds to a new climax, usually two thirds of the way through the instrumental interlude, at the end of the sixteenth measure when the solo muse lasts twenty-four measures; very often the second climax is announced with long plaintive cries of his guitar on the quarter-tone between the sixth and flatted seventh of the scale. At the conclusion of the opening solo, he begins singing in a relaxed tone, with the volume of the band much reduced. Now the lyrics lead toward a new climax, often in the form of a punch line: "Tell that slick insurance man (who's been around when I'm not at home) that he'd better write some insurance on himself," or, his most famous punch line from "How Blue Can You Get?," a song he borrowed from Louis Jordan's repertoire, "I gave you seven children and now you want to give 'em back."

B.B.'s sense of timing in running repeatedly through the cycle is crucial. Younger performers, especially rock musicians, fail to grasp the fact that climax is a state that cannot be prolonged; when they find the tension in the audience slipping from sheer fatigue, they push harder. B.B. learned from Reverend Archie that the performer must break the tension before fatigue kills it, allow the audience a respite, and then raise tension again, shooting higher the next time. If the respite is too long, the momentum is gone; if it is too short, emotional fatigue will prevent a proper climax. Timing the cycle is of the essence.

B.B. even goes so far as to incorporate the Pentecostal formula explicitly in his performance when he plays a tour de force which has no name and can not even be called a song. He introduces it by saying that it answers the question where gospel ends and blues begins, explaining that the instruments in the band will be the congregation, and his guitar will be the preacher. The drums and bass begin a low rumbling noise—the thumping of feet on the rough boards of the old church floor. He hits a sudden high note, and the horns rush in behind with a tonic chord on the same note—the congregation answering the preacher's cry. The rumbling continues during the silences between the preacher and his congregation. The guitar plays a slow, deliberate melodic figure which carries the instruments to a new chord (the subdominant) and the call and response continues. The pauses are of no set length and the rumble is uninterrupted.

Suddenly the organ takes off on a series of dazzling arpeggios—a sister from the congregation filled to overflowing with the Spirit. Thus the instruments proceed through the standard three-chord blues progression, and without pause B.B. leads the music back to the tonic chord, using his musical signature to glide into the next piece of music.

The musical conjuring act is of no overall set length; it has no tempo and no fixed melody. It is pure energy, and is one of the

The Famous St. John's Gospel Singers, Indianola, Mississippi, 1945.
Front row: Ben Carvin, John Matthew; standing: Birkett Davis, O.L.
Matthew, Riley King.

T-Bone Walker, 1969. *Photo by Charles Sawyer.*

Repairing Lucille. *Photo by Charles Sawyer.*

Photo by Charles Sawyer.

Photo by Charles Sawyer.

Photo by Charles Sawyer.

Photo by Charles Sawyer.

Pall's Mall, Boston, October 6, 1977. *Photos by Charles Sawyer.*

most impressive musical feats we can find anywhere. It may be presumptuous for an author to suggest a name for a musician's composition, but I feel that this piece might be called "Ode to Archie Fair."

The other component in the formula is the conversational mode. If B.B. was content to let his audience be strictly passive observers rather than active collaborators, he could never achieve the catharsis he aims for. He achieves the conversational mode by giving long, rambling introductions (usually spoken over the sound of the band playing softly) in which he expresses the premise of the song he is about to sing, thereby convincing the audience that while he sings he is expressing his own travail in a personal plea for sympathy and understanding. He tells stories, pokes fun at himself, occasionally plays the clown—all in an effort to draw the audience into the performance. His stories about love gone sour, about love betrayed, about love spurned all make a morality play of the lyrics to come which repeat the same theme: fear of rejection. In "Don't Answer the Door," he tells his lover that if she's sick she should "Suffer, suffer, till I get home/'cause I don't want a soul/Hangin' around my house/When I'm not at home," lest she fall for the doctor. In another, he sings, "I worked five long years for one woman/And she had the nerve to put me out." One song is a litany of the men whom his lover may prefer—the postman, the iceman, and that slick insurance man who had "better write some insurance on himself."

It is one of B.B.'s great resources that he can make an asset out of traits that others would find a shortcoming. One of his greatest accomplishments is the success he has in making his self-doubt the cornerstone of his art. Some artists succeed in spite of their insecurities; others succeed in order to banish theirs. B.B. takes his in hand and from it fashions his art. Self-doubt is his stock in trade, and he has made confessing it his profession. It is a measure of his skill as an artist that these public confessions are never acts of self-inflicted humiliation, nor do they ever leave him looking pathetic or foolish. Few others could stand before an audience and win their sympathy by declaring:

> Nobody loves me but my mother.
> And she could be jivin' too.

WHAT'S LEFT for B.B. in his music? He has one musical ambition as yet unfulfilled: to make a series of classic albums. These
consist of one album with a big band, one on which he would
play only familiar old tunes like "Don't Get Around Much
Anymore," one comprised of country blues of both the Nashville
and Delta varieties, and finally, an album made as a tribute to his
idol, Louis Jordan.

Epilogue

B.B. AND I had our last working session—with tape running—at the airport in Jackson, Mississippi. Interviews are hard work owing to the concentration required for both parties, so we were relieved to be interrupted by two black youths who passed our restaurant table and exclaimed, as if they'd discovered a diamond on the pavement, "This is B.B. King!" Then, drawing back as if dubious that any such treasure could be other than counterfeit, one of them added, "Are you *the* B.B. King?"

"How many are there?" asked the Blues Boy in reply. They grinned appreciatively.

Our concentration was broken. We switched off the machine and declared the strictly autobiographical research of the book complete. Passing out of the arrivals lounge into the midday sun, I felt as if we had stepped into a transparent soup, the air was so thick from the heat and humidity. I walked B.B. to his car, a misshapen, dull-brown station wagon he had borrowed for the day from Mayor Charles Evers. B.B. dawdled before opening the door and groped for words to express something of great personal significance. Taking me entirely by surprise, he switched to a mode of conversation that would be judged as deeply intimate by any two people. The exact details of our conversation are of no particular consequence to his life story or to understanding his character, and they didn't change my view of him one iota; they consisted of the sort of small confessions and expressions of emotion each of us makes in the rare moments when our defenses are completely down. The important thing about the episode is the fact that he had no fear in dropping the last screens that protected him from someone engaged in writing his biography. I was very conscious of the fact that our racial differences seemed absolutely irrelevant to his capacity to stand before me, emotionally naked.

"Right now I have a little while of rare pleasure ahead of me," he said changing his mode again, this time to make a robust but utterly relaxed declaration. "Tonight I'm not working, nobody knows where I am, and I'm not expected anywhere until tomorrow evening. It's hot, but I love the heat. With the windows down, the wind blowing through the car and my cassette playing Lonnie Johnson and Blind Lemon, I'll take my time and be right at home."

He eased behind the wheel and pulled away, leaving a faint sound of Delta blues that died in the soupy Mississippi air.

Appendix I: Requiem for Jim Crow

THE HILLS OF MISSISSIPPI

MY ODYSSEY in quest of B.B. King's past took me over 10,000 miles, but the significance of B.B.'s life story is better gauged by social change, for which there is no unit of measure like the mile or the year. In the course of my conversations with B.B.'s friends, relatives, benefactors, and business associates, I saw fleeting glimpses of a world that disappeared in a vortex created by the cross-currents of irresistible social forces. In that world lived Jim Crow, the symbolic personification of segregation with all its racist laws and social customs. Jim Crow, a character as real as the mythic figures of any culture, is dead now, but he is still recalled by some with vivid intensity. B.B. himself has said that as a child he hoped to meet Jim Crow one day.

My chronicle starts in Kilmichael, a tiny town in the hilly part of northern Mississippi to the east of the Delta. I came here hoping to find B.B.'s grammar-school teacher, Luther Henson, and Wayne Cartledge, the son of farmer Flake Cartledge (B.B.'s benefactor); if luck was with me, perhaps I might also find some of B.B.'s schoolmates. I approached Kilmichael from the part of Mississippi called the Delta, and driving east along Highway 82, I was startled by the way the terrain changes abruptly from the unrelieved level plain of the Delta to the steady rolling hills one finds just beyond the east bank of the Yazoo River. For miles between small towns the road is flanked by ridges covered with blankets of kudzu, a vine once imported to fight erosion, now a rampant nuisance that smothers everything in sight. Tall trees and telephone poles have long since disappeared beneath its creeping runners. Now they stand shrouded and mute, giving the landscape a forbidding, otherworldly atmosphere.

LUTHER HENSON, retired teacher of the Elkhorn School, lives in a newly constructed bungalow, painted a pink only a few shades lighter than the red clay of the surrounding earth. At a glance, he looks an unlikely character to be the man B.B. King most credits with his success in life. His speech is slack and slow; at the slightest pretext, he breaks out in a grin that is friendly but a little foolish. Meeting him for the first time, I was a little taken back by his servile manner of saying "Yassuh" and "That's right, suh" to almost everything I said. But I was struck at once by his quiet dignity. And the content of his speech soon revealed that he is no fool. He spoke of his years as a teacher with unabashed pride, yet without bragging.

"I tried to do all I could," said Henson characterizing his life's work. "If I hadn't been concerned about the betterment of our people, I couldn't have done the job I did. I did it as a sacrifice. . . . I started teaching before I was nineteen. When I was twenty-five, I had an offer to clerk in a dry-goods store in Tulsa. Things were so tough here I decided I'd go to some other place where I'd have some more freedom. They said I was spoilin' them [the schoolchildren], and I thought I'd quit spoilin' 'em and go on to somewhere else." A grin began spreading on his face. "After I got out there and worked awhile I decided to come back [to Mississippi] and spoil 'em a little more. I was taking a risk," he said, referring to the ever-present danger he felt was posed by resentful whites, "but I come on back and go like a man."

Our two-hour conversation was sprinkled with long, silent intermissions which neither of us seemed to find uncomfortable. The greatest ordeal of his life, he explained, was seeing two of his sisters die from pellagra, a form of malnutrition. He carried one of them to the madhouse in Jackson before she died.

"During the depression when the banks went broke, I had money in the Kilmichael Bank, but I couldn't pay my property taxes. I hadn't been paid what I was owed from the school. I would have lost my land if I hadn't got a loan from a lady. People were hungry. I took in ten extra children besides my family and with my farming we killed enough meat; we had lard, and a bunch of cattle there. I fed them bread, meat and vegetables for a whole entire year. Ten extras. The merchants had things in the stores, but they couldn't sell them because nobody had any money. You couldn't blame them for not selling on credit."

B.B.'s success is a source of personal satisfaction to Henson. So, too, is the more modest success of one of B.B.'s classmates, Walter Doris, Jr., who together with B.B. and his cousin Birkett Davis, sang gospel. "I told Doris that we could make Mississippi a better place together, if only he would stay," Henson said about him. "Now he's deputy sheriff of the county. . . . The last time I saw B.B. [in 1972], he said he wanted to give me a token of remembrance; he gave me a $50 bill, the first one I'd ever seen."

Before leaving Luther Henson, I asked him if he knew Edwayne Henderson, the Kilmichael farmer who, I had been given to believe, was the landlord to B.B.'s grandmother and kin when they were sharecroppers. "Yassuh. I know Mr. Henderson real well. My daddy drove the oxcart that brought Mr. Henderson's grandmother, Sarah, out here from Wilmington, North Carolina. When her husband, name of Henson, died, she come out here to Mississippi in a wagon with her son, Riley, and my father. When she remarried to a man named Henderson she gave my father to her boy Riley."

For a moment I was confused, thinking I hadn't understood the words properly. I asked him to repeat them, and then it dawned on me what he meant. "You mean it was before the War Between the States?" I asked to be sure.

"Yassuh. That's right, suh."

As a final question I asked Henson if he had any regrets in life. "Only one, suh. I believe if I'd had a decent education, I might of made something of myself."

I WENT DIRECTLY from Luther Henson to see Edwayne Henderson, the farmer-landlord to B.B.'s sharecropping family, who lives a mile or two from the feed store down Highway 82, the main road through Kilmichael. My interview with Henderson and his wife, the most vivid portrait of the old-style institution of sharecropping, was the most interesting and enlightening encounter in my whole odyssey in search of B.B.'s roots—so remote is he today from the child he was and so different the settings.

Edwayne Henderson aroused in me an instant liking: a man in his mid-sixties, straightforward and outgoing. There was something unusual and appealing about him that escapes precise characterization; there seemed to be more of the man's character displayed in his superficial behavior than one usually finds on first meetings, so that I got the impression that he was the kind of person content to let the world see him as he is. His wife was homey. Both spoke of B.B. with obvious affection since he had been so well-mannered and good-natured a boy when they knew him. I asked for specifics about B.B. and his kin; I particularly hoped they could tell me when B.B.'s grandmother died. Henderson struggled to remember the specific details and a brainstorm hit him: in those days—thirty-five years ago, it was—he used to keep detailed records on the finances of all his tenants. The ledgers now lay on a closet shelf. Without hesitation, he found the ledger for 1940–42 and offered it to me for browsing. Here I had stumbled on a bygone world. Yet the very success was also problematic. The contents of the ledger's pages and my evening with its owners raised a difficult social and moral question: how much could I blame them for the shameful social relations their ledger reflected, and how much could I exonerate them by letting them hide behind the existing economic order?

The pages of the ledger recorded the entire finances of individual providers—Elnora Farr, grandmother; Mimy Stells, aunt; and uncles, Jesse Davidson and William Pullian, even our hero himself for the first year after his grandmother died, here referred to simply by his Christian name: Riley. For each provider, a page for every year. A few jottings and the whole institution of sharecropping was transparently clear. There were notations for the monthly advance against the tenants' earnings from the coming crop: $8 for the big providers; $5 for Elnora Farr, since she had only herself and her grandson, young Riley, to provide for; $2.50 for fourteen-year-old Riley. There were also entries for the tenants' half share of expenses in raising the crop ("3 half bags of fertilizer") and credits for wage work. Near the bottom of each page there was also a place for the entries for the tenants' share of proceeds from the sale of the crop; in some cases these were pitifully poor. And there were the interest charges at 8 per cent. Nearly every page ended with a net debit for the tenant. This, we know was the distinguishing feature of the system: it kept them in debt.

What I saw seemed to me incredible. Henderson had so favorably impressed me with his openness in showing me the records that I ventured to ask him if he would allow me to borrow them to put in my book. Without hesitation he produced a razor and we cut the relevant pages from the book. He had only one proviso in giving his permission to include the records in this book: that the tenants' monthly furnish be placed in the perspective of the cost of living at the time.

Mimy Stells 1939

March 1   Cash $5.00
April 1   Cash $5.00
April 29 Cash $5.00
June 3   Cash $5.00
July 1   Cash $5.00 ⎱ Bank
Aug. 1   Cash $5.00 ⎰

Fertilizer ½ of 3 sacks @ $1.35
   per sack $2.05

acct.	$34.61*
bank	$10.00
	$24.61
credit acct.	− $16.30
pd. in full	$ 8.31

Mimy Stells 1940

account brought forward page 25		$ 8.31	
Dec.	Cash $5.00	$ 5.00	
March 1	Cash $5.00 (furnish)	$ 5.00	
April 1	Cash $5.00 (furnish)	$ 5.00	
May 1	Cash $5.00 (furnish)	$ 5.00	
June 1	Cash $5.00 "	$ 5.00	
July 1	Cash $5.00 "	$ 5.00	
		$38.31	
	Int.	3.08	
		$41.39	
Sept.	1 yd. cotton sack	.13	
		$41.52	
Nov. 9	cr. acct. for cotton sold		$16.21
	carried forward to page 35	$25.31	

* Includes 8% interest charge on principal of $32.05.

William Pullian 1940

Account brought forward from page 24		125.35	
Dec.	Cash $13.00 Cash $ .50	13.50	
March 1	Cash 8.00 (Furnish)	8.00	
Credit account with rental check			$18.81
March	Cash 5.00 to Midwife	5.00	
April 1	Cash 8.00 Furnish	8.00	
May 1	Cash 8.00 Furnish	8.00	
April	Fertilizer ½ of 2 sacks at $1.96 each	1.96	
Feb.	Credit account $1.87 (building fence)		1.87
April 20	Pd. City Drug Store for medicine	4.00	
June 1	$8.00 Furnish	8.00	
July 1	$8.00 Furnish	8.00	
		$189.31	$20.68
Sept.	9 yds. cotton sack @ 12½	1.13	
Nov.	By work in Joe McK. timber $2.00		
	By work in new [illegible] $12.50		14.50
	By work on bridge and Pasture		5.00
		$190.44	$40.18
	Int.	15.20	
		$205.64	$40.18
		$165.46	
Nov. 9	By cotton sold		7.60
		$165.46	
		7.60	
	Carried forward to page 34	$157.86	

Jesse Davidson—1941 Farm Acct.

Bal. Brought fwd. from—page 27—[1940 Bal.]		$ 49.26	
March 1	Cash 10.00		
April 1	Cash 10.00	$ 20.00	
April 1	By rental check		$22.70
May 1	Cash 10.00		
June 1	Cash 10.00 Shoes 2.00 Fertilizer 10.00	$ 32.00	
June 1	Glasses for Lorene 10.00		
July 1	Cash 10.00	$ 20.00	
		$121.26	$22.70
Sept. 18	By B/c wt 460 @ 17.85 = $82.00		$41.00

Oct. 1   Cash in Jackson 1.00—cash in
          Mphs. 1.00   2.00
                                                    ─────────
                                                    $123.26 $63.70
                            Int @ 8%   9.84
                                                    ─────────
                                                    $133.10 $63.70
                                                    ─────────   ───────
                                                    $ 69.40
Oct. 1   1 Pig
          4 Gal. Molasses 2.00   3.00
                                                    ─────────
          Paid in full by [illegible] $ 72.40
                                                    ─────────
          Jessie moved to Sunflower Miss.   72.56

They help fulfill Henderson's requirement. The following entries are eloquent: Jessie Davidson, October 1, 1941, one pig, $1.00; June 1, 1941, a pair of shoes $2.00, and October 1, 1941, molasses, $.50 for a gallon. It should be said, too, that the tenants raised most of their own food by planting vegetable gardens and keeping chickens. There is also an entry on Riley's record that has caught my eye: on June 1 Henderson purchased a pair of trousers for him and charged his account $1.00. But fair is fair: a pair of trousers should have cost Mr. Henderson no more than 80 cents. Moreover, Riley was allotted a mere $2.50 a month. Even though at that time and place tenant families grew much of their own food and the landlord provided housing and firewood to his tenants free of charge, half a month's allotment is too much for one pair of trousers.

Henderson got nearly as much excitement as I, thumbing through his old records. He certainly views his own past as fair and square. The dingy pages with their carefully itemized accounts written in his own well-schooled script, some in pencil, some in fountain pen, took him back to his own hard times. He called my attention to one page in particular, which showed a summary of his 1943 Income Tax Return. Without the slightest reluctance, he agreed to let me include this information, too; the total net income is $1,106.67.

Edwayne Henderson's Income Tax Return, 1943

I. INCOME AND RECEIPTS

Cotton sold	$2,048.35
*Milk sold	677.18

* Henderson had a herd of forty dairy cows, thirty of them actually milking at any given time.

Cotton seed sold		359.96
Poultry products		150.00
Salaries		1,303.31
	Gross Earnings	$4,538.80

II. EXPENSES

Tenants share of cotton and cotton seed sold		$1,204.16
Labor-Farm	163.50	
Timber	307.44	470.94
Repair to Equipment		87.00
Fertilizer		134.00
Feed		435.00
Taxes Advance	65.76	
Car Stamp	5.00	
Car Tag	6.27	
**Victory	36.00	113.03
Transportation, hauling cotton, feed and fert.		185.00
Interest Paid		162.00
Reroof and repair tenant houses		225.00
Small tools and misc. supplies		65.00
Dep. on Equipment		200.00
Seeds		75.00
Donations charity etc.		75.00
Total Deductible Expenses		$3,431.13

Net Taxable Income 1943: $1,107.67

The traditional sharecropping economy is descended from the Reconstruction era. It evolved by fits and starts, and more or less was over by the time the civil rights movement was in full swing. Between the two world wars it was probably at its peak. Henderson's tax return of that time gives us a sense of scale and a basis for comparing the economic station of a landowner with that of his tenants. In the early 1940s, Henderson usually had five tenant families farming on his land. Their share of the Henderson operation can be reckoned by adding the "tenants share of cotton and cotton seed sold" ($1,204.16) with the labor expenses ($470.94, on the assumption that he gave all his wage labor to his own ten-

** Probably a $50 War Bond.

ants). This gives a total of $1,675.10 thus paid out to his tenants, which was split five ways, making the base income of each tenant family $335.02. By comparison, Henderson's base income for the same period can be obtained by deducting his tenants' share of cotton proceeds ($1,204.16) from his gross earnings ($4,538.80); this deduction is necessary since he included his tenants' share of his crop in his own gross earnings for the year! This yields for him a base income of $3,334.64, roughly ten times the base income of any of his tenants. It is interesting to note that if we deduct Henderson's own wage earnings listed as "salaries" ($1,303.31), which were, presumably, received for his own labor working for others, from his gross earnings ($4,538.80) the result, $3,234.49, should reflect his gross income as a farmer. That figure is $7.61 less than his reported farming expenses ($3,431.13 minus the two deductions of $113.03 and $75.00— two deductions which appear to be unrelated to farm expenses— equals $3,243.10). Thus, his total gross income was positive, but his gross farming income from farming alone was below his deductible farming expenses. In 1943, then, farming was a losing proposition for Edwayne Henderson! Should I still be cross with him for charging Riley $1.00 for a pair of pants?

Yet one item in Henderson's records still troubles me: the 8 per cent interest he charged his tenants on their furnish. Before condemning Henderson as a heartless usurer, however, one might take into account that in some instances Henderson himself had to borrow the money which he advanced to his tenants as their monthly allowance (these entries are marked "Bank") and he, in turn, paid interest to the bank—surely at 6 per cent. For 1943 he reported $162.00 in interest paid out (to the bank, presumably) which is 5 per cent of his gross farm earnings and 15 per cent of his net taxable income. But, to repeat, charging high interest on the tenants furnish was universal practice then and remains so today: sharecropping was never meant to be fair by the standards of any other subculture.

Two features of the economy dominate the picture: the part of manual labor in the economy and the concentration of land in the hands of whites. The institution of sharecropping has not vanished, but one of these two features—the dependence on manual labor—has completely disappeared in the thirty-five years that have passed since the days when the preceeding figures were compiled. Today, Edwayne Henderson has only one tenant farmer sharecropping on his land, yet he has not enough land for that one tenant: he rents some at $25 an acre. That tenant now tends seventy acres of crop land as opposed to Riley's one, and he receives a monthly advance of $200, which has the real [1940] value of about $20, as opposed to Riley's $2.50. That tenant, an illiterate father of eight, also benefits from living rent-free in a house on Henderson's land and from farming with machinery owned by Henderson.

Nor is that the whole operation. In addition, he tends Henderson's livestock, in return for which Henderson allows him to feed his beef steer out of Henderson's crib. The Hendersons, who are childless, still regard their tenants with great paternal affection; Mrs. Henderson went recently to the maternity ward of the local hospital to see the latest addition to their tenant's family, referring to the new addition as "my eighth grandchild," and Mr. Henderson fills out his tenant's tax returns for him. [The tenant's adjusted gross income for 1977, incidentally, was 50 per cent higher than my own salary during my last year as associate professor of humanities at a small liberal arts college.] The last remaining feature of the sharecropper's lot in life will disappear soon, if Henderson and his tenant are any indication: Henderson's will provides for his tenant to receive the house he lives in plus ten acres of land.

The way Henderson and his wife spoke about black people was as revealing about race relations as were his farm records. On the physical differences between the races, he described the amazing tolerance of black people to working in the heat—far greater than that of whites, he emphasized. Their skin is different, he explained; for one thing, it's naturally oily. When he was a boy, he remembers, while swimming with his black chums, he saw how the water stood up on their skins in tiny beads "like fresh rain on a simonized car." Yet this did not serve as an argument for the view that blacks are more suitable for work; whereas in the heat black works better than white, in the cold, it is the other way around. Is this also related to oily skin, I wondered, but did not ask. He did not explain.

On the social differences between the races, Mrs. Henderson reported the difficulty she had when attempting to impress the current tenant with the great importance of education for his chil-

dren. On the economic differences, Mr. Henderson described the
utter dependence of his tenant on a landlord's protection; the case
in point was the tenant's recent purchase of a car (it was secondhand, of course) for which Henderson countersigned the car
loan. He showed me the loan agreement and the illegible scribble
that was the signature of his tenant beside his own.

Mixed into the conversation about sharecropping past and present was the story of Henderson's old mule, now toothless and
too old to work. Henderson feeds it a special soft meal which it
manages to gum up well enough to digest. Mrs. Henderson
chafed her husband, saying that if it weren't for his careful attention to the mule, it would have died of starvation long ago.
"Hell," said Henderson, "I made a living off that mule for over
ten years. Now I've got him on pension!" It struck me in the moment I heard him say it that nothing characterized his benevolent
attitude toward the black tenants who farmed on his land so well
as his story about putting his old mule on pension. I shuddered.

Perhaps not. I may well be unfair toward Edwayne Henderson
to report that his attitude to the mules and the blacks who
worked his land impressed me as strikingly similar. It suggests
that I saw in his attitude callousness or lack of sympathy toward
both. On the contrary, he has impressed me as goodhearted, and
concerned, and responsible. Yet he did see his duty to his tenant
and to his mule in similar ways, and the similarity is most discon-
certing to those who do not share the ease with which he accepted
sharecropping in all its variants. After all, in those bygone times
he was a free man; true, he was in debt to the bank, but he could
always sell his land, settle his debts, and move on. By contrast,
his tenants of the older days were not free: they constantly owed
him for back furnish (money advanced), and their only col-
lateral was their labor. That was the very idea of the sharecropping system—the transformation of the bondage of slavery to
capitalist-style bondage. Tenants could not move on, unless they
found another landlord who would pay their debt to their present
landlord—the modern version of old-style slave trade.

Before leaving the Hendersons, I want to address the distress-
ing moral questions I raised before. The dilemma raised by my encounter with the Hendersons is a very familiar one—not only for
social scientists, but for anyone with a social conscience; how
does responsibility for the social order fall on the individual? The

Hendersons were not the makers of the social order in which they made their lives. They did not introduce sharecropping; it was the conventional way of raising cotton in those days, perhaps the only one possible then. Nor did he get rich on the backs of his tenants. Indeed, the year 1943 was a losing year for him as far as farming was concerned.

On the other hand, the argument absolving the individual of responsibility for the social order in which he lives does not bear up under all conditions. What should we say about the responsibility of Henderson's grandmother for keeping the slave Syrus Henson, father of teacher Luther Henson, whom she gave to her son as a present? Indeed, the exact same argument, putting responsibility entirely on the system, is the one invoked by Lieutenant Calley for his defense of the My Lai massacre. For his part, Henderson is proud of his record as a landlord and cites the fact that none of his tenants ever exhibited any disloyalty toward him or expressed any grievance against him. So far as he knows, they all thought highly of him. He may well be entirely right, and, if B.B. King is a proper indicator, then indeed he is. With a dash of pride, he showed me a warm letter B.B. sent to him and his wife a few years ago.

I confess that I have no pat answers to the moral questions I have raised, beyond what I have hinted thus far: the system allows latitude, and within it Henderson was better than most; also, the system is improvable, and though I doubt he fought to improve it, he accepted the improvements with grace and flexibility. Surely this is not a full answer, but then the present report is not exactly a moral treatise, and I leave the reader to sort out the morality in private: all I say is, there is some sorting out to do here. I really was torn by this likable representative of the remnants of American slave ownership.

I FOUND Wayne Cartledge sitting on a tractor at his Kilmichael farm. To reach his 340-acre dairy operation, I had driven back and forth along a labyrinth of gravel roads which cut through severely eroded banks of red clay. Once I got to his simple white clapboard farmhouse, I parked in the yard and walked to the fence where he could catch sight of me from the high seat of his tractor. He made no overt sight of recognition, but drove the trac-

tor across the dirt road and parked it in front of the barn. When
he approached on foot, he gestured silently toward a bench beneath a shade tree. Gesturing for me to sit on the bench, he
pulled up a large, upended bucket, squatted down on it, and
began telling his personal recollections of B.B., who had been his
foster sibling for a short while forty years before. He spoke in a
high-pitched, nasal voice, and his Mississippi twang was too thick
for adequate metaphor. There was a gentle breeze blowing, and
the sound of birds singing and cows bellowing blended with the
rustle of the trees. He spoke about the hard times his family had
endured as a boy and the long, debilitating fatal illness of his father, Flake, which lasted eight years. There was no medical insurance, and the debt for the medical bills fell on Wayne, the only
child. He emphasized that his father had nothing to his name in
the days when he took young Riley as his ward. As a cash tenant,
his father had to get up the rent money—crop or no crop—even
if the landlord was a relative.

After an extremely terse account of his life as the son of a Mississippi cash tenant he offered to take me to the place where his
father had his farm and where young Riley had the little shed that
was his home in 1942. We adjourned from the pastoral setting
under the shade tree and climbed into his pickup. As he pulled up
beside a gate a few miles down the gravel road, he gave a wry
look and said, "Now I'm gonna do somethin' you wouldn't do
back where you come from . . . park and leave the keys in it."
We strolled into the pasture beyond the gate, past a collapsing
wooden farmhouse that was home for Flake Cartledge, his wife,
and son Wayne thirty-five years ago. Down the slope, Wayne
pointed to a slight depression in the ground and pronounced it
the spot where young Riley's cabin had stood. There was a small
herd of cows grazing a few yards further on among some willows,
a scene fit for nineteenth-century English landscape painters.

Before returning to the Wayne Cartledge farm, we stopped
briefly at the cottage of John and Lessie Fair. John Fair is the
brother of Sanctified preacher Archie Fair, B.B. King's primal
model of the cathartic performer. Archie is dead now, and
brother John is old and slightly infirm. Wife Lessie sat on the
edge of the porch, intermittently leaning forward to spit tobacco
juice on the sunburned grass, while her husband played us a tune
on his antique guitar. Cartledge and the Fairs spoke to each other

with the special intimacy that baffles Northerners who think that black and white keep their distance in the Old South. They argued the religious question of free will, a fundamental dividing line among Bible Belt Baptists, but their argument was more friendly banter than serious debate; at one point Wayne tried politely to draw me into the brief discussion, but my Yankee inhibitions got the better of me, and I declined.

On the way back riding in the pickup, I told Wayne that B.B. had repeatedly expressed indebtedness to his family for the good turn Flake Cartledge did young man Riley. "That's just the way we tried to live," said Wayne. "We don't do nobody any favors, but we don't take from anybody either. We just shoot straight." A moment later, he thoughtfully summed up his state in life and his main ambition. "All my life I been a broke person; never had any money. Just now in the last few years, I got up to where I can see daylight. Eventually I'd like to be able to say I don't owe anyone anything. I'd like to get even."

MY LAST STOP in the hills of Mississippi was at the courthouse in Winona, Mississippi where I met Walter Doris, Jr., deputy sheriff of Montgomery County. Junior Doris, a schoolmate of Riley, a year or two older than his now-famous boyhood chum, was waiting for me by the courthouse door. I was late because, expecting an old-fashioned courthouse, I mistakenly had driven to the center of town and marched up the steps of the most august building in sight—one with tall pillars. It turned out to be a church. The new courthouse, a one-story building of brick and glass, is away from the center of town on a large open space set back from a winding semiresidential street. Junior Doris is a slow-walking, slow-talking man of medium build and high forehead. He looked comfortable in his freshly pressed, short-sleeved deputy's blouse. My first question was how a black man came to be deputy sheriff in a rural Mississippi county. With no fanfare or boasting he replied that by the mid-1970s, black voter registration had reached a sufficiently high level to give an advantage to any candidate for sheriff who would pledge to appoint a black deputy Doris was appointed deputy in 1976 when sheriff Billy Costilow made good on his campaign promise. The whites of Montgomery County adjusted well to the new situation of having a black man in the uniform of the law, he said, but some blacks, by contrast, have refused to recognize his authority, a ticklish problem when he is making an arrest.

When they were boys, Walter Doris, Junior and Riley King were schoolmates at Luther Henson's Elkhorn School. Doris' family, like Riley's, farmed as sharecroppers in the Kilmichael area. The Dorises were better off than Riley's kin, however; they owned a mule team and were "fourth tenants"—which meant that they supplied their own equipment as well as the labor to raise their crop, and the landlord, who owned the ground they tilled, took only one quarter of the proceeds. Around the age of ten or twelve, Junior, Riley, and Riley's cousin, Birkett Davis, formed a gospel singing group. The group broke up when, first Birkett and then Riley moved to the Delta. Birkett still lives in the Delta town of Indianola, where he is a church elder. Doris remained in Kilmichael and directs a gospel group when he is off duty.

The details Deputy Doris gave about himself as we sat in the courthouse lobby, prompted me again to wonder what are the personal qualities that set one person on a life course that is a roller coaster and another on one which is a bicycle. (Perhaps the latter metaphor comes to mind because Riley sold his bicycle to Junior Doris after he peddled it sixty miles from Lexington, Mississippi, back to Kilmichael in 1942.) After serving a hitch in the service, Doris returned to the Kilmichael area and worked for wages at a sawmill while he did a little farming on the side. Around 1953 he moved to Chicago with his wife and two children.

For ten months he worked in a packinghouse, then moved back to Kilmichael with his family. He did not take to city life, but he might have stayed in Chicago if his wife and children had been content there; but, his children so disliked the Chicago schools that they refused to attend. Back in Mississippi, Doris worked for a while driving a school bus before he landed a job at a plant that manufactured concrete conduits. After five years at the conduit plant, he took a job at the J. A. Ocean Company in nearby Winona, Mississippi, a firm that produces picture frames. He remained at the Ocean Company from 1965 until he became deputy sheriff in 1976.

As Doris gave his particulars to me, it was very difficult to gauge his own attitude toward his progression through life, his delivery was so laconic, so low key; but gradually I got the impression that he regards his upward movement with self-satisfaction. It was lunchtime now and he suggested we drive over to his house in Kilmichael, seven miles away where he could give me a record of his gospel singing group. We climbed into his dilapidated sedan outside and we headed out. He looked very serious sitting at the wheel with his service revolver on his hip poking down into the seat cushion and his straw stetson brushing against the stock of the shotgun which hung just behind his head on the metal grate that converted the back seat into a cage. At his one-story house within sight of the highway on the outskirts of Kilmichael, Doris played me the 45-rpm record of his group singing his song, "Watergate Boogie," a mild satire on the Watergate affair, set to a gospel-style arrangement. He explained that the recording was made in Memphis at the expense of the group, which sells copies at its regular weekend performances around Mississippi. He told me somewhat shyly that since the recording was made he had revised the lyrics "so I've got them where I really want them." He expressed uncertainty and asked my advice: should he try selling the record *as is* to a major gospel label or go back into the studio to rerecord? Both, I told him, and advised him to consult B.B., who was scheduled the following month to play a few gigs in the area.

But he did not see B.B. when his old friend came to Mississippi to play later that month. Doris was probably on duty that night when B.B. played in the immediate neighborhood.

By local standards, Walter Doris, Jr., is a go-getter. He has raised himself up from poor tenant farmer to moderately prosperous deputy sheriff, a position of some respect in the community; he has a daughter in college. B.B. smiled with pride when I brought him the news that Junior Doris had made deputy. Yet, compared to B.B., who tore out of Kilmichael in 1943 and never looked back, Doris is a late-bloomer—a fact I couldn't escape noticing as he played me his satire on a political scandal five years old. B.B. said as much of him: "Junior was always slow in school—not dumb or stupid you understand, just slow. We wondered if he'd ever get married, but he did." Meeting Walter Doris, Jr., the late blooming, upwardly mobile deputy sheriff and gospel group leader, made me wonder: What makes some people slow and others fast?

DOWN IN THE DELTA

The Delta is as flat as a griddle. The soil there is a rich, dark brown, the color of molasses. The flatness of the plain is relieved by tree breaks and occasional tall cotton gins. Reclamation of the Delta from swampland and canebrakes began before the War Between the States and was finally finished in the early 1930s, when the Army Corps of Engineers finished taming the flood-prone Mississippi River. The fields are dotted with abandoned sharecroppers' cabins, and here and there along the road is a tiny one-room clapboard church, with a sagging cross atop, windows boarded up and paint peeling. Individual tractors have replaced the long lines of laborers in the fields. Almost every acre of free ground is under cultivation. The peculiar conditions of soil and weather here favor the growth of long-fiber cotton and make this probably the best cotton country in the entire world. Water is a constant source of worry to Delta planters: Will there be enough when it's needed, and will there be too much when it's not?

The spring of 1978 was a very wet one in the Delta, and when I drove east on Highway 82 toward Indianola in mid-May, I saw entire fields where the furrows were full of standing water, and creek banks submerged under a few feet of muddy water. The sun reflected off the stagnant water in long, silver ribbons. By that time, it was already late for planting, but so long as the fields were too sodden for heavy machinery, the planters had no choice but to wait before planting.

Today Indianola, located in the heart of the Delta, is a peaceful little Delta town of slightly less than 10,000 souls. Along the main highway running east and west, bypassing the center of town, are located numerous cropdusting airfields with stubby little planes whose raised cockpits—raised for better visibility while spraying crops—make them look like winged hunchbacks. Nearer town, the highway is lined with dealerships selling heavy farm machinery—huge cotton pickers and multi-purpose tractors. A near stagnant stream creeps through the middle of town right under the main street. There are no parking meters in town, and the day-cop on the main street has an artificial hand. Indianola is the county seat of Sunflower County.

My first order of business was to arrange an appointment with the widow of planter Barrett who employed B.B. in his late teens. Then I went looking for B.B.'s old chums. I found his cousin Birkett, sitting with the other elders, presiding over a church meeting. He was extremely warm toward me, inviting me to join him on the dais, where I was briefly an honorary elder of the Church of God in Christ. In the winter of 1944, when B.B. was a newlywed sharecropping on the Barrett plantation, Birkett and his wife shared their cottage with Riley and Martha King. Birkett has long since stopped sharecropping and now works in the local hardware store.

John Matthews, who sang with Riley and Birkett in The Famous St. John's Gospel Singers, now lives in a solidly middle-class brick ranch house within sight of the cotton compress. He is principal now of the Sunflower Elementary School, a large, clean one-story brick building of recent construction. The school, which was integrated in 1970, accommodates roughly 300 students, all but 28 of them black. Of the 17 teachers at the school, 13 are black, 4 white.

Nelson Dotson, who ran a fix-it shop with his brother Willie in the old days, made crude recordings of the St. John's Singers on an $80 Silvertone Recording Machine. I found him on a rocker on his porch, looking out on a yard full of broken lawn mowers which awaited his attention. Dotson is now secretary of the local NAACP. He expressed his frustration over the fact that now that the legal apparatus of segregation has been abolished, racial progress must come through more subtle means than going to federal court. "It's no longer the law we're fighting," Dotson told me. "Now it's the *system* and the *policy*." He described the "white flight" from the public schools to private academies. "It's hard on the poor whites who are too proud to send their kids to the integrated public schools and too poor to send them to the white private academies. They keep their kids out of school. Pretty soon they'll be as dumb as we were." When he spoke about the old days, he focused his bitterness on the plantation bell, which was usually struck an hour or more before sunrise to call field hands to work. A black man's life was run by the sound of that damn bell, he told me. "Things haven't changed that much. The white man still calls the black man to do his work for him—only now he uses Bell Telephone instead of the plantation bell."

It was time for my meeting with Mrs. Barrett. I said good-bye to Nelson Dotson and drove back across the tracks to the quite prosperous residential neighborhood where lives the widow of Johnson Barrett, Delta planter and Riley King's onetime big boss.

Mrs. Johnson Barrett was an elderly and somewhat frail widow, but still the mistress of the house. She received me graciously on the sun porch of her Indianola residence. We sat in white wicker rockers surrounded by potted plants. The white walls reflected the abundant midafternoon light. On a table to the side stood a copy of the Old Time Gospel Hour Edition of *The Open Bible*. Elsewhere around the room were numerous religious books and magazines including the Oral Roberts Association magazine, *Abundant Life*. Behind her on a bookshelf a few years' issues of *Reader's Digest* stretched beneath a row of books including a volume of poetry by Robert Frost.

With only the slightest prompting from me and not in response to any specific questions, Mrs. Barrett began telling yarns about her life. She had hardly begun when she interjected her endorsement of the changes in race relations instituted over the objections of most white Mississippians. She said that in her opinion it was a good thing that the Supreme Court forced some social changes on the Old South, although at the time she and many others didn't think so. Then, without elaborating on that opinion, and without any introduction, she began telling a story of how she was raised with two black children. It happened simply because her grandmother promised her dying cook that the cook's two children, Ike and Pearl, would be raised in her own house. An addition was built onto the house, but it fell to Mrs. Barrett's mother to fulfill the promise because the grandmother who had made the promise died not very long afterward. So Mrs. Barrett was raised with two black foster siblings. She described how her mother sat between the cribs and nursed the children, black and white, without any regard for color. Many years later, Mrs. Barrett was reunited with Pearl, who had made a rewarding life in Texas raising kids and cattle. When Mrs. Barrett invited Pearl to visit her home, Johnson Barrett cautioned her, saying that putting up a black guest in their house "might raise some eyebrows." He suggested that they reserve a motel room for Pearl. "My mother wouldn't have put her in a motel," Mrs. Barrett told her husband.

With a misty look in her eyes, she moved on to tell the story of her courtship with her husband, and of their early and unsuccessful attempts to found a plantation before coming to Indianola and making a go of it. With great pride, she led me out through the garden to view her treasure: the original bell from the Cockeral Plantation; the plantation itself was one of the failing operations that Johnson Barrett tried continually but unsuccessfully to revitalize. The bell had an inscription on it, reporting its purchase by A. B. Cockeral & Brothers in March 1898. She said it would eventually go to the Cottonlandia Museum in Greenwood, Mississippi.

We returned to the sun porch. She resumed her account of how the Barrett plantation was founded. As before, she emphasized the tradition of racial tolerance in her family which continued after her husband sold the plantation and still continues today, after her husband's death. As if to illustrate, she mentioned an old black man who has worked for her family for decades now. Years earlier, when Mr. Barrett built an addition on the man's house, he used the occasion to induce his employee to get a license for his common-law marriage of many years' standing. According to Mrs. Barrett, as her husband lay mortally ill from an aneurysm a few days before Christmas 1973, some of his last thoughts were about the welfare of that old black hand. Now that Mr. Barrett is dead, that man is one of Mrs. Barrett's few links with the past; it was clear from the way she spoke that she is devoted to him. In keeping with her husband's dying request she looks out for the welfare of the man, who gave his best years working for Johnson Barrett. Just the day before, in fact, she had managed to secure his claim for Social Security; he had been unable to produce a birth certificate and had no firm knowledge of his exact birthday, but by steadily pestering the authorities over the telephone, Mrs. Barrett had prevailed. Now he'll get his monthly social security check. Moreover, she said, adding more weight to her implicit argument, after her husband died the family accountant reported to her that in bad years, when the tenants ended up in debt to him, Mr. Barrett often marked their unpaid balances "paid." (Weeks later, a reliable source informed me that this generosity in bad years was balanced by a little cheating in good ones.) Finally, she declared unequivocally that whatever else one may say, any set of customs that deprive people of their dignity are decidedly wrong. To underscore this denunciation of social injustice, she gazed long, hard, and silently into my eyes.

The silence was broken by the arrival of one of Mrs. Barrett's reading pupils, a young white girl dressed in a spanking clean starched dress. We were introduced and Mrs. Barrett boasted about how the young girl had given a splendid reading during a garden party held the evening before in the adjacent yard. She further explained that she teaches part-time in the Indianola Academy, which I knew from Nelson Dotson is the all-white school in the community (private, of course).

It must be granted that much of what Mrs. Barrett said was both self-serving and yet entirely credible; let me also add that her sentimental attachment to an object, the plantation bell, so bitterly regarded by others as a symbol of servitude seems to me to be no more than a sad reminder: each of us has at best a very partial view of the world around. Still, it took courage for her to condemn, if only by implication, the injustice of the social order in which she made her life.

For doing so she won my admiration. Meeting Mrs. Johnson Barrett was like seeing a faded photograph of someone whose kind, sincere eyes look out from a past era with a plea: "Forget me not!"

ACROSS THE GREAT DIVIDE

From Mississippi, I flew to the West Coast to rendezvous with B.B. at Lake Tahoe, Nevada, where he was playing an extended engagement at Harrah's Casino. In my briefcase I carried the farm records loaned to me by Edwayne Henderson showing, in grim detail, the economic struggle of boy Riley and his kin. I was eager to discover, how B.B. would react to these artifacts from his youth. Would he be bitter? Would he find them amusing? Would he even recognize them?

There are no direct flights to Tahoe from the East, so I deferred satisfying my curiosity about his reaction long enough to stop in Los Angeles and call on two people who once knew him closely—his father and his ex-wife. Both proved to be people of substantial character. In his father I discovered the source of B.B.'s incredible durability (apparently it is genetic). In meeting his ex-wife I found the only conspicuously major error in his life.

It was a shock meeting Sue Evans in her office high up in the
Security Pacific Bank building in the heart of Los Angeles. Expecting a raving, dark-skinned beauty, instead I found a slightly
plump, slightly homey-looking, attractive woman in her mid-thirties with skin the shade of a lightly tanned Caucasian. They say
that often you can tell more about a man by meeting the women
in his life than you can by meeting the man himself, and I felt at
least partly confirmed in that opinion after two hours' conversation with the woman who had been married to B.B. King from
1958 to 1966. Since divorcing B.B. in 1966, the former Mrs.
King has made a new life for herself. She has done well by any
standard but spectacularly well for a woman born black in Mississippi. I use the term "black" here in the sense in which she herself used it—to denote cultural, social and economic background,
not skin color—for Sue Evans, born Sue Carol Hall, is the daughter of a white man who had a family across the tracks from the
colored neighborhood in Leland, Mississippi, where Sue's mother
lived.

Sue Hall was evidently precocious. She entered Howard University at age sixteen but didn't stay long before dropping out
and marrying B.B. King, the famous blues singer. She made it
clear to me however that her attraction to B.B. was strictly personal since she never cared much one way or the other for the
limelight. To her, show business was simply her husband's liveli-
hood. It seems that even as the teen-age bride of the entertainer
she had a head for business because she objected to his policy of
always meeting his commitments even when it meant working at a
loss, rather than canceling unprofitable engagements. When she
looked at his career, she saw a ledger; when he looked it over, he
saw his crusade to win respectability for blues, plus all the hungry
mouths of his band members.

Her descriptions of life on the road with B.B. brought home
how very forceful was his dual obsession with music and success.
She described how he would hibernate in his hotel room for days
poring over music books, practicing his guitar and listening to old
records, and how she, a healthy kid of nineteen and twenty was
run ragged by the pace he kept. Life was full of days when break-
fast was a Coke and a can of Vienna sausages. In 1965 B.B.
promised her he would reduce his schedule the next year and
spend more time at home; but when the time came, he pleaded

poverty because the IRS had just slapped a $78,000 lien on him. Sue King was not persuaded because she felt that B.B.'s tax problems were symptomatic of his work mania: he got into tax troubles at least partly because he refused to cancel jobs that paid less than they cost, while he made up his operating deficit out of tax withholdings for him and the band. She filed for divorce; he did not contest. In 1966 their marriage was dissolved.

The settlement with B.B was favorable to Sue King, but to say it left her set for life would be an exaggeration. Being a single mother—the child was born before she met B.B.—with no particular training she could not possibly find life very secure. She went back to college at California State at Los Angeles and finished her B.A. in business administration. After a few years working for the City of Los Angeles in 1970 she got a job in Security Pacific Bank and rose to the position of assistant vice-president, working in the "problem loan" department, where the business affairs of financially troubled commercial debtors are analyzed. The minimum indebtedness of the clients handled by her group is $100,000. Many of the client companies she handles are multinational. Along the way, Sue King remarried and became Sue Evans. At the time of our meeting, she had already given Security Pacific her resignation to accept a more challenging job.

It surprised me to hear the tenderness and concern in her voice when she spoke about B.B. I had been prepared for rancor, but I found none. Her concern came through most strongly when she spoke about B.B.'s persistent financial difficulties. If only he would *manage* his money, she pleaded, he would be well heeled, if not downright wealthy. I asked what she estimated his net worth to be. "Much less than mine," she shot back. Then after a long thoughtful pause, she gave her appraisal: "Probably negative."

Perhaps Sue Evans might have become a shrewd business manager of B.B. King's affairs rather than an adviser to trouble-plagued debtors of a large commercial bank if only things had turned out differently, but she explained that she had been rebuffed when she tried to get involved in B.B.'s business affairs.

"B. thought that his wife's place was in the home," she said dejectedly. "He didn't want me to work. He turned a deaf ear."

" 'Don't Answer the Door,' " I said. It is the title of one of B.B.'s old hits, in which he tells his restless lover he wants her to cloister herself in the house so that he can be quite sure he is the only thing in her life.

"There were days when I didn't."

Our interview was over. Gathering up my notes, I asked her if I could convey any message from her to B.B.

She took out a card and an envelope, wrote a message on the card, and sealed it in the envelope.

"Give this to the dirty old man," she said with a grin and walked me to the elevator.

B.B.'S FATHER, Albert King, is a real character. He speaks a kind of Mississippi English that can only be called patois. He loves to ramble on about the old days and he drinks rivers of whiskey with no apparent affect. He left Mississippi in 1943 when he moved to Memphis and got a job in the Firestone plant, where he worked until retirement in 1972. When B.B. began making good money as an entertainer, he bought a farm on the outskirts of Memphis and moved his father out there. Eventually he gave it to his father. In the mid-1970s the old man sold it and moved to the Los Angeles suburb of Gardena.

There is a word that describes Albert King: "feisty." It fits him because it combines qualities of pluck, roguishness, and good humor with a touch of arrogance. He tells tales the way his son plays the guitar: each tale a little verbal solo, with its own tempo, full of its own special licks.

"I call B.B. my baby brother 'cause we're only eighteen years apart. I call him B.B. like everybody else, but his real name's 'Riley.' Now he's got them two Bs up front of his name: one B for 'Blues' and one for 'Beale.' . . . B.'s been real good to me. He give me eight Cadillacs and three trucks. A brand-new tractor too. I've been drivin' fifty-six years, and I haven't got but three tickets. . . . Would you believe it, I was thirty-two years old before I ever talked on the telephone.

"Workin' on halves with the man, if you made six bales of cotton, he got three. He had his three to the good. You had to pay for everything out o' your three and sometimes he'd hit you with 'plantation expenses'; he'd hit you for sixty or seventy dollars. Then you'd have to go work in the woods cutting wood for fifty cents or six bits a day so you could get yourself a sack o' flour or a little lard or somethin' like that.

"In all those little Delta towns the siren would blow at 10:30 at night. That's when you'd better get your bundles, 'cause when it blowed at 11:00, why, then you got to clear out of town.

"You might have some relatives from Chicago or New York come to visit you. They haven't ever seen a plow or a hoe; you're wearin' raggedy old clothes and they're dressed in nice store-bought clothes. The white man don't like them to come visitin' you 'cause they might put a mess in your head. In the fall of the year when you're settlin' [accounts] they [whites] watch you just like police do. Any stranger come on the place, they know it. But when you learn 'em [white folks], they're all right."

On lynchings and killings:

"It wasn't just over white women, but they'd kill you over a colored woman. My boss had a rider who killed a colored man over the cook and she was colored. . . . When they kill a man they put a sinker on you—tie a big gin fan on you—drop you in the lake. They don't want you to be *seen*. You'll never be seen no more.

"That plantation bell, it would wake up the dead. . . . We were in the second slavery. . . . Back in those days [the 1930s] we didn't call it a depression, we called it a 'panic.' "

Before I left him, Albert King showed me with pride the last Cadillac B.B. gave him and his garden which was just the kind of garden a Mississippi farmer would grow—wild and unruly, not the usual well-manicured garden that most suburbanites keep.

THE APPROACH to Lake Tahoe Airport from the air is abrupt and frequently choppy. Tahoe is a glacial lake surrounded by snow-covered mountains, and the small airport nearby is set down in a depression. Incoming aircraft are often buffeted by strong updrafts.

The cool dry air was a sudden change from the hot, muggy mid-May weather I had left behind in Los Angeles. The road from the airport to the entertainment area where the casinos are located runs near the south shore of the lake through forests of tall pines. As you approach the casino section, the highway is lined with small motels bearing names that appeal to the romantic sentiments of gamblers—names like Lucky Lady and Straight Flush.

The Nevada state line runs through Harrah's parking lot, a fact that has caused some consternation to many people, Bill Harrah especially, since it was recently revealed that faulty surveying instruments may have mistakenly placed the boundary several hundred yards too far south of the agreed upon specification when the line was drawn late last century. California has laid claim to jurisdiction over the land where the biggest casinos in the lake resort area are located, and gambling is illegal in California. Nevada rejects the claim, and while the wheels of justice slowly turn processing the litigants' conflicting claims, the wheels of the slot machines in Harrah's Casino continue whirling.

Entering Harrah's Nevada game room from the California parking lot, I was assaulted by the din of hundreds of slot machines manned by glassy-eyed vacationers methodically dropping coins into the machines and working the levers like pump handles.

Backstage, I found my way through the kitchen and into the back of the cabaret where a kind of burlesque musical review was in progress. I slipped into a booth at the rear and watched the dozen-odd bare-breasted dancers dressed in scanty fur costumes prancing around the stage. These were not carnival strippers; there was no bumping and grinding. The staging and lighting were elaborate; the tunes and the dances were not particularly suggestive. I wondered to myself: if this is not a high-class edition of the bawdy runway routines that once graced the stage of the Old Howard, then what is it? Suddenly I had it: topless Ice Capades minus the ice. The revue was probably intended to look high-class but in fact it was straight Middle American Schlock.

The closing number ended, and the stage curtain came down. Simultaneously a small curtain at the rear rose revealing a view through glass out into the main gaming room. The rear curtain had been down presumably to block the view of the stage from the gaming tables. Apparently Bill Harrah didn't want the poor rubes at the tables to be distracted by the sight of the prancing topless, iceless ice capettes on stage.

After a respectable interval to allow the cocktail waitresses time to ply the tables, the curtain went up on B.B.'s band, and after the customary three warmup numbers B.B. stepped from the wings. The crowd here did as crowds world over nowadays do for B.B.: they rose to their feet and gave him a long ovation. B.B.'s appearance on this stage is one of the great achievements of his career, yet the performance itself—even the setting—were not out of the ordinary for him. He played all his standards and a few from the new album, and they loved him. Fifty minutes later, he left the stage—to the sound of another standing ovation.

When I met B.B. a few minutes later backstage, he invited me up to his room together with Leonard King, his son and new valet, and Bebop, his road manager, who was now carrying his guitar. We rode the elevator to the tenth floor of Harrah's Hotel and entered B.B.'s two-room suite, which ordinarily rents for $180 a day. Bebop stood the guitar in the corner of the room, which, as usual, looked like a littered workshop. As B.B. peeled off his suit, Leonard hung it up piece by piece, then laid out a fresh suit for the 1:00 A.M. performance. B.B. thanked them both and dismissed them. Leonard hesitated before leaving. B.B. gave him a sceptical look, then produced a few free drink checks for the casino bar, which he gave him. "Come back at 12:45, son," B.B. told him. Leonard grinned, baring his enormous lopsided row of gleaming gold teeth, and left us alone.

I handed him the note from his former wife. "My ex! Humph!" he said after reading it. He shrugged and tossed the letter on the nightstand beside the telephone, whose message light was flashing. "She and I aren't seeing eye-to-eye these days," he added. "The lawyers and accountants say I owe her about $30,000 in back alimony. I never objected to paying alimony when she was single but she's been married a while now, and I can't see why I should pay a woman who's got another man. They say it's money that should have been paid before she remarried. If they say I owe it, well I'll pay it—but I don't have to like it."

I passed him the pages from Edwayne Henderson's account book, offering no explanation of their origin. He stared at the pages a very long time without saying a word; then he asked where I'd come up with them. I told him. He continued staring. He turned them over, coming back to the page with his own Christian name on it. "I had forgotten how little . . ." he said, his voice trailing off. He sighed and looked up, a little bewildered. I called his attention to Henderson's notation showing his grandmother's death in 1939, when he was fourteen years old—fully four years later than he had previously fixed the date. At first he insisted on his own version but he relented after looking very hard again at his grandmother's page with the word "died" scrawled across the bottom and the year 1939 at the top. He turned to the records of his aunt Mimy and uncles Jesse and William, poring over the details, repeating aloud individual lines shaking his head. It was moving and somewhat eerie watching him mulling over the pages: here was a man meeting a former self and finding that person a relative stranger.

After an hour or so with the Henderson records, interrupted by numerous phone calls, B.B. changed into slacks and a sport shirt and we went down to the gaming room of the casino. At the keno counter, B.B. took a blank keno ticket and began studiously X-ing numbers and linking them up in combinations with encircling lines. Keno is a kind of very complicated bingo; to play you select one or more numbers from 1 to 80, which you then register with the clerk who places your bet of 70 cents or more. When the betting is closed, the game officials randomly select twenty numbers by using a bingo-type device that tumbles numbered Ping-Pong balls in a blast of air. As the numbers are selected, they are posted one by one on a light-board above the counter and simultaneously appear on several other light-boards displayed around the casino. When he had finished filling out his card it looked like a diagram for a complex football play. He reached in his shirt pocket, pulled out a roll of hundred-dollar bills, and plopped two down on the counter. The clerk registered his wager and gave him $70 change.

While he waited for the drawing to begin B.B. explained how he had marked his ticket. He had played what is called a "way ticket" because of the strange markings that show how the ticket is to be played several ways; his comprised over thirty separate wagers or "ways" to read the ticket.

The betting closed and the officials began selecting the dancing numbered balls. The drawing was over almost before it began. It took some complicated reckoning to determine his winnings; they came to about $25. His net loss for the ten-minute drama was a little more than $100. He scooped up another ticket and took a seat in the gallery.

"I was playing at Caesar's Palace in Las Vegas one night," he said, a little vacantly, "playing a way ticket they call 'kings,' where you circle every number you play. I played 19, 25, 49, and 71, because I was born in 19*25*, my first hit was in 19*49*, and the year then was 19*71;* I also played 46 for my age at the time and 10, 66 and 33 for my address, 10 West 66th Street, Apartment 33D. That makes eight numbers. I hit seven out of eight. It paid $24,890! Ever since then I've been hooked."

"What did you do with your winnings?" I asked.

"I gave some of it away. I tipped the keno writer [clerk], and the bellman $100 each. I gave everyone in the band $100. And there's taxes. I don't know exactly. I spent it."

The start of the next game was approaching and he turned his concentration again to filling in his ticket. The results of this round were a replay of the first round. And so it went for five or six rounds until showtime called him away for the 1:00 A.M. performance.

During the final week of B.B.'s Tahoe gig we met a few times for working sessions with the tape running, usually in one of the casino restaurants, never out of range of the keno runners who carried his wagers to the counter for virtually every game. At one meal the tab for the food ran about $15 (he graciously picked up the tab) and his gambling losses came to about $500, which he rationalized on the grounds that his last wager before sitting down to eat had netted him around $1,100, so he was playing with "Bill Harrah's money, not my own." He seemed stoic in the face of his own declaration that no matter how big his winnings he was reconciled to plowing them all back into the casino coffers.

Appendix II: Plantation Organization and Lynchings

THIS APPENDIX is compiled to give the reader greater background on two subjects: plantation organization and lynchings. The plantation has a long history in the Western Hemisphere, going back at least to the eighteenth century and not confined to North America. Only plantations in the Mississippi Delta during the period of B.B. King's youth will be considered here. The best single source of information on Delta plantations of this time is a technical bulletin published by the Department of Agriculture in May 1939 (*Plantation Organization and Operation in the Yazoo-Mississippi Delta Area,* by E. L. Langsford and B. H. Thibodeaux. Technical Bulletin No. 682). The following information is taken from that source:

> Plantation Size (1939)
>   70% of all Delta farms were 300 acres or less
>   56% of all Delta farms were 80 acres or less
>   5.6% of all Delta farms were 1,000 acres or larger
>   2% of all Delta farms were 2,000 acres or larger

Thus, by 1939, more than half the Delta farms were very modest in size and for every moderately large (1,000 acres or more) and very large (2,000 or more) farm, there were twenty farms smaller. However, it should be added that more than a fifth of the land under cultivation, 21.5 per cent to be precise, was in the hands of very large plantation owners (those holding 2,000 acres or more).

A five-year average of all Delta farms for the period 1932–36 showed an average area under cultivation of 738 acres, an average annual capital investment of slightly less than $60,000, an average gross income per Delta farm of slightly more than $26,000, with average total expenses at slightly over $18,000, for a net income of almost precisely $8,000.

GROWING SEASON

The number of frost-free days in the Delta ranged from 200 to 230, with very few exceptions since the time the Weather Bureau began keeping records. Agricultural experimentation to reduce risk of damage to cotton crops from frost has yielded best results in the area of developing strains of cotton that require shorter times to come to maturity.

DIVISION OF LABOR

The statistics for the breakdown of acreage tilled by the four types of labor-sharecroppers—working on halves (sharing half of the proceeds with the landlord), share tenants working on quarters (sharing one quarter of the proceeds with the landlord), cash tenants (paying cash rental and sharing none of the proceeds) and wage laborers—show the following five-year average for the period 1932–36:

    47% of crop lands tilled by sharecroppers;
    10% of crop lands tilled by quarter tenants;
    1% of crop lands tilled by cash tenants;
    42% of crop lands tilled by wage labor

(These figures apply to *all* crop lands, not just those planted with cotton.)

TENANTS (1936)

In 1936 the average tenant family (sharecroppers plus quarter tenants) farmed 10.8 acres producing 10 bales of cotton. The average "furnish" (money advanced by the landlord against the tenant's earnings from the coming crop) per family was $161.56 for the year. From the standpoint of the planters, the furnish was a sizable capital item. A planter with 50 tenant families would thus lay out a sum in excess of $8,000 in furnish money, roughly 15 per cent of the total annual capital investment. For the five year period 1932–36, the average annual investment per plantation in tenant housing (the landlord's responsibility under both the sharecropping and quarter-tenant systems) was slightly over $8,000. Thus the combined furnish and housing investment for a typical plantation owner to maintain the tenant farmers working his ground was in the neighborhood of $16,000—roughly 30 per cent of the total annual capital investment.

The total number of sharecroppers in the Delta in 1936 was set at 56,703, down 10 per cent from the figure for 1935. The decline was undoubtedly due to increased mechanization as reflected in tractor sales, which were doubling every two years in the 1930s.

OF ALL THE INJUSTICES of the Jim Crow era, lynching stood out as a symbol that blacks did not have equal protection under the law. To black people, lynching meant that whites could inflict even the most violent crime against them with impunity. Now that lynching is a thing of the past, the word "lynch" has become almost synonymous with the murder of blacks by white mobs, yet many whites have been lynched in the United States. In the United States, after 1881, 28 per cent of lynch victims were white. In the Deep South, though, a great preponderance of lynch victims were black; nine out of ten people lynched in the Deep South since 1881 were black.

The main source of information concerning lynchings in the United States is the Tuskegee Institute. The records of the institute are summarized in a compilation titled *Eight Negro Bibliographies* (New York: Kraus Reprint Company, 1970) compiled by Daniel T. Williams of the Tuskegee Institute. According to institute records, from 1882 until 1968 a total of 4,752 people were lynched in the United States, 3,448 of them black and 1,307 of them white. A great majority of lynchings (over 90 per cent) in the United States took place before 1925, though during the depression there was a slight rise in the annual rate. Only the six New England states are lynch-free; every other state has had at least one lynching. Mississippi, with 581 (539 blacks, 42 whites), has had more lynchings than any other state. According to Tuskegee Institute records, the alleged offenses of the victims breaks down as follows:

Homicide	1,937
Rape	912
Attempted rape	288
Robbery	232
Felonious assault	205
Insult to a white person	85
All other alleged offenses	1,084

A detailed annual report of lynchings can be found in *The Negro Year Book* from 1912 to 1954, also published by the Tuskegee Institute. (See, for instance, *The Negro Year Book, 1947*, pgs. 304–7.)

This history of efforts to secure passage of an anti-lynch law in the U. S. Congress is one of protracted blockage by coalitions of Southern congressmen with other interest groups in the House and Southern filibuster in the Senate.

In 1922, and again in 1924, the House defeated an anti-lynch law sponsored by Missouri Representative Leonidas Dyer. The defeat of the Dyer bill in 1924 was engineered by a coalition of Southern and Western congressmen; the Southern congressmen pledged to support a tough immigration bill that restricted the entry of Orientals in exchange for the support of Western congressmen in opposition to the anti-lynch law.

In early 1937, two separate anti-lynch laws drafted by NAACP lawyers were defeated. A third anti-lynching bill, sponsored by Rep. Joseph A. Gavagan of Harlem, was under consideration when two black men were lynched at Duck Hill, Mississippi, on April 12, 1937. (Duck Hill, near Winona, Mississippi, is about ten miles from Kilmichael, Mississippi, where twelve-year-old Riley King was living at the time of the incident.) The victims, Roosevelt Townes and "Boot Jack" McDaniels, were accused of murdering a white man. A crowd estimated at 500 people abducted the two black men. A cavalcade of fifty or so automobiles drove to a wooded area with the two men and there the victims were burned with blow torches and hung from a tree.

The incident was reported in the international press, and many American newspapers gave it prominent coverage. Three days after the Duck Hill lynching, the House passed the Gavagan anti-lynch bill by a vote of 272 to 120. Many months elapsed before a version of the Gavagan bill came to the floor of the U. S. Senate for debate. There the supporters of the bill met a Southern stone-wall. A major filibuster was mounted in which Louisiana Senator Allen J. "Bellowing Bill" Ellender held the floor for six full days running. Senator Bilbo of Mississippi opened his effort in the campaign to block the bill on January 21, 1938, with a speech packed with racial innuendo. Finally, on January 30, 1938, the bill was set aside, and its supporters admitted defeat.

A more complete account of efforts to secure a federal anti-lynching law can be found in Robert W. Dubay's article, "Mississippi and the Proposed Anti-Lynching Bills of 1937–1938," published in *Southern Quarterly,* VII, *1,* 73–89.

Appendix III: Toward a Historiography of Oral History

OF THE TWO SOURCES of historical information, written records and eyewitness accounts, historians generally prefer the former, and with good reason. Documents may deteriorate with time but they do not alter in content, whereas our recollections are extremely malleable; without our quite realizing, they tend to change in time. Mental pictures seem to ferment, so that what was in reality confused and bland in recollection becomes aromatic and effervescent, or pungent and bitter. Inevitably this leads to distortions of fact. By the same token, the written records pertaining to a given historical incident or person usually lack exactly those subjective qualities that make eyewitness accounts so notoriously unreliable, and the results of the historians' efforts may be dry and lifeless. Ideally, then, the historian should have both kinds of source available and should combine them to write history with maximum accuracy and vitality.

The advent of inexpensive, highly portable tape recorders capable of great acoustic sensitivity has changed the writing of oral history and, in turn, the character of our language. It has changed the recording of oral history in a positive way by making it more accurate and in a negative way by encouraging pedantry. The positive change comes about because it is now possible to record the exact words of every historical account spoken, thereby enabling precise cross-checking of different sources. The negative change is a natural consequence of the sudden embarrassment of riches provided by the incredible capacity of pocket recorders to catch every last word which so many folklorists unabashedly spew onto the page with no thought for relevance or interest level.

The specific change in our language affected by the new technology is the gradual narrowing of the gap between the written and spoken word. The gap has existed as long as the two languages, written and spoken, have coexisted, and from the very beginning the gap has been closing. Moving slowly at first, perhaps like creeping glaciers, and then more quickly, with the invention of the printing press and the dramatic spread of literacy, written language and spoken language have been steadily converging as they developed. Now, with electronic media, more and more authors dictate their books on tape, and office workers on different continents exchange gossip via Telex.

Similarly, scholarship, which began as an extremely esoteric discipline confined to the study of ancient texts, has grown to cover a wide range of contemporary and popular subjects. For example, both *The Whole Earth Catalogue* and *Blues Records January, 1943 to December, 1966,* a comprehensive discography by Slavin and Leadbitter, are part of the scholarly tradition. Oral history, too, should be counted as part of that ever-expanding tradition. Whether the historian is taping jigs and reels in the hills of Kentucky, or examining the financial records of a Mississippi farmer, the process still counts as scholarship. Yet tapes are only raw data. The trick is to make minimal changes while maintaining maximal authenticity. Oral history, done well, contributes to closing the gap between written and spoken language—from both sides—making our written language more conversational and our conversation more literate.

The problems confronting the historian who has to resolve conflicting oral accounts with only scanty written sources is well illustrated by citing some details of my effort to confirm the account given me by Leslie "Greasy" Simmons about the Mississippi Gold Coast murder of a white man by a high-rolling black tavern owner, Leo "Jumpin' Jack" Jackson. According to Simmons, Jackson freely admitted to committing the murder when confronted by his friend, the high sheriff of the county, J. B. Stone, and Stone allowed him eight hours' head start before putting out an All Points Bulletin for his arrest.

To confirm Simmons' account I visited the sheriff's office in the county where the now-defunct Gold Coast was located. I had

hoped to find details of an investigation on record there, but the
present sheriff informed me that prior to 1970, when he took
office, no records whatsoever were preserved. He himself knew
nothing of the alleged murder, but he was able to refer me to ex-
sheriff J. B. Stone. In a telephone interview with me, Stone denied
that Jackson ever killed a white man, or that any white man was
ever killed on the Gold Coast while he was sheriff. Asked if Jackson was ever connected to any murder of any man, Sheriff Stone
replied that Jackson did kill a black man by shooting through a
closet door where the victim was presumably hiding, after which
Jackson fled Mississippi. Stone said he pursued Jackson and
finally caught him, but only after the witnesses, on whose testimony the case against Jackson was to be built, had themselves
disappeared. Stone was obliged to drop the case against Jackson
and set him free. So he said.

The records of the county court proved to be inconclusive in
resolving the conflict in testimony, partly because fire had destroyed all bills of indictment brought by the grand jury prior to
the mid-1950s. However, the handwritten minutes of the court-
room proceedings survived in a mammoth leather-bound book.
The minutes of the court show that a warrant for Jackson's arrest
was issued when he failed to appear to face a charge of murder,
and that his bail of $500 was thereby forfeited.

The other written record which I found pertaining to the case
was an item in *The Advocate,* a weekly tabloid reporting on
affairs in the black community. Appearing on the front page a
week after Jackson's failure to appear in court the item reported
that Jackson, a notorious big spender and celebrated nightclub
owner, had left town with angry creditors on his heels; of his
many escapades, the five-inch column ended by saying the latest
was a shooting fracas involving a serviceman. Nothing about a
murder, nothing about jumping bail. Several weeks later an item
in the gossip column of *The Advocate* exclaimed, "Don't ask us
where is Leo 'Jack' Jackson. He has vanished."

When I presented all this new information to Greasy Simmons,
he stuck steadfastly to his story, saying that it was entirely possible that Jackson killed a black man, too. The sum total of evidence is inconclusive. Only two things can be said with any cer-
tainty: first, no black man openly accused of killing a white man
in Mississippi in 1949 would have been released on as little bail

as $500; second, the need to suppress scandal over either Sheriff Stone's corrupt practice of tolerating illegal gambling in Jumpin' Jack's or the alleged illicit affair between the victim's (white) wife and black Jack, would be compelling, perhaps even thirty years after the fact, particularly if the woman in question is still alive. In presenting the incident, I have chosen to record Greasy Simmons' version of the story without the complications entailed in citing the public record of Sheriff Stone's denials because the other evidence does not conclusively falsify Simmons' story, and the telling of the story gives an accurate picture of how the social landscape of Jim Crow Mississippi looked through his eyes. The reader must decide which version—if any—to believe, and whether I am at fault as a historian for including one oral account while omitting a conflicting one.

A major obstacle which the historian must contend with in compiling a history where the written record is sparse is the sheer difficulty of finding participants in the events in question. In the case of this book, I was extremely lucky to have the help of Polly Walker, B.B.'s personal secretary in Memphis. I came to rely on her to locate the hard-to-find, long-since scattered members of B.B.'s entourage from his days on the chitlin circuit. In one case when all other methods had failed to locate Evelyn Johnson, B.B.'s former booking agent from Houston, Polly told me, "Call 'Slack Rack' in Houston and ask for 'Booker.' He'll know how to find her." Slack Rack is B.B.'s tailor and Booker, with a little arm-twisting, gave me Ms. Johnson's unlisted number.

Another of Polly's hot tips led me to a former drummer from one of B.B.'s early bands, a man named Solomon Hardy, known to musicians around Memphis as "Sparrow," from his days as a WDIA jock when he had a program called "The Sparrow's Nest." The story of my meeting with Sparrow is a shaggy-dog story on the methodology of compiling oral history. My conversation with Sparrow was the most colorful of the many talks I had in the course of all my researches, and, when for reasons that will soon be apparent, I found that I could not possibly use his account of the fiery crash of Big Red, I was crestfallen. (Fortunately, I was able to obtain other highly reliable testimony from another source.) Thus, I am greatly pleased to be able to close this appendix on the peculiar demands of writing oral history by relating my charming encounter with Sparrow, a genuine rogue and self-proclaimed bosom pal of B.B. King.

Sparrow works for the Owens Funeral Home in Memphis, Tennessee, and is known as one of the best body snatchers in town. The morticians of Memphis are extremely competitive—so much so that often the one to get the job of handling a given funeral is the one whose man is the first to arrive on the scene after the spirit has left the flesh. Therefore it is a great advantage to a funeral director to have someone on his staff with a reserve of goodwill in the community and a good intelligence network to inform him the moment someone has died. Sparrow is just the man for the job. He is full of good cheer, smooth talk, and plain hype. When he gets a tip that so-and-so just passed on, Sparrow turns up at the hospital or at the home of the grief-stricken family, expresses his deepest sympathy and asks "Won't you let me take care of everything?" A quick phone call to summon the waiting hearse, and Sparrow has the body for his boss.

My appointment with Sparrow was at the funeral home, a one-story brick building in a not very prosperous neighborhood. He was late, and I waited for him in the reception room of the funeral home, which looked like the lobby of a shabby hotel. While waiting, I thumbed through the only reading material around—a mortician's catalogue. It contained long, detailed descriptions of various embalming fluids, comparing their relative properties at retarding tissue swelling and "blotching." There were illustrated ads for gadgets of all kinds: embalming tables, chrome-plated catafalques, variable-speed electric winches for lowering coffins into graves. There were headrests, eye cups, mouth sutures, and body bags. Sparrow was a very long time coming—so long that when he finally arrived, I had a case of the creeps. By then, I was very glad to see him.

Sparrow is a small, compact, dark-skinned man with a coarse face and a crooked grin. He gave me at once the feeling that we were old friends. It was no chore persuading him to talk about the days of twenty-five years ago, scuffling around Tennessee, Arkansas, and Mississippi in cars leased by WDIA for B.B. and his musicians. The names of clubs he mentioned along the way had a romantic ring to them—Loftie's Place, Black Willie's, the White Swan and the Casablanca; the towns too, had their own allure—

Covington, Tennessee; Osceola, Arkansas; and Balstrop, Louisiana. He mentioned with obvious pride his guest appearance in 1945 as a percussionist with the Memphis Symphony on a program for talented high school students; he was the first black musician to play with the symphony. When I mentioned Johnny Ace, he quickly offered an analysis of his fellow Memphis musician and the tragic end of his whirlwind career: sudden, easy money is what had ruined him, he said; it made him lose his common sense so he became a dope-smoking, limelight fanatic.

We had been talking nearly an hour and I had forgotten the somber setting until a truck delivered a large floral display on a stand. Sparrow carried it through the door at the far end of the reception room. I followed him into the parlor where he set the display beside an open coffin in which lay a bearded black man in his thirties. The parlor, like the reception room, was sparsely furnished; four or five rows of folding metal chairs stood on a threadbare carpet. The room was more like the meeting hall of a poor church than my idea of a funeral parlor. I commented to Sparrow on the youth of the dead man and asked how he died.

"Shotgun," replied the famous body snatcher. "He was a mean dude. Gave a lot of people a hard time. Won't be bothering anyone now."

"Who shot him?" I inquired.

"Brother-in-law," Sparrow answered, motioning me back toward the reception room.

I turned the conversation to the subject of the crash of Big Red, and Sparrow took my lead as we returned to our places in the reception room. With high drama, he described the grisly scene on the bridge in Texas. It all happened because the brakes failed, he said; he gave a vivid account of how the driver of the bus shouted out that the brakes were going, complete with sound effects to indicate the driver pumping the failing brakes.

"We kicked out the windows at the back of the bus, and some of the band began jumping out. Some people freeze in a situation like that, you know, and one fellow, name of 'Birdeye,' froze in his seat. We had to drag him out and practically pushed him out the window. It was terrible, I tell you. You ask Cato, he'll tell you about it. He was driving when it happened."

The man named "Cato" in Sparrow's account is Polly Walker's husband, Cato Walker, B.B.'s driver, valet, mechanic and gofer of twenty-five years' service. By coincidence I saw Cato later that same day after Sparrow glad-handed me out the front door of the funeral home. I asked Cato when I saw him to tell me about the accident with Big Red.

"I'll tell you what I know about it, but that's not much since I wasn't there," Cato replied. "I was in Memphis when it happened."

"I thought you were on the bus," I said, a little confused. "Sparrow told me that you were driving."

"Sparrow?" Cato said, screwing up his face. "Shee-it, man! Sparrow wasn't there either. He was in Memphis, too."

Appendix IV: Analysis of a B.B. King Guitar Solo

B.B. KING is a consummate soloist. Each of his improvised solos has an internal logic and a progressive development of its own. In this they compare favorably for their sense of unity and balance with those of the best jazzmen around. Sticking strictly to the harmonically sparse blues scale, he relies heavily on subtle rhythmic variation to fashion distinct musical phrases which he links together in a musical grammar of his own. All his technical virtuosity is impressive—the fluid tremelo of his sustained notes, the use of "bent" notes pushed up onto pitch from half-tones below, the uniquely rich voice of his instrument achieved by his original picking and fretting techniques, plus control of his electronic amplification. Yet these features are strictly and permanently secondary devices in his grammar: they are embellishments, similiar to those found in baroque music. And the strength of each of his solo pieces derives from his conception of the whole solo piece as a musical design, not simply a string of dazzling hot licks. The following analysis of one B.B. King guitar solo recorded in 1966 (Bluesway BL-60001, Side II, ≠5 "Gonna Keep on Lovin' You") aims to show the musical design or overall architectonics behind his playing. In some ways, this solo is not quite typical of his playing: the allegretto tempo is faster than most songs on which he takes more than the short, twelve-bar instrumental breaks, and the subtonic or sixth degree of the scale (E natural in the key of G in which this piece is played) is used only a few times in passing. I chose this piece because it concentrates the aspects of his style that I wish to illustrate: in more important ways, it eloquently displays his style as an architect. It is a broken line packed with mounting tension, which meets final resolution, a broken line of halting, and stammering, an intense struggle to achieve full articulation. These qualities together are the key to virtually all of his guitar playing.

THE SOLO is played at allegretto tempo ($\downarrow$=106) and is 48 measures long, lasting 1 minute, 48 seconds in all. It follows the standard twelve-bar blues progression. This provides a natural division of the solo into four parts, 12 measures each. The opening part is an establishing prelude, played an octave lower than the other three parts. Its prelude style is established by its broken chords and simple play on accepted rhythms, by its simple hesitant structure: it consists of six musical phrases (beginning with the five-note musical signature that opens nearly every B.B. King guitar solo); each of the phrases is uncomplicated, devoid of sudden flurries or long sustains; they are clearly separated by pauses, and the rhythmic emphasis is squarely on the beat. The overall character is one of unhurried clarity with plenty of breathing space. Indeed, the fourth figure (measure 7) consists of a single eighth note preceded by 4 ½ beats of silence and followed by 8 ½ beats of silence. The last phrase (measures 10 and 11) makes a brief entry into the register where the phrases of the three main parts of the solo will be played. A single sixteenth note at the end of measure 11 serves as a binder to tie off part one and clear the way for part two.

The body of the solo—the two middle quarters, crammed together within a one-octave range—is confined to a six-tone blues scale—chromatized in the traditional blues manner—consisting of the notes G, B♭, C, D, F♮, and G (known as the Hypophrygian mode). Beginning in measure 13 with the opening phrase of part two come two tension-building elements: a marked tendency to syncopate, and a gradual focus on the top note of the scale as the final objective in the development. The accumulated tension of parts two and three (measures 13-36) meets final resolution at the beginning of part four (measure 37), where both the top note and the re-established rhythm are celebrated. The last 12 measures constitute the coda, a very tonal one, thereby emphasizing the resolution achieved at the ¾'s mark, ending on the dominant, thus harking on the opening bars.

Kudzu. *Photo by Charles Sawyer.*

A creek bank at floodtime, Mississippi Delta. *Photo by Charles Sawyer.*

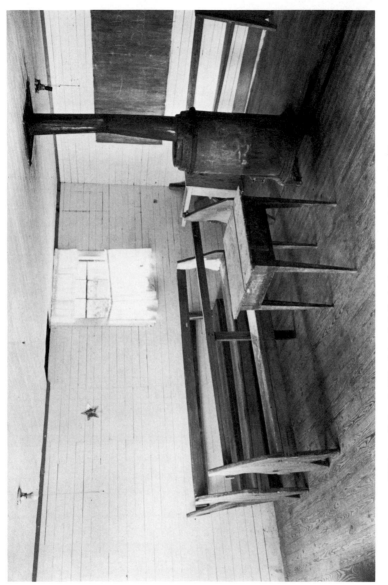

Elkhorn School, Kilmichael, Mississippi. *Photo by Charles Sawyer.*

Luther Henson (1978). *Photo by Charles Sawyer.*

Wayne Cartledge, son of Flake Cartledge, Riley King's benefactor. May 1978, Kilmichael, Mississippi. *Photo by Charles Sawyer.*

The Cartledge House, Kilmichael, Mississippi, where in 1942 Flake Cartledge lived as a cash tenant farmer with his wife, son Wayne, and his ward, Riley King, who slept in a shed nearby. *Photo, 1978, by Charles Sawyer.*

Elder Birkett Davis (in white) beside Pastor I. Flack of the Jerusalem Church of God in Christ, Indianola, Mississippi. Elder Davis and his cousin Riley (B.B.) King sang together in the St. John's Gospel Singers. *Photo by Charles Sawyer.*

Walter Doris, Jr., boyhood chum of Riley King, now deputy sheriff, Mongomery County, Mississippi, at the courthouse in Winona, Mississippi, May 1978. *Photo by Charles Sawyer.*

Sue Evans, the former Mrs. Riley B. King. *Photo, 1978, by Charles Sawyer.*

Albert King (1978): "I call B.B. my 'baby brother' even though he's my son, because there's only eighteen years between us." *Photo by Charles Sawyer.*

B.B. King in his suite at Harrah's Hotel, Lake Tahoe. *Photo by Charles Sawyer.*

Harrah's. *Photo by Charles Sawyer.*

B.B. is assisted by his son Leonard. *Photo by Charles Sawyer.*

Farming records of landlord Edwayne Henderson show the year's transaction (1939) with his sharecropping tenant Elnora Farr, grandmother of Riley King. *Courtesy of Edwayne Henderson.*

Farming records of landlord Edwayne Henderson show the year's transactions (1940) with his sharecropping tenant Riley King who tended one acre of cotton on Henderson's land. The monthly living allowance advance to Riley was $2.50. The "rental check" by which the account was paid was a government subsidy for the crop. *Courtesy of Edwayne Henderson.*

Indianola, Mississippi. *Photo by Charles Sawyer.*

Relics of the Chitlin Circuit, the Club Handy, Beale Street, Memphis, closed by urban renewal. *Photo 1978 by Charles Sawyer.*

Relics of the Chitlin Circuit, an abandoned roadhouse near Kilmichael, Mississippi. *Photo 1978 by Charles Sawyer.*

III

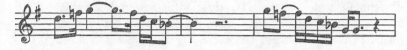

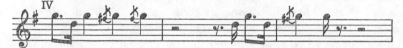

IV

gliss.

So much for the overall clear-cut structure of the piece. The center of the piece, however, consists of the two central quarters, and each has a clear structure of its own. The six phrases of part two (bars 13-24) are all linear descents of the six-tone scale, isolated by clear silence. In successive phrases, the execution of the descending scale is progressively retarded while embellishment and dissonance are piled up. Thus the following patterns fall into place. In the first phrase (measure 13) the descent from high G begins between the first and second beats. The first and second phrases are then separated by a measure's rest. The descent in the second figure begins between the second and third beats of the measure (15), with the addition of two embellishing notes, a grace note and the whole tone of C, between the D and B♭ of the six-tone scale. All the notes of the scale are played between beats, shifting the rhythmic emphasis off the beat. The second figure concludes with an amendment to the scale (measure 16), which ends on B♮, a distinct departure from the Hypophrygian modal scale, in which the B is flatted, thereby adding brightness and luster. The descent of the third figure is retarded until a moment after the third beat of measure 17 and a new tonal element is introduced by adding the dissonant combination of G and F♮ together. The dissonance is repeated in each of the last three phrases of part two with growing tension created by extending its duration from ⅓ beat on first sounding (measure 17) to 1¾ beats (measure 21). Descent on the scale is further retarded until by the fifth phrase (measure 21) we have come full circle to where being late has become being early, and descent now begins again on the second half of the first beat, as in measure 13.

By measure 21, the tension of retarding the scale has been replaced by the tension of harsh dissonance sustained without variance of tremelo or diminution of volume (thanks to the electronic amplifier) over nearly half the measure. In the closing figure of part two (measures 22 and 23), the tension is increased further by a series of three rapid attacks on the dissonance, all played off the beat. The effect is both to emphasize the harsh sound even more and to struggle with shaking it off, giving a push/pull impression—harsher still, yet nearly free of the harsh sound.

So much for the second quarter. At this point in the solo, the halfway mark (measure 24), the music cries out for a solid, clean high G, right on the beat, without the usual leading tone F♮

preceeding it, since here it would deflect and sound harsh. Rather, it is preceded by the dominant D, that stresses its role as a tonic. Thus, the first phrase of part three (measure 24 and 25) effects a partial resolution of the tension of the second part by sounding three clean high Gs free of dissonance. Yet the attack point of each is syncopated and falls between beats, to open the road to new tensions around which to build the third quarter.

The relations between the second and third quarters, then, is this: where the second part offers clear tension, the third offers hesitance. The third part, then, is a hesitant echo of the tense second part.

Having shyly announced the resolution in a syncopated way, the succeeding phrases of the third quarter avoid the anticipated resolution in favor of dawdling, teasing, syncopated, rhythmically complex sallies up and down the six-tone scale. Once in the third phrase of part three (measure 29), we are allowed the brief, passing sound of a high G played solidly on the first beat of the measure, followed by a brief, lucid, unsyncopated phrase that reasserts the unadorned six-tone scale. Yet this brief respite from the tension inducing devices does not dispel the elusive mood of previous phrases: a syncope at the end of the phrase is ambiguous in that while reintroducing the ambiguity it stresses the tonic but leads to highly syncopated passages whose rhythmic emphasis is more than ever placed off the beats; this continues for the rest of part three, whose last three phrases (measures 30-36) move emphasis one way and another around the beat where it is "expected."

The hesitance is further shown in the last phrase (measures 34-36), an extended figure, 2½ measures long, which rushes down the scale, turns momentarily (last beat of 35, first beat of 36) climbs back toward the long-anticipated focus of the first 36 measures—all the while still avoiding the beat—and, at last the hesitance is resolved, in measure 37, when four clean high Gs are played solidly on the four beats of this measure.

The concluding phrase of part three, which is the launching platform of the resolution, runs continuously into the grand resolving phrase that opens part four, and hence by contrast with the transitions between the previous parts with their polite pauses separating them, the rush from part three to part four further enhances the musical climax achieved in that resolution.

Thus, the clear structure of part two, where scales are progressively syncopated, is contrasted by the hesitance of part three, where syncopation is not unidirectional, scales do not fall increasingly into a pattern, but rather play around it. Of course, the patterns, both rhythmic and of broken chords, are established in part two, so that part three can hesitate around them without hesitance threatening to reduce clarity.

The remaining phrases of the final twelve-bar segment of the solo constitute a coda that celebrates the resolution of measure 37, first by echoing the resolution in measures 38 and 39 and then by giving a reprise of the devices of the first three parts of the solo with added bravura gestures (the down-up-down execution of the scale in measures 42 and 43, and the glissando of measure 44). The solo closes with a fillip (end of measure 47 and measure 48) that returns to the opening note.

SUMMARY

Opening Prelude

Part I: Simple, transparent figures, played on the beat in a lower register with plenty of breathing space between, establish a relaxed mood.

Body of the Solo

Part II: Tension Mounts. Progressively retarded descents on the blues scale, played behind the beat, are followed by dissonances of increasing duration, which finally break down in stammering attacks, further enhancing tension.

Part III: Hesistance. The relief anticipated in Part II is deferred. After shyly announcing the resolution in a syncopated way, the third quarter dawdles amid the notes of the six-tone scale creating a new tension: the uncertainty of wondering if the shadowy resolution glimpsed here must serve as the final resolution. The new and old tensions are resolved by a headlong rush to unequivocal resolution in measure 37.

Coda

Part IV: The accumulated tensions of the second two quarters are resolved in an unequivocal assertion of the top note of the scale. A bravura reprise of the earlier figures celebrates the triumph of measure 37. The solo ends on the dominant note, harking back to the opening.

Three more things need to be said to grasp the full significance of this one particular solo for understanding B.B. King's style of improving solos. First, the use of small nuances to make variations within a very narrow framework give his playing the appearance of diversity while never straying far from the basics. Compare, for instance, the descents of the scale in measures 17, 21, and 29. Second, the marked tendency to play off the beat succeeds in divorcing his playing from the relentless rhythm in precise tempo set by the supporting musicians, which accounts partly for the speechlike character of his melodic lines; at times his guitar sounds like the "voice-over" which narrates a film. (Over the years the drummers who have backed B.B. King have been known for their unusual ability to hold a faultless tempo. Yet when the recording of this solo, made in 1966 in a Chicago nightclub, is played at half or quarter speed, it reveals drummer Sonny Freeman making micro adjustments to the tempo at crucial points; approaching the transitions between succeeding twelve-bar parts he can be heard to slightly retard the tempo, thereby heightening anticipation.) This characteristic blending of speech and song is done by B.B. the same way in his singing as in his playing. The hesitant approach of the spoken to the sung word and its reflection in his instrumental solo is a hallmark of B.B. King's music.

Finally, a feature of Part II needs highlighting. As a child, Riley was afflicted with a stammer, a fact that B.B. King recalls with visible pain. He overcame his stammer by learning to speak slowly with extra deliberation. In commenting on his style of playing, he has said that sometimes he hears his boyhood stammer coming from his guitar. With this fact in mind, look again at the three phrases in Part II, measures 17-23, and you will detect the tongue-tied effort at articulation which finally breaks down (measures 22 and 23) in a flurry of stammering. Moreover, the hesitance in Part III has already been noticed. Furthermore, the super-deliberate execution of the resolving phrase in measure 37 then becomes the triumphant breakthrough to full articulation. Small wonder B.B. King's playing is emotion-laden, considering his music is a metaphor for his own quest for redemption by way of self-expression that brings about self-respect—a quest won by his triumph over the humiliating affliction of a stammer.

Appendix V: A Note on the Photographers

THE IDENTITY of some of the photographers whose work appears in this book remains a mystery to me. I don't suppose I shall ever learn who took the three sensitive, naïve photos of young Riley King, or even if they were taken by the same photographer. Nor will I likely learn the name of the photographer who made the touching portrait of Robert Henry, loaned to me by his widow.

Some of the photos from Memphis were probably taken by Ernest Withers, a lifelong resident of Memphis, who was among the first eight blacks hired for the Memphis Police Department in 1948. Withers was caught in an interdepartmental political crossfire, left the force, and became a photographer. He had a photography shop on Beale Street until urban renewal came to the downtown area; when the wrecker's ball finally crashed in through the back side of his studio, Withers relocated his business. He lost interest in the business at his new location in a shabby neighborhood and devotes most of his energies instead to his other job as a member of the County Liquor Commission. I saw some of his photos in the files at B.B.'s Memphis office and some of the prints that came into my hands along the way may well have originated in his camera.

I don't know what to say about myself as a photographer that might interest readers except to note that I think reporting in print is best handled by a combination of words and pictures and that in my view the process is best informed when the same hand guides the shutter and the pen. From the very beginning, I saw photographs as an important part of this biography. For the technically minded, I should add that all the photos I took for this book were made on black and white, either Tri-X or Kodak Recording Film 2475 (ASA 1000), the latter film serving me well when taking pictures in poorly lit nightclubs. Most of my photos that appear here were taken with a Leica M-2, though some were taken with an Olympus OM-1 and a few were taken with a Nikon F.

The really interesting story behind the photographs concerns the photos that depict life in the South during the 1930s and 1940s. They were taken by photographers working for a government agency known as the Farm Security Agency, an office established by the Roosevelt Administration to create propaganda for the New Deal. Some of the very best American photographers including Walker Evans and Dorothea Lange did their best work when they were employed by the FSA director Roy Stryker, a bold and innovative man with an uncanny knack for attracting talented artists. Stryker's story has been told a few times in a few places, but he was such an unusual character that it bears retelling.

Roy Stryker was a mere Colorado farmboy and son of an evangelical populist. But World War I took him from his setting, and he grew into an ambitious man with bold ideas of his own. His ambition brought him to Columbia University in the 1920s, where he studied economics for a Ph.D. and taught undergraduates. One of his bold ideas was that it is more important for his students to see a manure spreader than to open a book. It was a crazy idea that landed him in trouble with most of his professors, though, fortunately, not with all of them. He was stubborn. He sent his students to labor meetings and into mills and factories while he gathered photographs of less accessible sights of American agriculture. Soon his Ph.D. was hopelessly sabotaged by his unorthodox ideas of education and his passionate interest in photography which derived from them.

But meanwhile, he had made an impression on one professor there: Rexford Guy Tugwell, a speechwriter and adviser to Franklin Roosevelt. When Roosevelt formed a brain trust to rescue the shattered American economy, Professor Tugwell was appointed Assistant Secretary of Agriculture in charge of the brand-new Resettlement Administration, an agency for helping poor farmers become productive land owners and revitalizing the land itself. Tugwell looked for talented academics to join his staff. He wanted to teach the American people how their own economy worked and to gain public support for the New Deal. To overcome resistance to government management of the economy, it would be necessary to dramatize the depression.

Tugwell needed a propagandist. Stryker was a cinch for the job. Ten years before, when they were both at Columbia, Tugwell had written an economics textbook and given Stryker the chance to employ his crazy idea about learning-through-seeing when he asked him to choose the illustrations. In recognition for his contribution he gave him equal billing as co-author. In 1935 he appointed Stryker head of the Historical Section of the Farm Security Administration, the reorganized successor to the Resettlement Administration.

Stryker arrived in Washington without the vaguest idea of how to proceed. He knew it was his big chance, and Tugwell prodded him. Slowly he began recruiting photographers. First was Arthur Rothstein, who had caught Stryker's photomania when he took a course from Stryker at Columbia. Next was Carl Mydans, who had found it tough getting work as a journalist because he used a Leica camera, then regarded as a toy by professionals. Then came Walker Evans, who insisted on using a giant 8×10 view camera, and later Evans' painter-friend, Ben Shahn, who was no technician but was adept at moving about unnoticed with his Leica. Stryker saw some photographs by Dorothy Lange and hired her. Later came Russell Lee, John Collier, Jack Delano, Theo Jung, John Vachon, Marion Post Wolcott, and, near the end, Gordon Parks, a talented young black photographer. Together, under Stryker's guidance, the FSA photographers took 270,000 photographs of America between 1935 and 1943. It was a stunning collection.

The original FSA negatives are now on file at the Library of Congress, and prints are available to the general public for a very modest sum. All one needs to order a print from the Photo Duplication Service, Library of Congress, Washington, D.C. is the negative number. Roy Stryker left the American people an impressive legacy.

Annotated Discography of B.B. King Recordings, 1949–1980

DURING his thirty year career as a recording artist, B.B. King has recorded with two companies: Modern Music, a cluster of three rhythm and blues labels owned by Jules and Joe Bihari, and ABC Records, once known as ABC-Paramount, then ABC/Dunhill. Now ABC has been purchased by MCA Records, and MCA is B.B.'s nominal label. Recordings for Modern Music were released on the RPM, Kent and Crown labels and later rereleased on the Modern Oldies label (listed here simply as "Modern"). The following discography is compiled from two main sources: B.B. King's own personal record collection and the monumental discographic reference work by Mike Leadbitter and Neil Slavin, *Blues Records January, 1943 to December, 1966* (London: Hanover Books Ltd., 1968. Distributed in the United States by Oak Publications, 30 West 60th Street, New York, New York 10023). It is supplemented by cross-checks made from record shops specializing in out-of-print blues and rhythm and blues records. Information on unissued masters retained by Modern Music was supplied by Jules Bihari.

With a body of work so large as B.B. King's (over 100 singles and more than 30 albums) compiling an accurate discography is a formidable job made all the more difficult by the absence of any central repository of information corresponding to the Library of Congress Card Catalog and the Cumulative Book Index for bibliographic work. It is a regrettable fact that the archival concern common to the worlds of books and classical recordings is only just taking hold in the world of popular music.

The following discography is necessarily neither absolutely complete nor completely accurate. Still, it is as complete and accurate as the state of the art permits. Later scholars will improve on this version just as I have expanded and made more accurate the Leadbitter and Slavin version.

B.B. King Singles*

1949		Highest Chart Position†
Miss Martha King When Your Baby Packs Up and Goes	Bullet 309	
Got the Blues Take a Swing with Me	Bullet 315	
1950/51		
Mistreated Woman B.B. Boogie	RPM 304	
The Other Night Blues Walkin' and Cryin'	RPM 311	
I Am Worry, Worry	RPM 317	
My Baby's Gone Don't You Want a Man Like Me	RPM 318	
B.B. Blues She's Dynamite	RPM 323	
She's a Mean Woman Hard-Working Woman	RPM 330	
Three O'Clock Blues That Ain't the Way to Do It	RPM 339	R&B 1
1952		
Fine-Looking Woman She Don't Love Me No More	RPM 348	

* Recordings are grouped by label and listed sequentially according to label numbers which in most cases follows chronologically. All dates are approximate.

† Chart position taken from *Joel Whitburn's Record Research, Top Rhythm and Blues Records 1949–1971*, derived from *Billboard*'s hit record charts.

1952			Highest Chart Position
	Shake It Up and Go My Own Fault, Darling	RPM 355	
	Someday, Somewhere Gotta Find My Baby	RPM 360	
	You Didn't Want Me You Know I Love You	RPM 363	R&B 1
	Story from My Heart and Soul Boogie Woogie Woman	RPM 374	R&B 9
1953			
	Woke Up This Morning Don't Have to Cry	RPM 380	R&B 5
	Please Love Me Highway Bound	RPM 386	R&B 2
	Neighborhood Affair Please Hurry Home	RPM 391	R&B 8
	Why Did You Leave Me Blind Love	RPM 395	
	Praying to the Lord Please Help Me	RPM 403	
1954			
	Love You Baby The Woman I Love	RPM 408	
	Everything I Do Is Wrong Don't You Want a Man Like Me	RPM 411	
	When My Heart Beats Like a Hammer Bye! Bye! Baby	RPM 412	
	You Upset Me, Baby Whole Lot of Love	RPM 416	R&B 2
1955			
	Sneaking Around Everyday I Have the Blues	RPM 421	R&B 10

			Highest Chart Position
1955			
	Lonely and Blue	RPM 425	
	Jump with You, Baby		
	Shut Your Mouth	RPM 430	
	I'm in Love		
	Talkin' the Blues	RPM 435	
	Boogie Rock		
	What Can I Do (Just Sing the Blues)	RPM 437	R&B 12
	Ten Long Years (I Had a Woman)		
1956			
	I'm Cracking Up Over You	RPM 450	
	Ruby Lee		
	Crying Won't Help You	RPM 451	R&B 15
	Sixteen Tons		
	Cryin' Won't Help You, Baby	RPM 451‡	
	Can't We Talk it Over		
	Did You Ever Love a Woman	RPM 457	
	Let's Do the Boogie		
	Dark Is the Night Part 1	RPM 459	
	Dark Is the Night Part 2		
	Sweet Little Angel	RPM 468	R&B 6
	Bad Luck		
	On My Word of Honor	RPM 479	R&B 11
	Bim Bam Boom		
1957			
	Early in the Morning	RPM 486	
	You Don't Know		
	How Do I Love You	RPM 490	
	You Can't Fool My Heart		
	I Want to Get Married	RPM 492	R&B 13
	Troubles, Troubles, Troubles		

‡ RPM 451 issued in two versions with two different flip-sides.

1957		Highest Chart Position
(I'm Gonna) Quit My Baby Be Careful with a Fool	RPM 494	
I Wonder I Need You So Bad	RPM 498	
The Key to My Kingdom My Heart Belongs to You	RPM 501	

1958/59		
Why Do Everything Happen to Me You Know I Go for You	Kent 301	
Don't Look Now, But You Got the Blues Days of Old	Kent 307	
Please Accept My Love You've Been an Angel	Kent 315	R&B 9
The Fool Come By Here	Kent 319	
A Lonely Lover's Plea The Woman I Love	Kent 325	
Time to Say Good-bye Every Day I Have the Blues	Kent 327	
Sugar Mama Mean Old Frisco	Kent 329	

1960		
Sweet Sixteen Part 1 Sweet Sixteen Part 2	Kent 330	R&B 2
(I've) Got a Right to Love My Baby My Fault	Kent 333	R&B 8
Please Love Me Crying Won't Help You	Kent 336	
Blind Love You Upset Me, Baby	Kent 337	

1960			Highest Chart Position
Ten Long Years (I Had a Woman) Every Day I Have the Blues	Kent 338		
Did You Ever Love a Woman Ten Long Years (I Had a Woman)	Kent 339		
Woke Up This Morning Sweet Little Angel	Kent 340		
Good Man Gone Bad Partin' Time	Kent 346*	R&B 8	
You Done Lost Your Good Thing Now Walking Doctor Bill	Kent 350	R&B 23	
Things Are Not the Same Fishin' After Me	Kent 351		
Bad Luck Soul Get Out of Here	Kent 353		
Hold That Train Understand	Kent 358		
1961			
Someday Baby Peace of Mind	Kent 360	R&B 7	
Bad Case of Love You're Breaking My Heart	Kent 362		
1962			
Lonely My Sometimes Baby	Kent 365	R&B 24	
Hully Gully (Twist) Gonna Miss You Around Here	Kent 372	R&B 17	
Mashed Potato Twist Three O'Clock Stomp	Kent 373		
Mashing the Popeye Tell Me, Baby	Kent 381		

* Slavin and Leadbitter also list Kent 346 for Sweet Little Angel/Did You Ever Love a Woman.

1962

Going Down Slow When My Heart Beats Like a Hammer	Kent 383	
Three O'Clock Blues Your Letter	Kent 386	
Christmas Celebration Easy Listening (Blues)	Kent 387 (Also Kent 412 in S/L)	
Down Now Whole Lot of Love	Kent 388	
Trouble in Mind Long Nights	Kent 389	
The Road I Travel My Reward	Kent 390	
The Letter You Better Know	Kent 391	
Precious Lord Army of the Lord	Kent 392	
Rock Me, Baby I Can't Lose	Kent 393	
You're Gonna Miss Me Let Me Love You	Kent 396	
Beautician Blues I Can Hear My Name	Kent 403	
The Worst Thing in My Life Got 'em Bad	Kent 415	
Please Love Me Look at You	Kent 421	

1965

Blue Shadows And Like That	Kent 426	R&B 25
Just A Dream Why Do Everything Happen to Me	Kent 429	

		Highest Chart Position
1965		
Broken Promise Have Mercy Baby	Kent 435	
1966		
Eyesight to the Blind Just Like a Woman	Kent 441	R&B 31
Five Long Years Love, Honor and Obey	Kent 445	
Ain't Nobody's Business I Wonder	Kent 447	
I Stay in the Mood Every Day I Have the Blues	Kent 450	R&B 45
1967		
Blues Stay Away It's a Mean World	Kent 458	R&B 49
The Jungle Long Gone Baby	Kent 462	R&B 17
Growing Old Bad Breaks	Kent 467	
1968		
Blues for Me The Woman I Love	Kent 492	
Shoutin' the Blues The Fool	Kent 510	
Please Love Me Cryin' Won't Help You	Modern 1	
Woke Up This Morning Bad Case of Love	Modern 3	
When My Heart Beats Like a Hammer You Upset Me	Modern 11	
You Know I Love You Ten Long Years (I Had a Woman)	Modern 19	

		Highest Chart Position
1962		
	I'm Gonna Sit in Till You Give In You Ask Me	ABC 10316
	My Baby's Coming Home Blues at Midnight	ABC 10334
	Sneakin' Around Chains of Love	ABC 10361
	Tomorrow Night Mother's Love	ABC 10367
	Guess Who By Myself	ABC 10390
	Young Dreams On My Word of Honor	ABC 10455
	Slowly Losing My Mind How Do I Love You	ABC 10486
1963		
	How Blue Can You Get Please Accept My Love	ABC 10527
1964/65		
	Help the Poor I Wouldn't Have It Any Other Way	ABC 10552
	The Hurt Whole Lot of Lovin'	ABC 10576
	Never Trust a Woman Worryin' Blues	ABC 10599
	Please Send Me Someone to Love Stop Leading Me On	ABC 10616
	Every Day I Have the Blues It's My Own Fault	ABC 10634
	Night Owl Tired of Your Jive	ABC 10675

1964/65			Highest Chart Position
	I Need You Never Could Be You	ABC 10710	
	All Over Again The Things You Put Me Through	ABC 10724	
	I'd Rather Drink Muddy Water Goin' to Chicago Blues	ABC 10754	
	You're Still a Square Tormented	ABC 10766	
1966			
	Don't Answer the Door Part 1 Don't Answer the Door Part 2	ABC 10856	R&B 2
	Waitin' for You Night Life	ABC 10889	
	I Don't Want You Cuttin' off Your Hair	BL 61004†	
1968			
	Payin' the Cost to Be the Boss	BL 61015	R&B 10, POP 39
	Losing Faith in You I'm Gonna Do What They Do to Me	BL 61018	
	The B.B. Jones You Put It on Me	BL 61019‡	
	Get Myself Somebody Don't Waste My Time	BL 61022	
	I Want You So Bad Get Off My Back, Woman	BL 61026	
1969			
	Why I Sing the Blues Friends	BL 61029	R&B 13

† BL is the designation for "Bluesway," the now defunct ABC record label devoted to blues music.

‡ BL 61019 issued with two different labels, one "B.B. Jones" b/w "You Put It on Me," one "B.B. Jones" b/w "Stop Putting the Hurt on Me."

		Highest Chart Position
1970		
The Thrill Is Gone You're Mean	BL 61032	R&B 3, POP 15
So Excited Confessin' the Blues	BL 61035	R&B 14
Ask Me No Questions Go Underground	ABC 11268	R&B 18, POP 40
Chains and Things King's Special	ABC 11280	R&B 6, POP 45
1971		
Nobody Loves Me but My Mother Ask Me No Questions	ABC 11290	
Help the Poor Lucille's Granny	ABC 11302	R&B 36
Ghetto Woman Seven Minutes	ABC 11310	R&B 25
Sweet Sixteen (I Believe) I've Been Blue Too Long	ABC 11313	
I Got Some Help I Don't Need Lucille's Granny	ABC 11321	
Summer in the City Shouldn't Have Left Me	ABC 11339	
Who Are You On to Me	ABC 11433	
Philadelphia Up At 5 A.M.	ABC 12029	
My Song Friends	ABC 12053	

B.B. King LP Record Albums*

1956		
Three O'Clock Blues You Know I Love You	Crown 5020	

* Album titles not available in every case.

Woke Up This Morning
You Upset Me, Baby
Please Love Me
Blind Love
Every Day I Have the Blues
Ten Long Years (I Had
  a Woman)
Did You Ever Love a Woman
Sweet Little Angel
That Ain't the Way to Do It
Cryin' Won't Help You
Bad Luck

Boogie Woogie Woman   Crown 5063
Don't You Want a Man
  Like Me
What Can I Do (Just Sing
  the Blues)
Ten Long Years (I Had
  a Woman)
Ruby Lee
Early in the Morning
I Want to Get Married
Why Do Everything Happen
  to Me
You Know I Go for You
Past Day
When My Heart Beats Like
  a Hammer
Troubles, Troubles, Troubles

The Fool   Crown 5115
Time to Say Good-bye
Sweet Thing
I've Got Papers on You, Baby
Tomorrow Is Another Day
I Love You So
We Can't Make It
Treat Me Right
The Woman I Love

Precious Lord   Crown 5119
Army of the Lord
Save A Seat for Me
Ole Time Religion

Sweet Chariot
Servant's Prayer
Jesus Gave Me Water
I Never Heard a Man
I'm Willing to Run All the Way
I'm Working on the Building

Sneaking Around   Crown 5143
What Can I Do (Just Sing
   the Blues)
Ten Long Years (I Had
   a Woman)
(I'm Gonna) Quit My Baby
Be Careful with a Fool
Days of Old
Sweet Sixteen   Part 1
Sweet Sixteen   Part 2
I Was Blind
Whole Lot of Lovin'
Someday Baby
I Had a Woman

(I've) Got a Right to Love   Crown 5167
   My Baby
Good Man Gone Bad
Partin' Time
What Way to Go
Long Nights
Feel Like a Million
I'll Survive
If I Lost You
You're on Top
I'm King

My Kind of Blues   Crown 5188
You Done Lost Your Good
   Thing Now
Walking Dr. Bill
Hold That Train
Understand
Someday Baby
Mr. Pawnbroker
Driving Wheel
My Own Fault, Baby
Catfish Blues
Please Set a Date

My Kind of Blues is B.B. King's personal favorite. He has said that it comes closest to his ideal of blues. Doubtless it is the purity of this album with its clean, transparent sound, that appeals to B.B. It was recorded in one evening-long, trouble-free session using only drums, bass and piano as accompaniment. It is the purist's B.B. King.

Bad Luck Soul	Crown 5230
Get Out of Here	
Bad Case of Love	
You're Breaking My Heart	
My Reward	
Shut Your Mouth	
I'm in Love	
Blues for Me	
Just Like a Woman	
Baby Look at You	
Easy Listening (Blues)	Crown 5286
Blues for Me	
Night Long	
Confessin'	
Don't Touch	
Slow Walk	
Walkin'	
Shoutin' the Blues	
Rambler	
Hully Gully (Twist)	
Your Letter	Crown 5309
You're Gonna Miss Me	
Let Me Love You	
I Can't Explain	
Troubles Don't Last	
Got 'em Bad	
I Need You, Baby	
So Many Days	
Downhearted	
Strange Things	
The Wrong Road	
Going Home	Crown 5359
You Never Know	
Please Remember Me	
Come Back, Baby	
You Won't Listen	

Sundown
You Shouldn't Have Left
House Rocker
Shake Yours
The Letter

Three O'Clock Blues   Kent 5012
You Know I Love You
Woke Up This Morning
When My Heart Beats Like
   a Hammer
You Upset Me, Baby
Sneaking Around
Ten Long Years (I Had
   a Woman)
Sweet Little Angel
Why Do Everything Happen
   to Me
Every Day I Have the Blues
Sweet Sixteen   Part I & II
Bad Case of Love
Rock Me, Baby
Please Love Me
Just a Dream
Did You Ever Love a Woman

The Jungle   Kent 5021
Blue Shadows
Eyesight to the Blind
Five Long Years
Ain't Nobody's Business
The Jungle
It's a Mean World
Long Gone Baby
Beautician Blues
I Can Hear My Name
The Worst Thing in My Life
Got 'em Bad

Whole Lot of Love   Kent 5013
(I'm Gonna) Quit My Baby
You're Gonna Miss Me
Let Me Love You
I Can't Explain

Troubles Don't Last
Walking Doctor Bill
Hold That Train
Mr. Pawnbroker

From the Beginning†   KST 533

Please Love Me
Rock Me, Baby
Everyday I Have the Blues
Woke Up This Morning
My Own Fault
Five Long Years
You Upset Me
Blue Shadows
The Woman I Love
You Know I Love You
Sweet Little Angel
Treat Me Right
Sweet Sixteen
Eyesight to the Blind
Beautician Blues
Bad Luck
Troubles, Troubles, Troubles
Sneakin' Around
Sweet Thing
Three O'Clock Blues
The Jungle
Let Me Love You
The Worst Thing in my Life
Shotgun Blues

The Incredible Soul of B.B. King   KST 539
A New Way of Driving
The Other Night Blues
B.B.'s Boogie
Walkin and Cryin'
Everything I Do Is Wrong
She Don't Move Me No More
I Gotta Find My Baby
My Own Fault Darlin'
That Ain't the Way to Do It

† This two-record anthology of Modern Music releases is an excellent representation of B.B. King in his days as a chitlin circuit rider.

B.B.'s Blues
She's Dynamite
Questionnaire Blues

Turn On to B.B. King   KST 548
Looking the World Over
Worried Life
Bad Luck Soul
Goin Down Slow
Please Set a Date
Shut Your Mouth
Baby Look at You
You Done Lost Your
  Good Thing
Walkin' Dr. Bill
Recession Blues

B.B. King Better than Ever   KST 561
I've Got a Right to Love
  My Baby
Partin' Time
Feel Like a Million
If I Lost You
Good Man Gone Bad
I'll Survive
Long Nights
What a Way to Go
That Evil Child
You're on Top
I'm King

Anthology of the Blues   KST 9011
  B.B. King 1949–1950   (Archive
    Series
    Volume II)

I've Got Papers on You, Baby
Tomorrow Is Another Day
A Fool Too Long
Come By Here
The Woman I Love
My Silent Prayer
I Love You So
Sweet Thing
We Can't Make It

Treat Me Right
Time to Say Good-bye
I'm Cracking Up Over You

1962

Mr. Blues	ABC 456

Young Dreamers
By Myself
Chains of Love
Another Love
Blues at Midnight
Sneaking Around
On My Word of Honor
Tomorrow Night
My Baby's Comin' Home
Guess Who
You Ask Me
I'm Gonna Sit in 'til You
   Give In

1965

Live at the Regal	ABC 509

Every Day I Have The Blues
Sweet Little Angel
It's My Own Fault
How Blue Can You Get
Please Love Me
You Upset Me, Baby
Worry, Worry
Woke Up This Morning
You Done Lost Your Good
   Thing Now
Help the Poor

This is the classic B.B. King in-concert album. Recorded before a live audience on November 21, 1964, at the Regal Theater in Chicago, it captures the pure vitality and conversational mood that characterize B.B. King's performances. Blues music is a live genre and B.B.'s music, more than that of any other bluesman, must be heard in performance to be fully appreciated. In the transition to the studio some essential qualities are inevitably lost and hence this live performance before a black audience at one of the most renowned stations along the chitlin circuit is a jewel. If one album is to stand alone as representing B.B. King's achievement, this is it. Steady demand for the album has persuaded ABC/Dunhill to reissue it (ABCS–724).

1966

Confessin' the Blues	ABC 528

I'd Rather Drink Muddy Water
Goin' to Chicago Blues
See See Rider
Do You Call That a Buddy
Wee Baby Blues
In the Dark
Confessin' the Blues
I'm Gonna Move to the
   Outskirts of Town
How Long, How Long Blues
Cherry Red
Please Send Me Someone
   to Love

This album is a clumsy attempt to convert B.B. King into a new kind of blues singer, combining the earthiness of Ray Charles and the silkiness of Joe Williams. All that was achieved was losing the vitality of B.B.'s voice and the virtuosity of his instrument.

1967

Blues Is King	BL 6001‡

Waitin' on You
Gambler's Blues
Tired of Your Love
Night Life
Buzz Me
Don't Answer the Door
Blind Love
I Know What You're Putting
   Down
Baby, Get Lost
Gonna Keep on Loving You

This album is my own favorite. More than the Regal performance, recorded in a cavernous theater, this performance, taped in a Chicago nightclub, catches B.B. at the height of his powers as a performer. All B.B.'s studio cuts miss one thing which is pivotal in his live perform-ances: the unique voice of his instrument. The rich, sonorous sound

‡ BL=Bluesway (ABC Records).

of his sustained notes and the harsh edge of his attack seem to disappear before studio microphones. This recording has them both, full-blown, and the intimate atmosphere of a nightclub is thick in every groove. B.B.'s guitar solos are among his very best, marred only slightly by the use of reverb in places (an uncharacteristic choice for him).

The choice of material is classic and shows B.B.'s ability to best advantage. "Don't Answer the Door," one of his better-known songs shows the defensive, insecure self-doubt that permeates much of his repertoire; "Gambler's Blues" has a tour-de-force guitar introduction and idiomatically dazzling lyrics ["I don't know much about the dice/ But my baby knows I'm not the kind to crap out twice."]; "Tired of Your Jive" conveys the irresistible momentum B.B. can achieve when he is riding on top of the cushion of sound laid down by his sidemen; "Gonna Keep on Loving You" opens with a guitar break (analyzed in careful detail in another appendix to this book) which shows B.B.'s full bag of tricks; and the album closes with a blues rendition of the old standard, "Night Life," by country singer Willie Nelson.

1968

Blues on Top of Blues	BL 6011
Heartbreaker	
Losing Faith in You	
Dance with Me	
That's Wrong, Little Mama	
Having My Say	
I'm Not Wanted Anymore	
Worried Dream	
Paying the Cost to Be the Boss	
Until I Found You	
I'm Gonna Do What They Do to Me	
Raining in My Heart	
Now That You've Lost Me	

Lucille	BL 6016
Lucille	
You Move Me So	
Country Girl	
No Money No Luck	
I Need Your Love	
Rainin' All the Time	
I'm with You	
Stop Puttin the Hurt	
Watch Yourself	

His Best—The Electric B.B.
   King   BLS 6022
Tired of Your Jive
Don't Answer the Door
The B.B. Jones
All Over Again
Paying the Cost to Be the Boss
Think It Over
I Done Got Wise
Meet My Happiness
Sweet Sixteen
You Put It on Me
I Don't Want You Cuttin' Off
   Your Hair

1969

Live and Well   BL 6031
I Want You So Bad
Friends
Get Off My Back, Woman
Let's Get Down to Business
Why I Sing the Blues
Don't Answer the Door
Just a Little Love
My Mood
Sweet Little Angel
Please Accept My Love

Completely Well   BL 6037
So Excited
No Good
You're Losin' Me
What Happened
Confessin' the Blues
Key to My Kingdom
Cryin' Won't Help You Now
You're Mean
The Thrill Is Gone

1970

Indianola Mississippi Seeds   ABC 713
Nobody Loves Me But My
   Mother
You're Still My Woman
Ask Me No Questions
Until I'm Dead and Cold

King's Special
Ain't Gonna Worry My Life
    Anymore
Chains and Things
Go Underground
Hummingbird

B.B. King Live in Cook   ABCS 723
    County Jail
Introduction
Every Day I Have the Blues
How Blue Can You Get
Worry, Worry, Worry
Medley: Three O'Clock Blues
            Darlin', You Know I
              Love You
            Sweet Sixteen
            The Thrill Is Gone
            Please Accept My
              Love

1971

B.B. King in London   ABC 730
Caldonia
Blue Shadows
Alex's Boogie
We Can't Agree
Ghetto Woman
Wet Haystack
Part-Time Love
Power of the Blues
Ain't Nobody Home

1972

L.A. Midnight   ABC 734
I Got Some Help I Don't
    Need
Help the Poor
Can't You Hear Me Talking
    to You?
Midnight
Sweet Sixteen
(I Believe) I've Been Blue
    Too Long
Lucille's Granny

Guess Who   ABC 759
Summer in the City
Just Can't Please You
Any Other Way
You Don't Know Nothin'
    About Love
Found What I Need
Neighborhood Affair
It Takes a Young Girl
Better Lovin' Man
Guess Who
Shouldn't Have Left Me
Five Long Years

To Know You Is to Love You ABCX 794
I Like to Live the Love
Respect Yourself
Who Are You
Love
I Can't Leave
To Know You Is to Love You
Oh to Me
Thank You For Loving the
    Blues

Back in the Alley—The Clas- ABCD 878
    sic Blues of B.B. King   (previously
                                issued as
                                BLS 6050)

Sweet Little Angel
Watch Yourself
Don't Answer the Door
Paying the Cost to Be the Boss
Sweet Sixteen
Gambler's Blues
I'm Gonna Do What They Do
    to Me
Lucille
Please Love Me

The Best of B.B. King   ABCX 767
Hummingbird
Cook Country Jail
    Introduction
How Blue Can You Get

Caldonia
Sweet Sixteen
Ain't Nobody Home
Why I Sing the Blues
The Thrill Is Gone
Nobody Loves Me But My
   Mother

Lucille Talks Back   ABC ?
Lucille Talks Back
Breaking Up Somebody's
   Home
Reconsider, Baby
Don't Make Me Pay for His
   Mistakes
When I'm Wrong
I Know the Price
Have Faith
Everybody Lies a Little

Blues on Top of Blues   ABC ?
Heartbreaker
Losing Faith in You
Dance with Me
That's Wrong, Little Mama
Having My Say
I'm Not Wanted Anymore
Worried Dream
Paying the Cost to Be the Boss
Until I Found You
I'm Gonna Do What They Do
   to Me
Raining in My Heart
Now That You've Lost Me

1976

Together For The First Time   DHL 6-50190*
Three O'Clock Blues
It's My Own Fault
Don't Cry No More
Driftin' Blues
I'm Sorry

  * *Together For The First Time* features B.B. King and Bobby "Blue"
Bland.

Why I Sing the Blues
I'll Take Care of You
I Like to Live the Love
Don't Answer the Door
Goin' Down Slow
That's the Way Love Is
Medley

Bobby Bland and B.B. King   ASD 9317
  Together Again . . . Live
Let the Good Times Roll
Medley: Stormy Monday
          Blues
        Strange Things
          Happen
        Feel So Bad
Medley: Mother-in-Law
          Blues
        Mean Old World
        Everyday
Medley: The Thrill Is Gone
        I Ain't Gonna Be the
          First to Cry

1977

King Size   AB 977
Don't You Lie to Me
I Wonder Why
Medley: I Just Want to Make
          Love to You
        Your Lovin' Turned
          Me On
        Slow and Easy
Got My Mojo Working
Walkin' in the Sun
Mother for Ya
The Same Love That Made Me
  Laugh
It's Just a Matter of Time

1978

Midnight Believer   AA 1061
When It All Comes Down
Midnight Believer

I Just Can't Leave Your Love
  Alone
Hold On
Never Make Your Move Too
  Soon
A world Full of Strangers
Let Me Make You Cry a
  Little Longer

1979

Take It Home   MCA 3151
Better Not Look Down
Same Old Story
Happy Birthday Blues
I've Always Been Lonely
Secondhand Woman
Tonight I'm Gonna Make You
  a Star
Story Everybody Knows
Take It Home

Live! B.B. King on Stage   KST 515
Please Love Me
Everyday I Have the Blues
Sweet Sixteen
Three O'Clock Blues
Rock Me Baby
Sweet Little Angel
Baby Look at You
Woke Up this Morning
You Upset Me Baby
I've Got a Right to Love My Baby
Let Me Love You

1980

B.B. King Now Appearing at Ole Miss MCA2-8016
Intro-B.B. King Blues Theme
Caldonia
Blues Medley:
  Don't Answer the Door
  You Done Lost Your Good Thing
    Now
  I Need Love So Bad
  Nobody Loves Me But My Mother
Hold On

I Got Some Outside Help (I Don't
    Really Need)
Darlin' You know I love You
When I'm Wrong
The Thrill Is Gone
Never Make Your Move Too Soon
Three O'Clock in the Morning
Rock Me Baby
Guess Who
I Just Can't Leave Your Love Alone

In addition to the released recordings listed above, the following unreleased recordings are known to exist. The recordings for Peacock and Chess probably reflect B.B.'s intermittent dissatisfaction with the Bihari Brothers' policies which led him to periodic flirtation with other blues-oriented record companies such as Chess Records in Chicago and Don Robey's Texas-based operation. (Robey's booking agency, "Buffalo Booking," booked B.B. for many years on the chitlin circuit.)

Unreleased masters held by Modern Music:

Don't Go, Pretty Baby
All of Me
Yesterday
How Long
She's Yours, She's Mine
Why Must You Accuse Me
So Much Trouble
Prove Your Love to Me
Don't Let It Shock You
Evil Child
My Love Will Never Die
Don't Care Anymore
Long Gone Baby
Changing My Ways
Your Good Lovin' Man
Love My Baby
My Baby's An Angel
Ain't Gonna Keep on Being Your Fool
Loving You in Vain
My Baby's Dynamite
My Baby Ask Me Not to Leave
What Have I Done

Worrin' Crazy
How Much You Hurt Me
Young Dreamers
Mean Old World
Sunny Road
Running Wild
Blues at Sunrise
Somebody Has Changed the Lock on My Door
Dust My Broom
Don't Look Now
My Heart Belongs to Only You
And Like That
Nothing But a Fool
Give Me a Chance
You've Got My Hands Tied
Love My Baby
My Baby's an Angel
Heartaches and Pain
Sometime Baby
Looking the World Over
Trouble in Mind
Confessin' the Blues
Lonely Lovers Plea
Baby Please Don't Go
Do the Boogie
Tell Me, Baby
Going Home
Long About Sundown
Mercy, Mercy Baby
Green and Lucky (Blue and Lonesome)
Drifting Blues
Why Not
Hey Little Girl
Don't Look Now
Long Nights (The Feeling They Call the Blues)
Making Me Blue
A Woman Don't Care
Love, Oh Love
I'm In Love with a Woman
You Won't Listen (Action Speaks Louder Than Words)
Whole Lotta Meat
Looking the World Over
I've Got the Blues

Explain
Cheatin' on Me
I Need You
You've Been So Mean
How Blue Can You Get
Love Me Or Leave Me (Strange Things Happening)
Hard Way to Go
I Want to Write a Letter
Along About Sundown
Action Speaks Louder Than Words
How You Hurt Me
I'm in Love
Love, Oh Love
In The Middle of an Island
I've Got to Love
B.B.'s Boogie
Walking I Do Is Wrong

Unreleased recordings made for Peacock Records, recorded in Covington, Tennessee, 1953.

Vol. & Gtr. w Johnny Ace, piano.

Remember Me	Peacock unissued
What a Difference	—
I Don't Believe It	—
I Can't Put You Down	—
I Did Everything I Could	Peacock unissued
I've learned My Lesson	—
Come on Baby Take a Swing with Me	—

Unreleased recordings made for Chess records (1958):

Don't Keep Me Waiting
Recession Blues
Tickle Britches
Don't Break Your Promise

Index